The Adobe Photoshop Layers Book

The Adobe Photoshop Layers Book

Harnessing Photoshop's Most Powerful Tool, covers Photoshop CS3

Richard Lynch

ELSEVIER

AMSTERDAM • BOSTON • HEIDELBERG • LONDON • NEW YORK • OXFORD
PARIS • SAN DIEGO • SAN FRANCISCO • SINGAPORE • SYDNEY • TOKYO
Focal Press is an imprint of Elsevier

Focal
Press

Focal Press is an imprint of Elsevier
Linacre House, Jordan Hill, Oxford OX2 8DP, UK
30 Corporate Drive, Suite 400, Burlington, MA 01803, USA

First published 2007

Notice
No responsibility is assumed by the publisher for any injury and/or damage to
persons or property as a matter of products liability, negligence or otherwise,
or from any use or operation of any methods, products, instructions or ideas
contained in the material herein. Because of rapid advances in the medical
sciences, in particular, independent verification of diagnoses and drug
dosages should be made

British Library Cataloguing in Publication Data
A catalogue record for this book is available from the British Library

Library of Congress Number: 2007930479

ISBN: 978-0-240-52076-6

For information on all Focal Press publications
visit our website at www.focalpress.com

Printed and bound in Canada

07 08 09 10 11   11 10 9 8 7 6 5 4 3 2 1

Dedicated to

Vivian Lynch (1933–2005)

CONTENTS

ACKNOWLEDGEMENTS

This has been the best and easiest book project I've ever worked on, not in small part due to the efforts of the publisher and other current partners and friends. Thanks to the crew at my new publisher, Focal Press: Paul Temme for taking his email seriously; Emma Baxter for having the good sense to see the value of my proposal; Asma Palmeiro for calling to keep me on time, out of trouble and for adjusting my mood; and all those behind the scenes who did the great job with layout and soft hands in editing (Mark Lewis, Lisa Jones, Mani Prabakaran, David Albon). Thanks to all the folk at betterphoto.com (students and staff) who helped me establish my online courses that helped me refine the concepts for the book, especially: Jim Miotke and Kerry Drager. Even more thanks to those few trusted sounding boards I have in the book business: Greg Georges (gregorygeorges.com) and Al Ward (actionfx.com). Thanks to people and organizations who helped with equipment and information: Joyce Fowler (permissions) at Adobe, Keri Friedman at Lens Babies, Mark Dahm (the answer man) at Adobe, Nils Christoffersen (foreign legion), ColorVision (Spyder does it!), amvona.com and wacom.com. Additional thanks to others at the fringes: Doug Nelson (retouchpro.com), Todd Jensen (thefineartoriginals.com), Fred Showker (60-seconds.com), Barbara Brundage, Katrin Eismann and Luke Delalio (lukedelalio.com).

Thanks to home support for their extreme patience, ability to plan around, occasional input and inspiration: the lovely Lisa, the ghetto Julia, the good-humored Isabel and the affectionate but noisy Sam.

Special thanks … For those who gave me the chance in the past: Mitch Waite, Stephanie Wall, Beth Millett, Bonnie Bills and Pete Gaughan. For being wrong: Dave Cross and Jeff [the Ax] Shultz (Contract? What contract …). For delay: Dan Brodnitz and Steve Weiss. Robert Blake for the 'F'.

Tokens for tons of other characters that roll in and out and affect the ebb and tide: Alan R. Weeks, Kevin Harvey, Larry Woiwode, Tony Zenos, Joe Reimels, Hagen-Dumenci, Rexetta, Grandma97, Stephen (aka. KENNY), Murphy (1988–2007), AT, VDL, TV, SB, P-G, TC, DL, and various Lynches, Nardecchias and Hongs.

INTRODUCTION

Sometime in early 1993, I was working for a how-to photography book publisher as an editor/designer. We had Photoshop 2.5 and I used it to make adjustments to scan the images and illustrations to make them ready for print. Photoshop was fairly new at the time; it didn't yet have all of the features that would, not much later, make it the industry standard in image editing.

One particular project I remember working on was scanning topographic maps for a book on various New York waterfalls. The book had been self-published by an author who added the maps to the book to give the reader an idea of the landscape around each of the falls. We were planning on redoing it and bringing it to a larger audience.

For the original book, the author had public domain maps scanned and placed in the book at the original size. They accounted for a significant number of pages in the original book. We made the decision to size the maps for each of the falls into a single page or set of facing pages to make the whole landscape visible at a glance. When the author had the maps scanned for the original book, he didn't ask for the image files. We had to rescan the maps for the new book.

It sounded like it should have been an easy thing. We had a decent flatbed scanner, and scanning the maps was easy enough. I fit as much of a map as I could onto the scanner glass and scanned each map in even columns and rows, leaving a little overlap, and saved the scans to separate files. I'd planned to assemble them all later in Photoshop. Like making a puzzle using numbered pieces, it would be easy (see **Figure 1**).

After I made all the scans, I opened the scanned map files, made a new file large enough to hold all the scans and then started placing them in the image one at a time via copy and paste. Placing the first image was easy, and everything at that point was working as planned. The next image wasn't nearly as easy. The lines for the topographic maps didn't line up very well. I tried doing some rotation, but I couldn't get all the lines to match up at

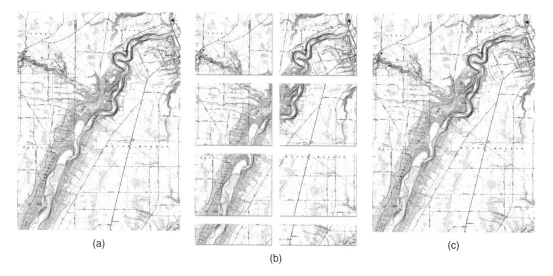

FIG 1 (a) The topographical map was far to big to fit on the flatbed scanner. (b) The plan was to scan the map in pieces and fit them all together. (c) When reassembled the new map would look like the original whole – at least that was the plan.

one time, no matter what I did and how I fussed. When I got the lines near the bottom to align, the ones at the top would be off, if I nudged right or left, it would fix one thing and goof up something else.

As it turned out, lining up the pieces of the map was a nightmare. I did the best I could in aligning that second piece, and finally decided it would never align perfectly – it seemed I was a victim of scanner distortion besides lacking perfect alignment between scans. When I deselected the pasted piece, it merged with the original, misaligned gradation lines and all (see **Figure 2**). All I could do was Undo and try it again, or move on. I went on to the next puzzle piece, the first in the next row, hoping I wouldn't have the same problem. It was just as hard to get it to align correctly. The fourth piece was even harder as I had to try and align to two edges (top and left) of the piece. None of the subsequent pieces aligned perfectly, and I was left with many disconnected gradation lines.

I continued putting the pieces together and after I was all done I went back and painstakingly corrected every line by patching. It took many hours of additional time to make, finesse and blending all of the repairs.

Several months after the map project, Adobe came out with Photoshop 3. I read about the new version, which featured layers

FIG 2 The gradation lines mismatched every time a piece was put in place.

as the key new addition. Layers were a way to let you store parts of your image independently in the same image, letting you stack your changes without committing them. In a way, I surmised that layers could act like selections, but with more permanence. Instead of the situation you had before where selected parts of the image would automatically merge into a single image plain when deselected, you had the option of keeping the area separate. Layers offered the opportunity to reposition the objects you had on separate layers at any time.

I thought back to the maps and how even that simplistic view of layers would have saved me hours of time. I could have pasted the separate scans to their own layers so I could move each independently even after I had all of the scans in one image (see **Figure 3**).

There were many other advantages to layers that I would discover in the coming months that went far beyond the simple way I first thought of them. I would have power over opacity and could lower it for any given layer (say to 50%) to see through to the content of the layers underneath and see better how the layers might align. I would be able to erase areas of the map that I was adding to blend the overlap optimally, and lessen the need for patching. I could have made patches for the gradation lines in new layers

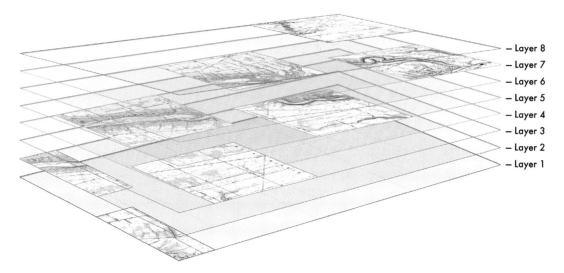

— Layer 8
— Layer 7
— Layer 6
— Layer 5
— Layer 4
— Layer 3
— Layer 2
— Layer 1

FIG 3 Layers would allow image areas to remain separated as if each were placed on its own pane of glass in the image

and greatly simplified blending in those adjustments. In all, the advantages of layers would have cut the work I had to do on the map by days, not just hours.

Over the years and through the next seven-plus versions of Photoshop, I would discover many other uses for layers, including:

- using layers as an organizational tool for image corrections and the center of workflow;
- using layers for storing multiple versions of an image in one file;
- using layers to set up complex adjustment scenarios that allow more flexibility and power than standard Photoshop tools like Channel Mixer or Calculations;
- using layers to imitate other color modes (Lab and CMYK) without converting from RGB;
- using layers to create custom CMYK and duotone separations for print;
- using layers to develop powerful techniques for color and tone enhancement, sharpening and effects;
- using layers to enhance control of the application of any tool in Photoshop;
- leveraging layer power to allow completely non-destructive image editing throughout the process of image editing.

Layers have seen some enhancement, though they were remarkably well matured in that initial release. Layer functionality includes some extraordinary powers that I have still barely seen mentioned in tutorials and books, and even when these features are mentioned, they are never explored to their potential.

Layers – what I consider the most powerful tool in all of Photoshop – a feature in Photoshop used so extensively that it will affect the correction of *every* image – has never been the subject of a book.

This is very surprising considering more esoteric features such as Channels and Actions have books written about them. Every Photoshop book mentions layers, and some have dedicated chapters to them, but no book has focused on and explored the advantages of using layers as the core of obtaining the best images with the least amount of work until now.

The Goal of This Book

The goal of *The Adobe Photoshop Layers Book* is to give the reader a complete approach to editing images using Layers as a springboard. Layers will be used as a catalyst to organize corrections and solidify workflow (the holistic process of editing images), and act as the central component to corrections in every change. The reader will learn professional correction techniques that can be applied to any image, and they will become familiar with the power of layers as an organizational, correction and revision tool. The ultimate goal is to portray layers as the heart and soul of image correction, and build a foundation of good practices to help approach correction and enhancement of any image.

Achieving the Goals

The process of discovering layers starts with the essence of learning what layers are and exploring the layers interface and commands in detail. Exploration continues by applying layers in real-life image editing situations using images found on the CD. The approach looks at the fundamentals of images and image editing, and shows how layers enable users to make any adjustment to an image in a non-destructive fashion using essential tools and concepts.

The techniques provided in this book help you take your corrections to a professional level without hocus-pocus or steps that are impossible to comprehend. You'll see what happens behind the scenes in step-by-step procedures, and you'll be given the tools – customized actions created just for this book – to move through those steps quickly to set up image editing scenarios.

This book will divulge

- A process of approaching image corrections (a workflow) centered on layered development with proven methods and a proven, core tool set.
- High-powered editing techniques and scenarios that leverage the power of layers to enhance your ability to make any image adjustment.
- Realistic image editing situations with real images by using realistic expectations to get real results.
- Timeless techniques that span many versions of Photoshop based on good core fundamentals and essential understanding that can be used with any image.

This book will *not*

- Show you fleeting techniques that emphasize the newest tools just because they are new.
- Examine a plethora of rarely used tools in excruciating detail just because they are there.
- Show you how to create crazy effects that you may use once in a lifetime, if ever.

Who Should Read This Book

This book is for anyone who is serious about enhancing their Photoshop skills and getting better results from all of their digital images. It applies to those using either a digital camera or scanner with Mac or PC computers.

Readers of this book should not be absolute beginners with Photoshop. This book is for intermediate and advanced Photoshop users who have at least dabbled in using layers, perhaps knowing they could make more of them.

It is assumed that the reader is familiar with the basic Photoshop tools (or that they are competent to research these in Photoshop Help). This book is written for:

- Intermediate and advanced users who want to understand how to use layers optimally for non-destructive adjustment and organizing image corrections.

- Serious hobbyists who want to get more from their investment in Photoshop by leveraging the power of its most potent tool.
- Those with some rudimentary experience with Photoshop who are looking for an organized approach to editing any image and getting consistently better image results.

How This Book Is Organized

As you go through this book, you will discover a mixture of practical theories, examples of the types of changes you'll make in images daily, and projects to work on to help you understand the process as well as why it works. Projects are devised so that you don't just complete an exercise or press a button and ogle the result, but so that you see what goes on behind the scenes to help understand what you have done. When you understand, you can apply that understanding to other images predictably, either by using tools provided to drive the processes or by manually applying learned techniques.

A routine is established so that you set clear goals, and establish a method of approaching your images consistently. The examples provided ensure that you can see the changes when they have achieved the desired result. This understanding will enable you to apply the techniques you learn to other images so that your images can be improved consistently.

In Photoshop, many tools and functions can be accessed by more than one method. When following along with this book's step-by-step instructions, use the suggested steps for accessing the tools. Using other methods may cause sequences to behave unpredictably. For example, opening Levels with the keyboard shortcut (Command+L / Ctrl+L) will open the Levels dialog box but will *not* produce an adjustment layer, and this can affect the outcome of a procedure that depends on the adjustment layers being created.

You will learn multiple color-separation methods to take apart image color and tone, as well as different ways to isolate color components, image objects and areas. When you can isolate colors and image areas, you can correct those areas separately from the rest of the image and exchange, move, and replace elements to make better images. Actions included on the CD are introduced in the exercises and will reveal functional scenarios that can be used with any image and simplify the process of applying what you learn.

The chapters build from one to the next, each using some ideas from the previous chapter(s), building to chapters which follow image process from beginning to end by using a single image. Chapters will incorporate mini exercises that invite the reader to Try It Now, using a hands-on approach to learning. All images used in these exercises can be found on the CD, so the user can work along. No book of any length can completely explore every facet of every concept that they present, but they should give you a pretty good idea. Each chapter ends with a segment that considers possibilities for using the techniques and concepts you've learned in each chapter. The purpose and content of each chapter is listed below:

Chapter 1 – The Basics of Layers: Layer Functions and Creation

Understanding how to work with layers starts with understanding some basics about what layers are, what their capabilities are, what functions are in the layers palette, and how to locate all that you need to apply basic layer power. Readers will explore the layers palette, see how all the basic functionality fits into the layers palette and menus, learn how to create layers, access and apply basic layer functions, and how to adjust the layer viewing preferences. We'll run through a hands-on no-knowledge-necessary example of using layers and see some simple effects that can be achieved in the world of layers.

Chapter 2 – Layer Management: Concepts of a Layer-Based Workflow

Exploring practical application of layers shows the flexibility that layers offer and organization they provide, and leads to using layers most effectively. There are reasons to create layers based on the scope of layer capabilities and the changes you want to make; in a similar vein, there are reasons not to create layers, reasons to delete or combine layers, and means of managing layer content such as merging, linking and grouping. Effectively managing layers and layer content will help keep image corrections on track, will allow users the flexibility to step back in corrections, and will also keep images from bulking up to ridiculous sizes unnecessarily. This discussion will include a brief discussion of layer types, such as type and adjustment layers, linking, alignment and activating (multiple deletes and duplication). Readers will test out all the layer creation and combining features, and will be introduced to the steps of a digital workflow.

Chapter 3 – Object and Image Area Isolation in Layers

For users who have ever wanted to change just one small part of an image, this chapter begins to look at how to do that effectively with layers. Sure you can isolate areas with selection, but selection has disadvantages in that changes are all or nothing and selected areas are only temporarily isolated. Layers enhance your freedom to correct image areas by isolating areas completely from the rest of the image. Once areas are isolated, users can make adjustments, and then fine-tune adjustments in ways that are impossible with simple selective change. We'll look at using layers to isolate image areas and objects using copy and paste, and applying a simple layered effect using layer styles and manual effects. We'll also look at blending layers using Opacity, and the idea of adding external components to an image to look at how layers offer flexibility to control composition.

Chapter 4 – Masking: Enhanced Area Isolation

Even more advanced means of isolating image areas exist in the form of masking. Masking allows users to hide areas of a layer without actually removing those areas from the image; masked areas are hidden in the image rather than permanently erased. We'll look at masking as it applies to layer transparency, layer clipping, Adjustment layers, and proper layer masks. We'll use layer masking to paint in effects, affect image sharpness selectively, and change image color selectively.

Chapter 5 – Applying Layer Effects

With the ability to isolate image areas comes the advantage of applying layer-based effects. We will look at the effect possibilities, practical uses and application. We'll consider the difference between Fill and Opacity. We'll peek around the corner to Chapter 6 by using layer modes and revisit examples from Chapter 1. Then we'll look at how you can create layer effects manually, using concepts from Chapters 3 and 4 to isolate and mask image areas. Global settings will be explored for applying effect direction.

Chapter 6 – Exploring Layer Modes

People that get involved in using layer modes often just apply them willy-nilly like filters, and experiment till they see something that they like. There is a better approach to layer modes: actually knowing what they do and when they can be helpful. Not all layer modes are really useful for everyday correction but some are, and they are very powerful tools. We'll look at ways that users can use layer modes everyday for image enhancements and improvements. Calculations will be explored in making some simple separation of image components into color and luminosity to see how components of an image can be separated to allow useful change. Manual effects like dodge and burn, image comparison, contrast enhancement and more will be explored.

Chapter 7 – Advanced Blending with Blend If

Photoshop has several advanced blending modes that allow users to blend layers based on components/channels, qualities in the current layer and qualities in layers below the current layer. This capacity is mostly encompassed by Blend If and component targeting. These powerful tools are often great to use as adjuncts to more familiar layer tools, but we will explore examples of more than one type, in practical examples that use Blend If for image change.

Chapter 8 – Breaking Out Components

This chapter looks at ways to leverage the power of layers to separate out image areas by tone or color. These powerful methods of separating images into components can lead to a plethora of advantages in creating layer-based masks based on specific image qualities, and can open the door to a world of creativity in manipulating tone, color, shape and composition. Custom tools will be provided for users to create involved image scenarios that allow layer-based channel mixing of different sorts and targeting tone and color change in a more powerful way than other channel mixing options or controls offered as standard Photoshop tools.

Chapter 9 – Taking an Image through the Process

Now that we have explored the parts of layers and what they can do, we will look at applying layers as a complete process to an image from beginning to end. This chapter offers the opportunity to review every preceding chapter as part of an actual application in image correction. It offers the opportunity to focus on the workflow, it reinforces the idea of outlining what to do with an image before approaching corrections, and it shows how to keep everything organized during the process.

Chapter 10 – Making a Layered Collage or Composite Image
As an exercise in creativity and an opportunity to break out all the tools that readers encountered in the course of this book, the final chapter is devoted to exploration of compositing and collage work. The emphasis will be on considering the idea of collage, and then how changes and additions are implemented using the power of layers. Source images will be provided from the examples in this book for looking at panorama stitching, composites and collage. Readers will be encouraged to exercise their layer muscles by using techniques from previous chapters to make a creative collage from a variety of source images.

The CD

One of the most important parts of this book is the CD. First, the CD contains all the images from this book so that readers can work through the corrections exactly as they are portrayed. Second, the CD contains a set of custom actions that will help readers set up scenarios in their images and to repeat long sets of steps that are in this book but would otherwise be tedious to apply. To use the actions and simplify procedures you'll have to do nothing more than load and run an action. These actions/tools are meant for readers of this book only and should not be shared freely with other Photoshop users. The actions must be installed into Photoshop via the actions palette to be accessible. The CD, images and actions will operate on Windows and Macintosh computers.

To install the actions, first locate the actions folder on the CD. Actions in this folder can be dragged directly to the actions palette in Photoshop, or they can be loaded through the Load Actions function on the Actions palette menu (see **Figure 4**).

After you've installed the actions, you'll be able to access them in the Actions palette. Open the Actions palette by choosing Actions from the Window menu. The usage of the actions is discussed in this book, and all are described in the readme file for the actions on the CD. Please make use of the website for this book and use the online forum to discuss any problems you may

FIG 4 Open the Actions palette from the Photoshop Windows menu, then choose Load Actions from the palette menu.

be having with the CD. Find links for the forums on the website http://www.photoshopcs.com

The images used as practice files in this book are provided on the accompanying CD so that readers can work along with the exercises. They are mostly provided as .psd files (Photoshop documents) but may be in other formats as appropriate to a particular exercise. These images are copyrighted and for educational purposes only; please use them only in the context of the exercises. Work with the images by opening them with Photoshop directly off the CD, and save them as you need them to your hard drive. The images are all compatible with Macintosh and Windows computers.

Mac and PC Compatibility

The actions and images on the CD are completely compatible with Mac and PC platforms, and they work in the same way within

Photoshop across platforms. The greatest difference a user will note in this book is that shortcuts differ between Mac and PC. For example, to open the Levels palette on PC, the user would press the Ctrl+L keys; on Mac the user would press the Command+L keys (Command is sometimes known as the apple key). Keyboard equivalents on Mac and PC are:

Macintosh	Windows	Example
Shift	Shift	Shift+X
Option	Alt	Option+X / Alt+X
Command	Ctrl	Command+X / Ctrl+X
Control+click	Right-click	Control+click / Right-click

All keystrokes are included in their entirety in this book, first Mac, then PC, separated by a slash '/'.

The Leveraging Photoshop Layers Newsletter and Blog

The *Leveraging Photoshop Layers* Newsletter and Blog (web log) keeps you up to date on frequently asked questions, tips and troubleshooting. I send the newsletter and Blog to all subscribers, and they will also be available online. The frequency of the newsletter should be once every 2 months; the Blog will be updated about once a week.

All you have to do to get the newsletter is subscribe by submitting your email address on the subscription page. Subscription is free, and the newsletter is available to anyone who wants to join. You can sign up on the website http://www.photoshopcs.com.

The Blog is available online, and you can subscribe with a feed subscription service (e.g., http://www.feedblitz.com), RSS or Atom reader.

Contacting the Author

I have been in the practice for years of supporting my books through the internet via my websites, forums and through email, and I visit various forums online regularly. I am glad to answer reader questions, and consider it an opportunity to add to explanations in this book and note areas that could use enhancement in future editions.

On the website, I maintain a newsletter and Blog to keep readers abreast of questions that I get asked and have the opportunity to answer, and I post errata (or a list of any errors and typos found after publication). All this is meant to help you through any troubles you might have with this book and techniques. I provide these resources so that you can get legitimate answers direct from the source, rather than having to fish around in other forums or on other websites where there is likely no one who knows the materials better than I do. However, you'll need to seek me out, as it is much more difficult for me to find *you*. If you have questions, it is likely that other people will have those same ones, too. Please feel free to ask as the need arises.

To catch up on any information having to do with this book, please visit the official website http://www.photoshopcs.com. You will find links there to all the resources (forum, newsletter, Blog, troubleshooting, errata, etc.). While you should visit the website first as a primary resource, readers can also contact me via email using the following address: rl@ps6.com or thebookdoc@aol.com. Depending on volume, I respond personally to email as often as possible, and I look forward to your input.

Bread

The Basics of Layers: Layer Functions and Creation

Understanding how to work with layers starts with understanding some basics about what layers are, what their capabilities are, what functions are in the layers palette, and how to locate all that you need to apply basic layer power. In this chapter we explore the layers palette, see how all the basic layer functionality fits into the layers palette and menus, learn how to create layers, access and apply basic layer functions, and look at how to adjust the layer viewing preferences. We'll run through a hand's-on no-knowledge-necessary example of using layers and see some simple effects that can be achieved in the world of layers. Even if you feel comfortable with layers, this chapter will help make sure we are all starting off with the same basic familiarity with layers and how they are accessed as tools. With that under our belt, we can look forward to applying layers to images.

📖 Please note that while this book will look at many tools and features, it will focus on the explanation and exploration of using layers. Photoshop Help can provide more depth or information about tools and their application not provided by the text. To find Photoshop Help, click Photoshop's Help menu and choose Photoshop Help, or press Command+/ or Ctrl+/ [Mac or PC].

What is a Layer?

Images are usually considered to be two dimensional. That is, when images get printed on a piece of paper or displayed on a screen, they have a height and width only. Although there may be an appearance of depth, there is no actual depth. The images are flat, and lack a third dimension.

Whenever you view images fresh from a digital camera, the image is flat and two dimensional on your screen. This is true, even though the image may actually be stored as separate Red, Green and Blue (RGB) grayscale components in the file (see **Figure 1.1**).

FIG 1.1 Though your color RGB images have separate RGB components, they appear merged as a two-dimensional color image on screen and in print.

The components of your RGB image that are combined by the computer when the image is displayed, and the result is a two-dimensional color image rendered on your computer screen.

Layers are similar to RGB color components, in that multiple layers can be added to an image and the result is still an image in two dimensions. Layers act as additions to your image that overlay one another as you add them to the layer stack (see **Figure 1.2**). These additions can be full color as opposed to grayscale RGB components. When an image with layers is displayed in Photoshop (or Elements and other programs that can recognize images stored with layers) the result is still a two-dimensional image made from a composite of the layers (see **Figure 1.3**). Individual layers can store complete RGB color that will combine in two-dimensional display of the image, as if you were looking down through the layers from the top of the layer stack.

FIG 1.2 The 'layer stack' is the stacking of layers in the layer palette.

Adobe called the virtual stacking of images 'layers' because they resemble a layered stack of transparent images. New image content is added to the original image and creates alterations to the image by layering, or building on changes over the original image content. It does this without changing the content below the new layer. This ability to make additions to the image in layers

FIG 1.3 Separate layers appear merged as a two-dimensional image on screen and in print.

keeps changes and alterations more fluid and movable, allowing you to finesse and sculpt the image result.

Layering allows you to work on distinct image areas while retaining original image information in the layers and background below. This ability to retain original image information is known as non-destructive editing; you retain the original image information undisturbed as you make changes by adding image layers. Each change is incorporated as if they were made on transparent sheets over your image that can be removed or re-ordered. The layers are stored separately in the working image file and when saved to layer-friendly formats (TIFF, PSD, PDF). During editing, layer content can be viewed and managed using the Layers palette (see **Figure 1.4**).

Layers can be created as needed and used for infinite adjustments to your images, and they can be stored with the image, copied both in the current image and to other images. They can be adjusted and revisited for further changes at any time. Each layer is a distinct visual object that can fill the entire image plane, though the visibility of individual layers and layer content is affected by

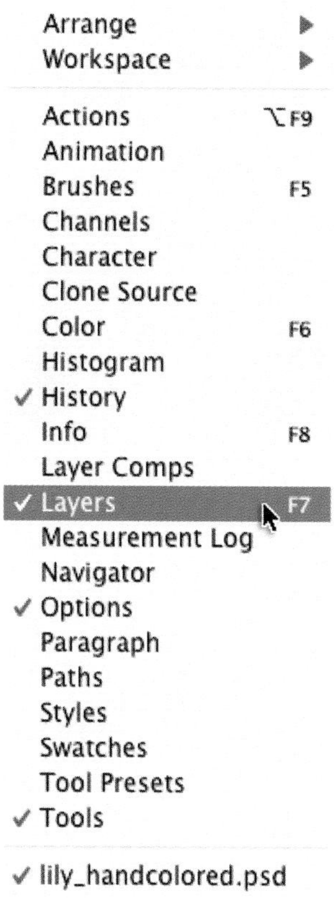

```
Arrange              ▶
Workspace            ▶

Actions            ⌥F9
Animation
Brushes             F5
Channels
Character
Clone Source
Color               F6
Histogram
✓ History
Info                F8
Layer Comps
✓ Layers            F7
Measurement Log
Navigator
✓ Options
Paragraph
Paths
Styles
Swatches
Tool Presets
✓ Tools

✓ lily_handcolored.psd
```

FIG 1.4 To open the Layers palette, choose Layers from the Window menu or press F7 to toggle the Layer palette view.

many other layer properties such as layer mode, layer opacity, layer masking, layer clipping and layer visibility.

While the basic functionality of layers is simply allowing you to keep image content and changes separate, the separation allows you the advantage of customizing how image areas combine. Control gives you advantages that allow you to achieve results that would otherwise be impossible or extremely difficult in an image without layer capabilities. Each of these capabilities will be explored through the examples and exercises in this book.

Layer Palettes and Menus

One of the keys to making use of layers is knowing how to access layer functions. Layer functionality can be found in several places in Photoshop, with the bulk of layer functions found between the layer palette, the layer palette menu, the Layers menu and Layer Styles.

📖 NOTE: Menus are listings of functions and features by name that can be selected with a click. These menus may be on the main program menu bar, but they may also be attached to palettes or other menus as submenus. Palettes (and dialogs) differ from menus in that they are floating windows that may have buttons or other graphical interface options that go beyond just a listing of features by name.

The layers palette (see **Figure 1.5**) is really a command center for controlling layer views and how layers combine. Open the layers palette by choosing Layers from the Windows palette.

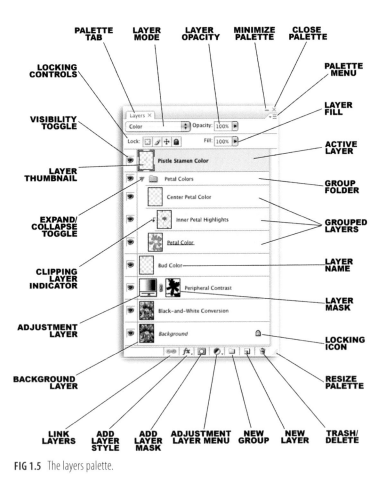

FIG 1.5 The layers palette.

Simple buttons on the palette allow you to access many powerful features at a click. For example, you can toggle the visibility for individual layers on or off, you can add effects, create new layers, duplicate layers and delete them. Other button features allow you to lock layer transparency, color and transparency, position, or the entire content of the layer (transparency, color and position) (see **Table 1.1**).

TABLE 1.1 Features of buttons.

Icon	Button	Function
▬	Minimize Palette	Toggles the view for the palette expanded/collapsed.
✕	Close Palette	Closes current palette, or hides palette tab.
Normal ⬍ Normal Dissolve Darken Multiply Color Burn Linear Burn Lighten Screen Color Dodge Linear Dodge (Add) Overlay Soft Light Hard Light Vivid Light Linear Light Pin Light Hard Mix Difference Exclusion Hue Saturation Color Luminosity Lighter Color Darker Color	Blending Mode	Blending Mode allows you to select how layers will react with layers below by choosing a mode type from the menu.
Opacity: 100% ▶	Layer Opacity	Opacity will allow you to control the transparency of the entire current layer from 0% to 100%.

TABLE 1.1 (Continued)

Icon	Button	Function
Fill: 100% ▶	Layer Fill	Similar to Opacity, however changing fill will effect only the content of the layer; layer styles are not affected by Fill, but can be controlled separately with the Opacity.
▼ ≡ New Layer... ⇧⌘N Duplicate Layers.... Delete Layers Delete Hidden Layers New Group... New Group from Layers... Lock Layers... Convert to Smart Object Edit Contents Layer Properties... Blending Options... Create Clipping Mask ⌥⌘G Link Layers Select Linked Layers Merge Down ⌘E Merge Visible ⇧⌘E Flatten Image Animation Options ▶ Palette Options...	Layer Palette Menu	Accesses the context sensitive layers palette menu. Items on the menu will vary depending on the currently active layer(s).
▣	Lock Transparent Pixels	Locks layer pixel transparency. Allows change in color/tone.
🖌	Lock Image Pixels	Keeps layer pixel transparency and color/tone from changes.
✛	Lock Layer Position	Locks layer position. Transparency and color/tone can still be changed or adjusted.
🔒	Lock All	Locks transparency, color/tone, and position of layer content.
👁	Layer Visibility Toggle	Shows/Hides the content of the associated layer.

TABLE 1.1 (Continued)

Icon	Button	Function
	Link Layers	Allows layers to be linked so that you can move or transform the content of more than one layer at a time and maintain alignment.
fx. Blending Options... Drop Shadow... Inner Shadow... Outer Glow... Inner Glow... Bevel and Emboss... Satin... Color Overlay... Gradient Overlay... Pattern Overlay... Stroke...	Add Layer Style	Allows users to add a layer style to the active layer based on a selection from the menu that appears.
	Add a Mask	Adds a layer mask to the active layer if there is not one. If there is already a layer mask, adds a vector mask. If there are both or the layer is a Background layer, this is disabled.
  Solid Color... Gradient... Pattern... Levels... Curves... Color Balance... Brightness/Contrast... Black & White... Hue/Saturation... Selective Color... Channel Mixer... Gradient Map... Photo Filter... Exposure... Invert Threshold... Posterize...	New Adjustment Layer	Adds a new adjustment layer to the image based on your selection from the menu that appears.

TABLE 1.1 (Continued)

Icon	Button	Function
	Create a New Group	Makes a new layer group. If clicked it makes an empty group. If layers are dragged to the button, a new group is created with those layers.
	Create a New Layer	Adds a new layer above the currently active layer.
	Delete Layer	Deletes active/selected layer(s). Deletes layers dragged to the button.
	Resize Palette	Click-and-drag on this to change the size of the palette

Photoshop's Layer Palette Menu and Layer menu share much of the same functionality with a few exceptions depending on the current editing task. Both menus are context sensitive, adjusting functions and function availability depending on what features can logically be applied. Options are grayed out when not available. While functions on the menus represent the same things, access to those functions may affect how layers are created and handled in the image.

It is not necessary to memorize the functions and menus, there will be layer functions you rarely use and those you will perhaps never use. The graphic reference to the functions (**Figure 1.5**) will prove to be a handy guide if you are not very familiar with layers. What is more important than memorization is to know what type of functions are available and generally where they can be found and what type of access the program provides to those functions. That way even if you don't know the exact tool or function, you at least know where it can be located. Rolling over tools and icons in Photoshop will reveal tool tips that name the item/function, and using these actively in the program as you edit will help you get familiar with all the functions in context.

There will be occasional mention of version-specific features in exercises (including features in newer Photoshop versions), however, in most cases if you are using an older version, it will not impact working with your images or completing the exercises from this book or using the book's technique.

Types of Layers

There are several distinct types of layers that can be created in your images. All are visible in the layers palette, though some (Adjustment Layers, for example) have no visible content though they affect change in the image. The types of layers are listed in **Table 1.2**.

TABLE 1.2 Types of layers.

Layer Type	Description	Comments
Background layer	Specialized content layer that is the dedicated background for the image. The bottommost layer of an image; the result of a flattened image. These layers are always locked, have no mode, and are always 100% opaque. Can be converted to a regular layer by double-clicking.	Background layers have little to do with the photographic notion of 'background' in that the content is not necessarily just image background information and shouldn't be assumed to isolate this image area. Most images start with just a Background layer.
Type layer	Specialized content layer that contains editable type. Type layers are automatically added by application of the Type tool by clicking on the image or clicking and dragging (to form a type box). Type layers can be masked, used with applied blending modes and varied in opacity/fill.	The editable type in a type layer is what sets it apart. Once a type layer is rasterized (turned into a bit map) it becomes like any other content layer – it just happens to be in the shape of type, type that isn't editable, but has other advantages.
Fill layer	Layers that apply color fills, gradients or patterns. These are created using the Layer>New Fill Layer submenu. Fill layers can be masked, used with applied blending modes and varied in opacity/fill. Because they contain content, they can be converted to a Background layer.	Fill layers are closely related to Adjustment layers and type layers. They have content (color, gradient, pattern) which makes them distinct from Adjustment layers, yet the content can only be edited through a dialog which makes them much like Adjustment layers.

TABLE 1.2 (Continued)

Layer Type	Description	Comments
Adjustment layer	A layer that applies a specific function to underlying layers in the layer stack. These are specific functions created using the Layer>New Adjustment Layer submenu. Adjustment layers can be masked, used with applied modes and varied in opacity/fill. They cannot be converted to a Background.	Adjustment layers have no content of their own beside mask content. They are very useful for applying non-destructive adjustments in the form of Levels corrections, Color Balance, Hue/Saturation, etc., all of which can be adjusted or undone at any time during editing.
Layer Group (Set)	Layers that are grouped together in a folder in the layers structure (palette). Almost strictly an organizational tool. Grouping allows all layers to be treated like a unit so that they can easily be moved, viewed/hidden or masked as one.	Originally introduced as layer Sets with Photoshop 7, the name was changed to Groups with Photoshop CS. A Group is nothing more than the content of the layers that it contains.
Clipping Layer, Clipping Group	The bottommost layer in a clipping group. The solidity of the clipping layer controls what is revealed in the layers that are clipped (added to the clipping group). These work like cookie cutters where the bottom layer is the mold.	One of the most useful quick-targeting features in Photoshop. Allows users to instantly mask any layer with the solidity of another. Once you start thinking in layers, this is an oft-used tool.
Smart object	Smart layers group together and save selected layer(s) as another image (PSB (Photoshop Object) file type) that is referenced by the image. This can reduce image file size, but may be more useful for updating groups of files at one time.	An interesting use of Smart Objects is an example where you are doing portraits for a little-league team and you want to make them all look like they have their own team cards. You can create the graphic card component, then save and import to multiple images.
Video Layer	Allows incorporation of video clips into images. Works much like a Smart Object referencing an external video file.	New with Photoshop CS3. Not terribly useful for image editing.

The distinction between Background and normal layers is an important one. Background layers serve a distinct purpose as the image background and lose a lot of the functionality of free-floating layers. Certain tools will behave differently when applied to backgrounds and others cannot be applied at all. For example, the Eraser tool will erase to the background swatch color rather than transparency as it would in other layers. Similar masking issues apply: you cannot apply a layer mask to the background layer.

The above reference is just a quick look at the vast capability of layers. Hands-on experience with layers in realistic situations will familiarize you better with how to look at and control layer content and the advantages they provide for editing images. Before getting into creating your first layers, let's take a quick look at controlling what you see on the layers palette using the Layer Viewing Preferences, and then we'll practice making a few layers.

Layer Viewing Preferences

Layer viewing preferences determine how you see thumbnails in the layers palette. These preferences are set on the layer palette menu. To get to the layer palette menu, you will need the layers palette open; it may help to have an image open as well so you can see the difference in the setting results.

📖 Try It Now

1. Open any image in Photoshop.
2. If your Layers palette is not already in view, choose Layers from the Window menu.
3. Click on the menu button at the upper right of the palette.
4. Choose Palette Options from the menu that appears. The Layers Palette Options dialog will appear (see **Figure 1.6**).
5. Choose your preference for the size of the thumbnail that you prefer to view.

Either the second or third option from the top is recommended for thumbnail viewing. This will allow you to get an idea of layer content without taking up too much of your screen. No view will prove to be completely adequate when trying to distinguish layers. While the largest thumbnail gives the best view of the layer content, it may prove to be too large for many of the exercises in this book as the layers will cascade off the screen. The 'None'

FIG 1.6 The Layers Palette Options.

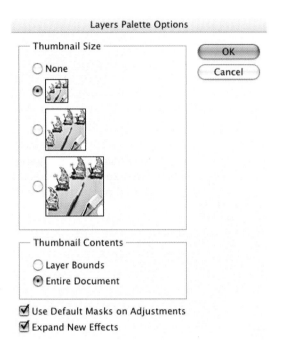

Layers Palette Options

option will take up the least amount of screen landscape, but will make you rely entirely on layer naming which negates the value of visual cues.

You can change this option at any time; it applies to the palette, and not to actual layer content.

Getting Started Creating Layers

There are many ways to create new layers in Photoshop, and the methods serve different purposes. **Table 1.3** describes various methods, and the most common ones.

TABLE 1.3 Methods to create new layers in Photoshop.

Function	How To
Duplicate Layer	• Drag any layer (including the background layer) to the Create a New Layer button. This creates a duplicate layer and adds the word 'copy' to the new layer name.
	• Choose the Duplicate Layer command from the layers palette menu or layers menu. Creates a duplicate and adds the word 'copy' to the new layer name.

TABLE 1.3 (Continued)

Function	How To
	• From the top menus choose Layer->New->Layer Via Copy or press Command+J / Ctrl+J with no selection active. Creates a duplicate and adds the word 'copy' to the new layer name.
	• With two images open, click on a layer in the layers palette and drag to the currently inactive image. Hold the Shift key on the keyboard while dragging to center the image in the image you are dragging it to. Creates a new layer in the second document with the same name as the layer in the originating document.
Blank layer	• Click the Create a New Layer button. Creates a new layer with the default name Layer # (where the number is sequential, starting with 1).
	• Choose the Layer->New-> Layer command or New Layers from the layers. Creates a new layer with the default name Layer # (where the number is sequential, starting with 1).
Layer via copy	• Create a selection, then Copy (Command+C / Ctrl+C) and paste (Command+V / Ctrl+V). Creates a duplicate of the selected area in a new layer with the default name Layer # (where the number is sequential, starting with 1).
	• Choose Layer->New->Layer Via Copy or press Command+ J / Ctrl+J with a selection active. Duplicates selected area to a new layer with the default name Layer # (where the number is sequential, starting with 1).
	• Press Command+Option+Shift+E / Ctrl+Alt+Shift+E. Merges visible layer content to a new layer with the default name Layer # (where the number is sequential, starting with 1).
Layer from Background	• Double-click the background layer in the layers palette. Converts Background to layer. The new layer will be created with a default name of Layer 0. Does not add to the layer count.
New Background Layer	• Choose Layer>New>Background From Layer. This changes the active layer to the Background layer. Does not add to the layer count.
Adjustment Layer	• Choose any of the New Adjustment Layer submenu options from the Layers menu (including Levels, Hue/Saturation, Invert, etc.). A New Layer dialog will open allowing you to change Name, Clipping, Color, Mode and Opacity. Once you accept the New Layer option by clicking OK, a function dialog will appear as appropriate.

TABLE 1.3 (Continued)

Function	How To
	• Choose any of the adjustment layer options from the Create New Adjustment or Fill Layer menu off the Layers palette. A function dialog will appear as appropriate to the function selected.
Fill Layer	• Choose any of the New Fill Layer submenu options from the Layers menu (Solid Color, Gradient, Pattern). A New Layer dialog will open allowing you to change Name, Clipping, Color, Mode and Opacity. Once you accept the New Layer option by clicking OK, a function dialog will appear as appropriate.
	• Choose any of the fill layer options from the Create New Adjustment or Fill Layer menu off the Layers palette. A function dialog will appear as appropriate to the function selected.
	• Choose the Shape tool, then be sure the Shape Layers option is selected on the Option bar (use mouse tool tip to find the button for the option). Click-and-drag on the image.
Type Layer	• Choose the type tool and click on the image. Use the keyboard to enter text once the cursor appears. The type tool can be used in combination with vectors to make type on a path and with shapes to make text in a shape.
	• Choose the type tool and Click-and-drag on the image. Makes a text box that will contain the text that is entered. Use the keyboard to enter text once the cursor appears.

📖 Try It Now

If you take a moment and sit down in front of the computer and run down the bullet list, you can test out creating all these new layers. Of course there are reasons to create layers, but right now gain some familiarity with the basic creation methods. This will help you locate them later when you need them, and play is a great way to become familiar and comfortable with creating layers. It won't be long till we are immersed in serious layer work!

If you do go through the exercise of creating the layers, you'll notice that different layer types can be identified by different layer icons in the layers palette. Table 1.4 shows icons and what they mean.

TABLE 1.4 Identification of different layer icons.

Icon	Layer type
	Black & White
	Brightness/Contrast
	Channel Mixer
	Color Balance
	Curves
	Exposure
	Solid Color
	Gradient
	Gradient Map
	Hue/Saturation
	Invert
	Levels
	Pattern
	Photo Filter
	Posterize
	Selective Color
	Threshold
T	Type

At this point we have dissected enough of the layers palette and the things that you will see there to have a reasonable orientation as to what to expect.

Exercise

Running through the bullet list and creating random layers in a stack may be interesting, but not nearly as interesting as working through a practical example. In this exercise, we will take an image, add a copyright, burn in the frame, and add a drop shadow using some simple layer creation and techniques. The exercise is a fairly easy, more or less practical run-through of some layer creation techniques that will take about 15 minutes and requires little or no understanding of layers. This is meant to be a glimpse into layer functionality; while there is some explanation of what is going on during the exercise, better understanding of the features we are looking at will come as we explore the possibilities of layers throughout the rest of the book.

📖 There is almost always more than one way to execute a set of steps to accomplish a result in Photoshop. Though you may usually use different methods, even for simple steps, it is suggested that you follow the steps as written the first time you run through any exercise in this book – especially when a specific means of accessing a function is suggested. Experimenting with other methods may yield somewhat different or confusing results. If an option or function step is not specifically mentioned, it is left up to you to choose.

📖 Try it Now

1. Open any image and flatten if necessary (Layer>Flatten Image). The image should have only a *Background* layer when viewed in the Layers palette.
2. Double-click the *Background* layer. This will open the New Layer dialog (see **Figure 1.7**).

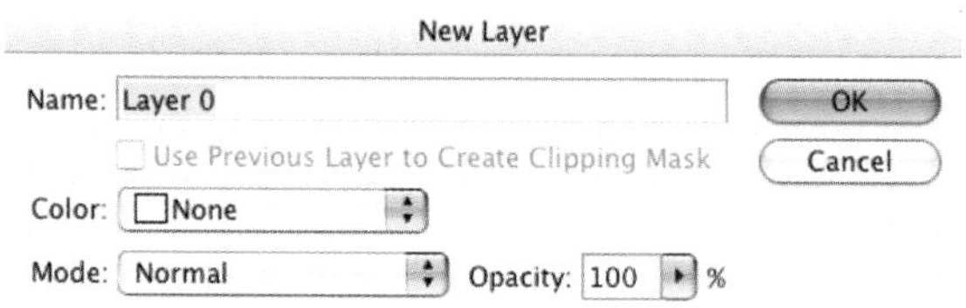

FIG 1.7 The New Layer dialog.

New Layer

Name: Layer 0   OK

☐ Use Previous Layer to Create Clipping Mask   Cancel

Color: ☐ None

Mode: Normal   Opacity: 100 %

3. Change the layer name of the Background Copy layer to '1 Original Background' by typing in the Name field. Click OK to accept the changes (**Figure 1.8**).

FIG 1.8 Change the layer Name.

4. Set the background swatch color to white. To do this press D on the keyboard (sets default colors). This color selection will affect the results of the next steps.
5. Create a new layer (click the Create a New Layer button on the Layers palette). This creates a new layer above the 1 Original Background layer.
6. Make the new layer into the background layer by choosing Background From Layer (Layer>New>Background From Layer). This will change the layer to a background and fill with white.
7. Choose Canvas Size from the Image menu. When the dialog appears, choose the following options: New Size: Width: 120% (Choose from the menu in the dialog box), New Size: Height: 120%, do not check the Relative box, leave the anchor (White box in center) at the default, Canvas Extension Color: Background. Click OK to accept the changes. This will create a white border around your image.

   📖 Canvas Extension Color is new to Photoshop CS3. 'Background' is the default for earlier versions, so there is nothing to change in CS2 and previous versions.

8. Choose the Type tool by pressing T on your keyboard.
9. With the type tool selected, choose a font and font color for a copyright from the Options bar. If you don't know what to choose, pick Arial, Regular, 12pt and black. These options can be found on the Options bar, just below the program menu.
10. Click on the 1 Original Background layer in the layers palette to activate it and then click on the image with the type tool. This will create a new type layer in the layers palette just above the 1 Original Background layer, and a blinking cursor will show on the image.

11. Type in 'Copyright © 2007 [your name]', click the Commit Any Current Edits button on the Type Options bar, and move the copyright to a place in the image that seems suitable using the Move tool. To choose the Move tool, click the Move tool on the toolbar, or press V on your keyboard.

✔	Commit Any Current Edits Button
⊘	Cancel Any Current Edits Button

📖 To get the copyright symbol, press Option+G on a Mac; on Windows, hold down the Alt key and press the following keys on the number pad in order: 0, 1, 6, 9, then release the Alt key. If this does not work immediately or if you have a keyboard with no number pad, turn on the Numlock feature from the keyboard (press the Numlock or similar button). For more information about Numlock on PCs, consult your computer's user manual.

12. Change the name of the type layer you just created by adding a '2' to the beginning of the name. To do this, choose Layer Properties from the Layers menu or the Layers palette menu. Once you have completed the name change click OK to accept the changes. At this point your layers should look similar to **Figure 1.9**.

FIG 1.9 Layers after step 12.

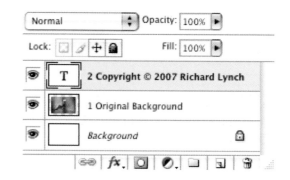

13. Create a new layer at the top of the layer stack, and name the layer '3 Frame Burn'.
14. Hold down the Command / Ctrl key [Mac/PC] and click directly on the thumbnail for the 1 Original Background layer. This will load the solid part of that layer as a selection.

⛿ Keystrokes will always be noted in the steps in the same way, and a reminder of the order will appear once in each exercise when the first keystroke appears. Mac keystrokes will always be followed by PC keystrokes, separated by a slash.

15. Invert the selection (press Command+Shift+I / Ctrl+Shift+I).
16. Fill the selection with black on the 3 Frame Burn layer. To do this, be sure the 3 Frame Burn layer is active, choose Fill from the Edit menu, and when the Fill dialog appears choose these options: Use: Black, Mode: Normal, Opacity: 100%, do not check the Preserve Transparency checkbox. See the dialog in **Figure 1.10.** Click OK to accept the changes. This will fill the frame area with black.

FIG 1.10 Layers after step 16.

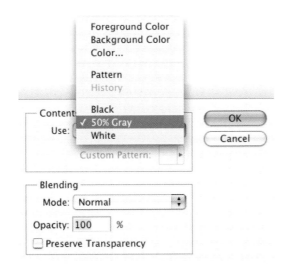

17. Deselect by pressing Command+D / Ctrl+D. Deselecting assures you will apply the next changes to the whole image.
18. Move the layer down in the stack by pressing Command+[/ Ctrl+[. This will switch the order of the 2 and 3 layers.
19. Apply a Gaussian Blur to the layer. Choose Gaussian Blur from the Blur submenu on the Filter menu (Filter>Blur>Gaussian Blur). Set the Radius to 50, and click OK to accept the changes.
20. Change the Opacity of the 3 Frame Burn layer to 40%, and change the Mode to Multiply using the Mode drop list and

Opacity slider on the layers palette. Lowering the Opacity will lessen the effect of the change.

21. Click on the Background layer to activate it.
22. Create a new layer, and name it '4 Drop Shadow'. Because you activated the background before creating the layer, it will appear in the layer stack just above the Background.
23. Hold down the Command / Ctrl key and click on the 1 Original Background layer thumbnail to load it as a selection.
24. Fill the 4 Drop Shadow layer with 50% gray. Use the Fill function from the Edit menu, and change the Use drop list under Contents to 50% gray. This will fill in color under the 1 Original Background layer and no change should be apparent in the image.
25. Deselect. Command+D / Ctrl+D. This will release the selection.
26. Choose Gaussian Blur from the Filter menu (Filter>Blur> Gaussian Blur). When the Gaussian Blur dialog appears, use a radius of 20 pixels, and click OK to accept the changes. This will soften the edges of the 4 Drop Shadow layer.
27. Choose the Move tool (press V), and move the 4 Drop Shadow by holding down the Shift key and pressing the right arrow on the keyboard twice and then the left arrow twice. Release the Shift key. This action will have moved the content of the current layer 20 pixels down and 20 pixels right. At this point, the layers should look like **Figure 1.11**.

FIG 1.11 Layers after step 27.

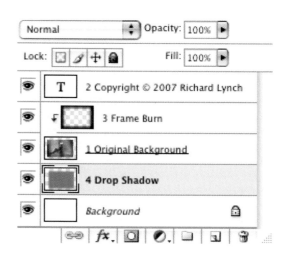

28. Make a Hue/Saturation adjustment layer by choosing Hue/Saturation from the New Adjustment Layer submenu on the Layers menu (Layer>New Adjustment Layer>Hue/Saturation). When the New Layer dialog appears, click the Use Previous Layer to Create Clipping Mask checkbox and change the name of the layer to 5 Shadow Color before clicking OK. The Hue/Saturation dialog will appear. Click the Colorize box and adjust the Hue, Saturation and Lightness sliders to adjust the color of the drop shadow to something pleasing. Moving the Hue slider (right or left) will change hues as if they are on a color wheel. Moving the Saturation slider to the right will increase saturation; moving it to the left will decrease saturation. Moving the Lightness slider to the right will lighten the shadow; moving the slider left will darken the shadow. Click OK to accept the changes.

📖 The use of Previous Layer to Create Clipping Mask checkbox has been named different things in almost every other versions of Photoshop. It is the only checkbox on the New Layer dialog, and it always does the same thing: it creates a clipping group from the layer you are creating. See the Types of Layers **Table 1.2** for more information.

FIG 1.12 Layers after step 28.

You should now have 6 layers: 1 Original Background, 2 Copyright Text, 3 Frame Burn, 4 Drop Shadow, 5 Shadow Color and 6 Background (see **Figure 1.12**).

If you really want to test out your understanding of layers thus far see if you can accomplish the following. Don't worry if you can't complete all the items in this list, some of this will be discussed in the coming chapter.

- Change the color position and face of the type in the copyright layer. Hints: double click the type layer in the layers palette to select all the type, use Hue/Saturation like you did in Step 28, or use the Options on the Options bar.
- Make a Group (or Set) from the six layers you created.
- Activate the 5 Shadow Color Adjustment layer, and merge down.

Summary

We looked at a lot of things in this chapter, from the basics of what a layer is, to how they are applied. You should have had the opportunity to explore the palettes and menus where layers are created and manipulated, and gained a more comprehensive visual conception of what layer functions look like as part of the palette. We've looked at the possibilities of adjusting how the layers palette displays, and have explored the initial possibilities of creating layers.

The core purpose of this chapter is introductory. Now that you have seen some of what layers can do, let's move on into learning how they help you manage your workflow and form the basis of your image editing process.

cabbage

Layer Management: Concepts of a Layer-Based Workflow

The greatest benefit to using layers is that you get tremendous flexibility in controlling image changes, and the ability to revisit, adjust and view changes at any time later in the correction process. You can also store the changes to see what you did, and create techniques by examining your process. The biggest drawback to layers – besides learning to harness t he tremendous number of options – is bulking image file size, and organizing an ever-lengthening layer stack. This chapter looks at how to use layers as a means of managing your approach to correcting images and keeping those changes organized by incorporating layers as the core of your workflow.

Talking about managing layers before talking about using them is really a chicken and egg scenario: it could be argued that it is more important to know what to do with them than how to manage them. However, my thought is simply this: start with good fundamental practice in using layers, and it will be more natural to use them in a way that is most beneficial to your images.

Managing layers starts with knowing how to create them – as we looked at briefly in the previous chapter – and continues with knowing how and when to combine them to save file size, and group and arrange them to keep them and your image corrections effective and organized. Making the effort to keep things organized may take a little more time at first, but, like all maintenance and organization, will help in the long haul to keep you on track, and becomes more natural as you do it consistently. For example, when you make a meal, you might follow a recipe. This can save you from goofing up dinner entirely. Along the way you might make some adjustments to taste depending on your level of confidence, or depart from the recipe entirely once you are more sure of what you are doing. The recipe acts like a fall-back or outline of a basic plan.

When you follow an organized plan for using layers, they end up being not only a means of correction and an organizational tool for those corrections, but a means of driving corrections, organizing the correction workflow and acting as a history of image correction. Effectively managing layers and layer content will help keep your corrections on track, will allow you the flexibility to step back and forward in corrections, and will keep your images from bulking up to ridiculous size unnecessarily. Just like a recipe, layers act as a plan for getting to where you want to go.

To look at layers as part of a total process, we'll begin with an outline of an approach to image editing and outline a basic tool set that you will use in conjunction with layers. Then we'll look at more theoretical applications of Layers for organization and image correction, and how layers factor into and direct the process of correction.

The Outline for Image Editing

For the sake of putting layers in the context of process, we'll look at a complete outline for processing images from beginning to end. Layers are crucial to every stage of correction. Our outline will look a bit beyond just the process of correction to be sure the process is considered from end-to-end: from monitor to print. Consider this outline as your plan for editing images and use it as a roadmap in making all your image corrections – especially if you do not have your own plan in place.

The steps to image editing are segmented into several distinct parts: setup, capture, evaluation, editing/correction and purposing/ output. *Setup* encompasses all necessary steps for preparing your equipment for capture, image editing and output. *Capture* is gathering your digital source images to use in editing and output. *Evaluation* is consideration of what you will be doing with the image and the steps you will be taking in correction. *Correction and editing* is manipulation of the source image captures according to your evaluations and in preparation for output. *Purposing and output* encompasses all manner of final use of images in display, in print to different media and processes (inkjet, offset, light process), or for a monitor (web pages, video). Though layers are only involved directly in the editing stage, the other stages all affect the choices you make in the correction and editing, so it is valuable to have a quick look at the entire process in more detail.

Setup

Setup is everything you need to do to prepare for image editing. Being sure your capture device, system and editing program are set up correctly and that you have considered the purpose or use of the image. This is important to ensure you will get the results you want.

- *Be sure your computer system is ready* for image editing with Photoshop. You will need to consider the requirements for running Photoshop, such as how much RAM your computer has and the speed of the processor. Check the requirements (find these on the packaging, or on the Adobe website). You will also want to have significant free disk space, and establish a backup routine (and have the appropriate media on hand). Concerns for your computer setup may extend to having a firewall in place, virus protection and image-editing input devices.

   You are not limited to using a mouse when editing images, and other devices may be more to your liking. Image-editing input device possibilities include trackballs (http://aps8.com/ trackball.html) and graphic pen/tablet combinations (http:// aps8.com/wacom.html). I rarely use a mouse for serious image editing.

- *Calibrate your monitor, and create a custom ICC profile*. The custom profile is usually made during the calibration process, and helps Photoshop compensate for color display. Calibration is an essential step in color management.

📖 Calibration devices such as the ColorVision Spyder 2 Pro (http://aps8.com/spyder.html) can simplify calibration, make it more accurate, help manage ICC profiles and make color management less of a chore.

- *Set up Photoshop*. This includes setting up color management preferences, preferences for scratch disks/memory usage, and testing output. Photoshop is a memory hog, and it is not unheard of to dedicate a drive to the sole purpose of being a Photoshop scratch disk. Giving Photoshop a lot of room to do what it does ensures your best chance of getting the results you intend consistently, and that your system functions optimally.
- *Have a system for archiving*. Be prepared to archive the original image files safely when you download them from the camera and before you begin work on them. This may require consideration of archiving media and equipment. Archiving is crucial to a safe workflow where you always work with a copy of an image to do all of your image editing. If any step in the editing goes awry, you will want to be able to return to the original image to start over. Working on copies will also give you the opportunity to repurpose the original in the future or take advantage of new and emerging technologies that might help you get more from the original image capture. DVD drives, CD-ROM, RAID arrays, tape backup, external drives and even online storage can all be considered in keeping your images safe.
- *Consider the final purpose of the image*: resolution, size, color, file type and purpose. This can affect your other choices in setup. You may work at different resolutions and in different color modes throughout the image-editing process for specific purposes, but knowing what you need from the outset of the project can help you work smarter, with less possibility of getting into situations where you compromise image integrity.
- *Be prepared to make the best use of your camera*. Know your camera settings and controls. Nothing will do more to help you get the best shot than knowing how to work your camera. This will include becoming familiar with your camara's unique settings. If you use accessories, knowing how they function is important as well. One of the most important camera accessories is the owner's manual. Be sure to put yours to good use, and read it several times from cover to cover – or at least those sections written in your own language! Remember to

bring all necessary equipment if you'll be shooting in the field: have ample memory on hand to take all the shots you want, and ample power (several sets of new or newly charged batteries).

📖 I have several 1 GB or 2 GB cards on hand whenever I shoot (see http://aps8.com/1gb.html, or http://aps8.com/2gb.html). In addition I carry a 80 GB Wolverine portable hard drive that reads 7 types of memory card and can be powered by battery (http://aps8.com/wolvarine.html). Between these, I can store about 12,000 shots without downloading to my computer.

• *Learn about scanner features and scanner software*. Software and features on scanners can often vary drastically between makes and models. Just like being familiar with your camera and settings, knowing what your scanner model can do and your options for scanning will help you get the most from the images that you scan. If using a scanner, again, make friends with your manual. Color calibration and profile building specifically for the scanner may also be appropriate steps to take at the point of setup.

Capture

With setup completed, you will want to take the utmost care in the actual capture of your images so that the result will be most useful and of the highest quality. Starting with the best source image leads to the opportunity to achieve the best result.

• *Take command of your camera to get the best shot*. This includes working with settings such as aperture and shutter speed, as well as controlling other qualities of capture such as depth-of-field and framing. Proper settings extend to use of other accessories such as flash, and also mechanics like holding the camera perfectly still as you depress the shutter, or moving evenly as you track the camera to follow motion or create special effects. Knowing the settings is only half the battle, practice using the modes and settings and creating interest in your captures will improve your photographic technique and enhance the improvements possible with Photoshop. There is nothing that can substitute for good source images.
• *Capture additional frames*. Don't be afraid to snap the shutter with your camera pointed at any subject that you might later use for retouching, compositional changes or enhancements. If you don't take a photo, you will not have the source to work with. For example, if shooting a group portrait you might take 3–5

shots of the group to be sure smiles are in place, eyes are open, poses are acceptable – you want to captured enough source images to make necessary enhancement and replacement easy. If shooting a high-contrast scene, you may want to make one exposure for the highlights and one for the shadows so you can merge the results later. Don't be too quick to delete potentially useful images just because they are not perfect in preview. You should have plenty of memory for more images (take a second look at your steps for preparation), and weed out the clunkers in Photoshop where you can give then a fair look.

• *Control scanner settings to get the best scans.* Settings for optimal scanning will often be achieved manually or via some manual intervention. In the case of scanning, resolution, color mode, white point and more, may be choices you will need to make to optimize results. Most scanners have auto modes, but the best scans are often made with scanners that allow manual adjustment during the process of scanning.

Evaluation

Actually looking at your images on screen and carefully evaluating them is what determines which steps you take in making corrections. You should take a moment to jot down some notes as to what you hope to accomplish with your changes. The result of the evaluation should be a short list of things you want to improve or change. A set plan has the additional benefit of keeping you on track and helping you make order out of the potential chaos of what tools and techniques to employ, and may also keep you from distracting and fruitless experimentation (Figure 2.1).

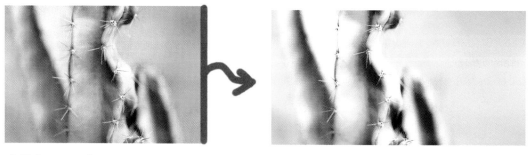

1. **Enhance color**
2. **Extend image to the right**
3. **Enhance contrast between blue/yellow**
4. **Sharpen needles**
5. **Soften color blotchiness and highlights**

FIG 2.1 Making notes on a rough print of your image may help your evaluation and keep goals in mind.

- *Consider tone and color*. This analysis can include determining qualities like the image type (high key, low key, high contrast), but more generally you will want to consider the dynamic range, how vivid the image is, the exposure, saturation and color balance/color cast.
- *Consider cropping and do a horizon check*. Cropping can be used to solve compositional problems as well as removing distractions or simply reshaping an image. A common problem in landscape photos is a tilted horizon, and this can often easily be fixed with a cropping adjustment.
- *Consider small scale enhancements and adjustments* to fix damage, eliminate dust or debris and possibly remove distractions.
- *Consider imaging heroics*. What I consider 'heroics' are corrections that go well outside the normal path of your workflow. Changing composition considerably (e.g., moving or adding a complex object to an image, compositing several images into something much different, and possibly some instances of HDR (High Dynamic Range) compositing), manually enhancing edge sharpness, recreating objects, etc., are all heroic efforts to make an image. These changes are usually very complex, require many steps in adjustment, a lot of skill and many layers. Experimentation also be considered heroics.
- *Consider image enhancements*. Once an image is refined through more obvious corrections, you may want to add softness, sharpening, saturation, other general qualitative adjustments to enhance the image, or add graphic elements, like framing. These enhancements may not be part of the original image.

Editing and Correction

At this stage of image editing, you will take specific steps to achieve the goals set during your evaluation. This is where you will actually employ layers as a core tool in organizing and executing the steps necessary to complete your corrections.

- *Make general color and tonal adjustments*. This means doing tonal and color adjustments that will not use selection or masking. Specifically you will rely on levels for most of this general correction. Other tools to consider are Hue/Saturation and Color Balance.
- *Make general damage corrections*, such as eliminating dust from scans, fixing cracks and holes in scanned images and reducing digital noise.

- *Make general compositional changes* including cropping, compositing and simple replacement or removal of objects.
- *Make heroic changes to the image.* This can include reshaping objects, broad compositional enhancement, experimentation or even collage.
- *Make targeted corrections* to the image using selection and masking. Usually you will want to exercise all general color and tone corrections before singling areas of the image for complicated masking correction.
- *Make enhancements to the image* for sharpness, softness, saturation, brightness and other generalized 'final touch' effects like framing, adding copyright, etc.
- *Save the layered Red, Green and Blue (RGB) version of the image* so you can return to the image for additional changes, repurposing, or to explore the techniques used. Be sure to give the file a new name when saving, so you do not save over the original.

Purposing and Output
Finalizing the image to target a specific output type. You may need to do this segment more than once if an image will be used on a website and in print.

- *Simplify the image* as appropriate for use in the medium you have selected. This step may include flattening the image or merging layers, altering the color mode, or removing extraneous image information (paths, channels, alphas, etc., don't worry if you don't know what all those things are). During the process of simplifying, be sure to retain all components that may be important to your output, like vectors for high-resolution offset printing.
- *Optimize the image* resolution and color for output/use. Make color, tonal and color space adjustments if necessary, and resize the image according to the target resolution. This step can include such changes as setting white and black points and making device-specific color changes.
- *Save the image in output file format.* Not all files are alike. Some services and output devices will require specific file types, and some file content will require file types that retain qualities you have created in the image (e.g., vector components). Make considerations for profile handling as part of your workflow and intended output, and be cognizant of whether or not you will embed a profile.

- *Package the image on proper media* for output use. Archive a copy of it along with the working version saved with layers so it can be reused if necessary.

This checklist may seem long, but each step will often not be very involved. Some steps you will do naturally, some take just a moment, and some are just reminders for maintaining a positive workflow. Practicing correction by following the steps in the list can ensure that you make all adjustments and corrections that you intend to do in achieving your goals for the image.

Photoshop's Essential Tools List

While it is still perhaps a little outside of the focus of the main focus of layers, a sort of master tool list can also be handy. This list is comprised of tools that you will want to be aware of and competent using in order to get the most out of your corrections with layers and Photoshop in general. When an electrician has to climb a telephone pole to fix a problem, he/she doesn't bring every tool. The practical, handy tools go in the belt, and up the pole they go, ready to handle any problem. The real trick is knowing what tools will handle any job so you can put those in your belt and to cut down to the essentials so you can focus on the task.

With a core set of tools you'll be able to focus on learning just those tools rather than trying to grasp the function, use and nuances of each and every tool on every menu. When you have less to remember, that leaves far less to get lost in by randomly exploring tools and functions. Exploration and experimentation can be left until you have more expertise, time or interest. With a lighter tool belt you'll have everything you need when you climb the pole, and you'll be sure to get the job done without coming down to waste time foraging around in the van for more tools.

The Mythical 'Read My Mind' and 'Do It For Me' Tools

In talking with people about Photoshop, one tool that they always seem to have thought they read about in a tutorial, or saw at a conference, or read about in a book is the Read My Mind tool or the Do It For Me tool, and sometimes even the Read My Mind and Do It For Me tool. One thing that users often seem to hope, and maybe never give up on, is that Photoshop will sometimes be able to do the thinking. It is terribly frustrating when you get an idea of how a result will look in your head and you use the buttons and functions you thought you should and then don't end up with the result you expected. If you are able to imagine how you want something to look, it means you have a good imagination and eventually Photoshop will work out well for you. However, the tools never do the thinking for you, and never know what you see in your mind's eye.

Really, you almost never want the computer to do it for you. The reality of using Photoshop is that automated tools for correction will usually make approximations. You are never hard wired to Photoshop, and the program itself isn't much of an artist – regardless of what you pay for it or what version you own. You may think you can depend on it to make images better, but really all it does is enable *you* to make images better. It never sees the images it works on, it just performs calculations that were developed by the designers, and sometimes what those tools will do to a particular image may be difficult to predict – even once you have a lot of experience. Most of the unpredictable tools are exactly the ones we steer away from in the tool list supplied here. To dispel the rumors: there are no tools that think for you. No matter how elegantly they work, tools will not not 'read your mind' or 'do it for you' and certainly none will do both – whatever the task. That is as it should be (**Figure 2.2**).

FIG 2.2 The only tools that attempt to automate corrections are those that you probably shouldn't use.

The following list is categorized into External Applications, Commands, Functions, Freehand Tools and Filters. Each is explained more fully by section. You can use other tools or additional applications as you explore Photoshop, consult tutorials, or develop your own workflow, but this list will be comprehensive in reflecting what you absolutely need.

External Applications
External applications are the additional software items that you add to your system to enhance processing. There are a plethora of add-ons you can install for Photoshop, some free and some for a cost, that claim to add on to what Photoshop already does. These may come in the form of plug-ins, actions, scripts, custom shapes and brushes, etc. Some of these additions may be valuable additions

(like those included with this book). Some will be good for users who are already very familiar with the tools in Photoshop, know what they want to accomplish with the program, and are looking for a specific enhancement. Generally, the wealth of available add-ons and plug-ins may seem tempting, but many plug-in and add-ons just duplicate or repackage functionality already in Photoshop, sucking in users on claims that they are the 'Do It for Me' tool.

There are really very few external software applications that you *need* to work with Photoshop. Those that you do need are mostly a given. You will need a computer that has operating system software capable of running Photoshop. You will also sometimes need drivers that are provided by the vendor of the additional equipment you purchase (for your printer, camera, backup systems/drives) or other manufacturer software to run hardware and devices. A few things you will need that are less obvious are software utilities to calibrate your monitor, and build an ICC profile. Some things you may *want*, like additional editing software, image management, etc. are not necessary, and they shouldn't be allowed to cloud the picture.

The best overall plan in managing peripheral applications is similar to the limiting your tool list: keep it simple to keep complexity and potential variables to a minimum. More software means more to learn, so put all the non-essential software aside. If you have trouble with your computer system, the first place to start troubleshooting is by eliminating extra software and peripherals – or simply not adding them as variables in the first place.

Adobe Gamma (PC) Display Calibrator Assistant (Mac) or another monitor calibration system	Adobe Gamma can be found on PC systems in the Control Panel; Display Calibrator Assistant can be found on Mac systems in the Displays System Preferences by clicking the Color and then Calibrate buttons. Both of these utilities do easy monitor calibration and ICC profile generation in one process.
	Alternatives to these free options already included with your existing software are calibration systems, like ColorVision Spyder, or other hardware calibration device for your monitor (see http://aps8.com/spyder.html). These devices are more reliable than software-only solutions.

	Monitor calibration and creating profiles can help you stabilize your workflow and get better color matching between your monitor and output. If you have problems with output color, the solution will likely start with good monitor calibration.
Device Software	Scanner, digital camera, printer, card reader, backup/DVD/CD/ RAID drivers and software that enables you to access additional hardware that you will be connecting to your system to access or store images. See user manuals and installation instruction materials for each device you add to the system for more information.
Photoshop Help	Help>Photoshop Help, or press F1. This can be a reliable resource for basic information on using Photoshop features and functions and is a great place to begin exploration of any Photoshop tool, and the price is right (free). Depending on your choices during the installation of Photoshop, this feature may require additional installation.

Commands

Commands are simple functions – essentially single step – used to achieve a result. I say 'essentially' because you may have to address a dialog to get the result accomplished. For example, if you open an image, you will need to use the Open command. In the Open dialog, you will have to browse to find the image you want to open.

Most commands will be found on the program menus, and can be invoked by shortcuts.

New	File>New, or press Command+N / Crtl+N [Mac/PC]. Opens a New image. In the New dialog, set the color, size and resolution to use for a new blank image. Creates a new image. You might use New to create a canvas where you would add other images to make a composite or collage.
Open	File>Open, or press Command+O / Crtl+O. Opens an existing image. You will use this command often to open images you have downloaded from your camera.
Save As	File>Save As, or press Command+Shift+S / Ctrl+Shift+S. Opens the Save As dialog. Save your image with a new name, file type or location. It is suggested you use Save As most or even all of the time to avoid file conflicts and potential for over-writing original files.
Save For Web	File>Save For Web, or press Command+Shift+Option+S / Ctrl+Shift+Alt+S. Save images for the Web using JPEG or GIF file types, limited color and

	transparency. Using Save for Web results in a smaller file than just saving as JPEG even with the same compression ratio. There are additional preview benefits as well.
Undo	Edit>Undo, or press Command+Z / Ctrl+Z. Reverses the previous action you took in editing an image. This is useful for all sorts of things, but mostly stepping back in the process when you don't like what a change achieved. To step back multiple steps, look to the History palette (Window>History).
Copy	Edit>Copy, or press Command+C / Ctrl+C. With a selection active in your image, you can copy the selected image area to the clipboard. Think of this like you might use copy/paste to move a URL to a browser, or edit text in an email. Copy can be used to duplicate custom selected image areas, or move image content to a new image.
Paste	Edit>Paste, or press Command+V / Ctrl+V. Paste the content of the clipboard that was stored using the Copy command into the current image. Copy and Paste are almost always used together to duplicate selected image areas to the same image or other images.
New Layer	Layer>New>Layer, or Command+Shift+N / Ctrl+Shift+N. New layers can also be created with the Create a New Layer button at the bottom of the Layers palette and the New Layer command on the Layers palette menu. This will create a new layer with no content.
Duplicate Layer	Layer>Duplicate Layer, or duplicate a layer in the Layers palette by dragging an existing layer to the Create a New Layer button at the bottom of the Layers palette. The Duplicate Layer command is also available on the Layers palette menu. This will create a new layer that is exactly like the one being duplicated but with the word 'Copy' appended to the layer name.
Create Adjustment Layer	Layer>New Adjustment Layer > and choose a selection from the New Adjustment Layer submenu. You can also create these with the Create New Fill or Adjustment Layer button at the bottom of the Layers palette. These help you keep adjustments distinct from layer content.
Merge Layers	Layers>Merge Layers (Command+E / Ctrl+E), Layers>Merge Visible (Shift+ Command+E / Shift+Ctrl+E). Merge layers in one of several ways to cut down on the number of layers in your image and be sure the file isn't unnecessarily large. Merging content should only be done where you don't expect to have to reverse the changes later; you can use Undo immediately following a merge, but you can't undo the changes in a later editing session (after saving and re-opening the image).
Flatten	Layers>Flatten Image (no shortcut). Very much like Merge, but this function specifically combines all layers and image content and flattens the image into a Background layer only.

Image Size	Image>Resize>Image Size, or press Command+Option+I / Ctrl+Alt+I. Allows the user to change the size and resolution of an open image. Usually this will be a step that you will take in preparing an image for output to a printer. Upsampling an image (making it bigger) by more than 10% or 20% is not recommended as you cannot re-create detail that you did not originally capture. Downsampling is less problematic. Use Bicubic resampling in most cases to get the best resizing result, and Constrain Proportions so the image does not distort horizontally or vertically.
Transform	Edit>Transform, or press Command+T / Ctrl+T allows you to reshape an object you have isolated with selection or by Copy/Paste so that it is in its own layer. This can come in handy when you have to patch an image area that is missing or damaged, or when you want to remove objects/people from a scene.
Inverse	Select>Inverse, or press Shift+Command+I / Shift+Ctrl+I. This will take a selection you have made and invert it; instead of the area inside the selection being selected, the selected area will change so that everything outside the original selection is selected. This is great for using a flatly colored background to make a selection of an object or in other instances where it is easier to make a selection outside an object than of the object itself.
Fill	Edit>Fill, or press Shift+F5. Will fill a whole layer in your image with a single color (foreground, background, black, gray or white). This is useful for color and tone adjustments, converting to grayscale, etc., but also for creating masks from selections.
Layer Opacity	Opacity slider on Layers palette (No shortcut). Adjust transparency/visibility of individual layers in an image to blend and combine layer content and effects. A variety of uses in blending layer content, and color and tone adjustments. Use up and down arrow keys for fine adjustments.
Layer Mode	The mode drop list on the Layers palette. In keeping with the common theme that everything isn't a necessary tool, of the 23 layer modes, only about 6 have every-day uses. These modes apply image content selectively. Normal mode is the default, multiply is used for darkening or creating shadows, screen is used for lightening, overlay has several enhancement properties for working with contrast, color applies layer color only, and luminosity applies tone sans color.

Functions

Functions are more complex than simple commands that have a definitive, one-step goal. Using functions you will have to determine how to apply settings achieve results, usually using multiple controls and function features to determine the final outcome. Adjustment of more than one control is usually necessary, and nothing can be achieved using the defaults.

Levels	Layer>New Adjustment Layer>Levels. Command+L / Ctrl+L opens a Levels dialog, but creates no adjustment layer. View image histograms as part of the Levels dialog box display. Use simple sliders to adjust tonal dynamic range and balance image color. Helps image contrast and color.
Color Balance	Layer>New Adjustment Layer>Color Balance. Command+B / Ctrl+B opens a Color Balance dialog, but creates no adjustment layer. Adjust color by balancing the influence of color opposites for highlights, midtones and shadows. Helps remove color casts and stubborn flatness in some images.
Hue/ Saturation Layer	Layer>New Adjustment Layer>Hue Saturation. Command+U / Ctrl+U opens a Hue/Saturation dialog, but does not create a Hue/Saturation adjustment layer. Adjust color by using slider controls to alter hue, increase/ decrease saturation, and affect general lightness and darkness. Most effective when used to enhance color saturation.
Layer Mask	Layer>Layer Mask>Reveal All (no shortcut). Customize visible image areas without permanently erasing content. Very useful for blending in pasted image areas, molding/fitting parts of a collage or composite. Often used in conjunction with Selection (Polygon Lasso, Magic Wand), Fill and/or the Paint Brush tool.
Blending Options	Layer>Layer Style>Blending Option, or double-click a content layer. Either action will open the Layer Style screen. From this screen you can control many options, like General Blending (Mode and Opacity), Advanced Blending (Fill Opacity, Channel Targeting), Blend If (conditional blending based on layer content) and Layer Styles (effects/styles assigned to the layer). This is a very powerful command center for controlling layers and how they interact. Can be used for a wide variety of content blending and effects.

Freehand Tools

The Toolbar has many freehand tools on it that you will use infrequently or not at all. By freehand, I mean that the application is controlled by your input device and the position of the cursor.

For all of these tools, be aware that options on the Options bar will affect the way the tools are applied. For basics about options for each of these tools, look them up by searching Help for '[tool name] options'.

Crop Tool	Press C on the keyboard. Used to change image size by permanently removing (cropping out) image edges. Use this to correct framing for your image, flatten horizons, remove objects at the edge of the image that shouldn't be in the frame, and to adjust perspective (make images 4 × 6 for example).
Polygonal Lasso Tool	Press L on the keyboard, and Shift+L to scroll the lasso tools. Create Selections of regular and irregularly shaped image objects by clicking at intervals around an object edge. Use short segments to select curved edges. Easier to control than the standard Lasso tool.
Magic Wand Tool	Press W on the keyboard. Create selections of areas of same/similar color quickly by clicking in the area. Great for making selections of large, similar colored areas (sky) or selecting objects with a single color background (select the background and Invert the selection).
Move Tool	Press V on the keyboard. Use to reposition objects on layers within your images, such as you might have when pasting replacement areas, or when working with collages or composite parts.
Clone Stamp Tool	Press S on the keyboard. Make brush-style corrections by sampling image areas to clone to another part of the image. Great for straight duplication of one image area to another. Excellent for all manner of spot correction such as dust or other simple debris.
Healing Brush Tool	Press J on the keyboard. Make brush-style corrections by sampling image areas to clone to another part of the image. Healing is similar to Clone Stamp, but this tool makes 'smart' corrections to your images by comparing the sampled area to the target and attempting to blend the correction with the surroundings. Perfect for making isolated corrections, like removing a stray eyelash from a cheek.
Paint Brush Tool	Press B on the keyboard, and Shift+B to scroll the brush tools. Used for freehand painting. Good for colorizing, adding manual shadows and highlights, as well as adding dodge and burn effects. An excellent tool for use with layer masks to create custom masking effects.
Eyedropper Tool	Press I on the keyboard. Sample to check color and tone values in specific image areas, or to set the foreground/background colors that can be used with Fill or Paint Brush. Also used in conjunction with the Info palette to display sampled color information.
Foreground/ Background Swatches	No shortcuts to open the Color Picker. Press D for default colors and X to exchange foreground and background. These color swatches store colors selected from the Color Picker or sampled from the screen using the Eyedropper Tool. To change the Foreground Color, use the Eyedropper tool and click anywhere on your image. To change the Background Color, press Option / Alt and click on your image.

Filters

Filters are an area of the program menus that get explored extensively by newer users, who often flock there to try out special effects and put some pizzazz into their images. The foray into filters is usually one that is hit or miss, and while you can spend innumerable hours applying different filters and settings, in reality, you get less pizzazz from filters than you get from shooting better images.

Filters listed here are few, because it is often difficult to predict exactly how some filters will behave and what benefit you will get from the result of applying it. These filters are the practical ones that you will use for image correction, fix damage and create simple effects. They are not 'wow' filters that will create instantly interesting effects. Before you do anything to make fantastic effects you want to have complete control of your image. These filters provide you with a means of control.

Add Noise filter	Filter>Noise>Add Noise. Adds digital noise to an image. Useful for roughening up tones that are unnaturally smooth, such as areas painted with a Fill or Paint Brush Tool. Sometimes used in conjunction with Gaussian Blur.
Gaussian Blur filter	Filter>Blur>Gaussian Blur. Blends adjacent pixels to create a blurring effect. Useful for smoothing out tones that are unnaturally rough, over-sharpened, or for creating focus effects (e.g., soft focus, depth-of-field).
Unsharp Masking	Filter>Sharpen>Unsharp Mask. Allows users to adjust both local and fine contrast in the image to affect the appearance of sharpness, improve edge definition and enhance contrast in color and tone.

Looking over these lists of tools and depending on how you count, there are just about 30 tools to keep in mind for editing your images. That may sound like a lot, but it is a fraction of the total number of tools yet it is a complete tool belt that will help you get through any image-editing situation. Be sure to become familiar with these if you are not already.

The Logic of Layers

Now that we have outlined a basic workflow and a basic toolbox, it is time to start wrapping the process of working with images around layers. As mentioned in Chapter 1, layers are a vehicle for instituting non-destructive change in images. In other words,

Exploring New Tools

One of the reasons users find Photoshop daunting is that they try to learn too much – or even all of it – at once. A better approach for most people will be to learn a tool at a time. If there are tools in the list here with which you are not familiar, note them, and give yourself the opportunity to explore them one a day, for half an hour. Read about the tools in Photoshop's Help (in Photoshop, press Command+/ or Ctrl+/), then open an image and explore the tool by applying it. Don't look so much for expert results as the opportunity to learn how the tool behaves. That experience will go a long way toward incorporating it into your workflow. Fifteen or twenty minutes a day for a month would cover this entire list, but chances are you are familiar with many of them already if you are reading this book.

you can keep the original image information intact while making virtual changes over it. Working with layers as a primary tool allows you to reverse any change. Used correctly, layers are a far more powerful tool than Undo or Histories. With Layers it is possible not just to undo or reverse sequential changes, but you can adjust the editing sequence and intensity of applied changes as you go by re-ordering layers, adjusting opacity and toggling visibility. The power of layers is greater if you approach them with a solid understanding of when to use them, and how to organize them with naming, grouping, merging, duplication, clipping and linking.

When to Create a New Layer

Some layers will force themselves on you. For example, when you use the paste command, Photoshop will create a new layer. This is usually as it should be. Ideally you will want to create a new layer for every change that you intend to make in an image. That is, if you are going to make a general color adjustment, make a new layer; if you are going to sharpen, make a new layer; if you are going to make a spot change to any image area, make a new layer; if you are making dust corrections to a scan, make a new layer (not one for each speck, but one for all of them).

The goal of layer creation is to keep each logical step in the process separated so you can return to the image in the future, see what you did, and perhaps reverse or re-create these changes and the process in another image. That is, layers can be used to archive your workflow in steps that you took to achieve the result, they can help you save time and effort if you want to make a change in the developed image without having to redo all the corrections, and they can provide a means of learning from your own efforts by reviewing your process – now or years from now.

Naming Layers

A very important means of keeping layers under control is being consistent with layer naming. When new layers are created, they are created with a generic name (e.g., Layer+number, or they may be named for the type of adjustment layer). Several practices can help you make better use of layer names: naming the layer by purpose, entering parameters used and numbering the order of creation.

Naming the layer by purpose is simply typing in a name that has to do with what you used the layer to accomplish.

For example, a layer used for dust removal would be named 'Dust Removal'; a layer used to isolate an object would be named for the object. When using functions like Gaussian Blur on a layer to soften an area, you may want to note the settings used in the layer name. Finally, you might also consider numbering the layers. Though you will often work from the bottom of the stack upward in order, that will not always be the case. See Figure 2.3 for a simple example of layer naming according to suggested practice.

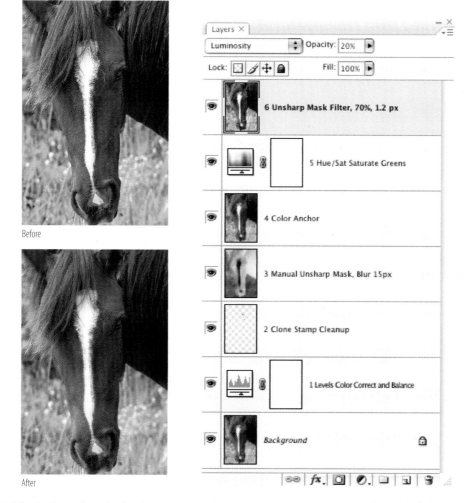

Before

After

FIG 2.3 Following the number order of the layers, you can track what was done to this image to achieve the result by looking at the layer names. All of these techniques are things we will touch on in later chapters.

This type of simple naming scheme has potential to be very helpful in that it can help you know what a layer is for without having to examine the content (e.g., shutting off other layers, increasing the size of the thumbnails, zooming in). Naming layers as you go to hint at what they are will help keep them organized and let them act as an outline or running history for your editing procedures. In that way, investing some time up front helps save lots of time later on in reproducing or duplicating results without extensive trial and error.

📖 While including some information in the layer name makes sense, including too much information can make the layer names bulky and difficult to read.

There are several ways to edit layer names. You can often change them when creating the layer, but you can also edit the names after the layers are created. It is time to take a look at working with layer names. The following exercise has no other goal than to explore the various opportunities for naming, there will ultimately be no change in the visual appearance of the image on screen.

📖 Try It Now

1. Open an image, and flatten it if it is not flattened already (choose Flatten from the Layer menu).
2. Choose Duplicate Layer from the Layers menu. This will open the Duplicate Layer dialog with the As field pre-named Background Copy (see Figure 2.4).

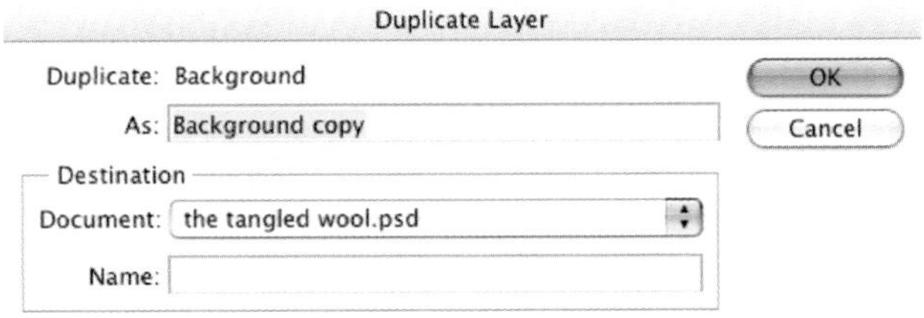

FIG 2.4 Duplicating a layer with the Duplicate Layer command creates an exact replica of the layer being duplicated but adds the word 'copy' to the name.

3. Change the As field by typing over the current default name. Change the name to 1 Duplicate Background, and click OK. This will close the dialog, and create a duplicate of the Background layer with the new name in the layers palette.

4. Hold down the Option / Alt key and then in the Layers palette, click-and-drag the 1 Duplicate Background layer to the Create a New Layer button at the bottom of the palette. This will open the Duplicate Layer dialog and allow you to rename the new layer. Name this layer 2 Duplicate of the Duplicate, and click OK. Clicking OK will close the dialog and create a new layer at the top of the stack identical to the other two, but in name.

📖 Had you not held down the Option / Alt key when dragging in the previous step, the result would have been to create the layer without opening the Duplicate Layer dialog.

5. Open the Layers palette menu (find the menu button at the upper right of the palette) and choose Layer Properties. The Layer Properties dialog will appear. Change the name of the layer to 2 Duplicate Background II. Click OK to accept the changes and close the dialog. Note the name will change for the current layer in the Layers palette.
6. Double-click the Background layer in the layers palette. This will open the New Layer dialog with the Name Layer 0. Click OK to accept the changes. You could have changed the name there, but you will change your mind shortly.
7. Double-click directly on the name Layer 0 in the Layers palette. The name of the layer will highlight in the palette (see Figure 2.5). You can type in a name change at this point. Call it Original Background, and then press Enter or Return on your keyboard to accept the changes.

📖 There are alternatives for getting to the Layer Properties. Option / Alt and double-clicking on a layer will open the Layer Properties. You can also open a menu for the layer: on Mac, hold down the Control key and click on a layer (not a Background); on a PC, right-click on a layer. Note that if you click on the layer or thumbnail, you will get different menus.

Any of these methods of naming your layers may come in handy at various points in the process of editing. You will develop favorites with experience. But the bigger point is to use layer naming opportunities to note what step(s) a layer contains at a glance.

Leave this image open, we'll use it in a moment for another quick exercise with layer grouping.

FIG 2.5 Directly changing layer names on the palette is possible as well by simply double-clicking directly on the name.

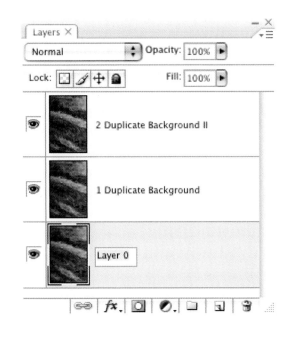

Grouping Layers

When you begin to work with layers extensively, things will start to get unwieldy. It may sound funny to those who currently don't use layers a lot, but you can easily end up with hundreds of layers in an image. For some of the advertising photography work I have done, which requires intense correction of models (changing face, body shape and contour, along with color correction, pore reduction, lens correction and the like), it often requires several submissions of an image, with revisions. I make a habit of saving every step in the hours of intense correction, so it is unnecessary to start over again when the revisions come back. Trying to repeat everything from scratch is not a very pleasant thought. The working version of images could end up with hundreds of layers and often several images in various editing stages that would be used for different parts of a composite. More recently I was designing a web interface for a web application, and the demo image had over 2000 layers. They almost become addictive.

One thing that happens when you get a lot of layers in an image is that they get confusing just to look at. Equally problematic is scrolling to the layers you need as you can't see them all on the screen at one time once you get over 25 or so – depending on the size and resolution of your screen and the Layer palette settings for the thumbnail size. To keep a bulking layer stack more manageable, you can store layers in layer groups. Groups work like folders in a file structure, they allow you to expand and collapse view of the content so you can choose to see what layers are in a group, or hide them (see Figure 2.6).

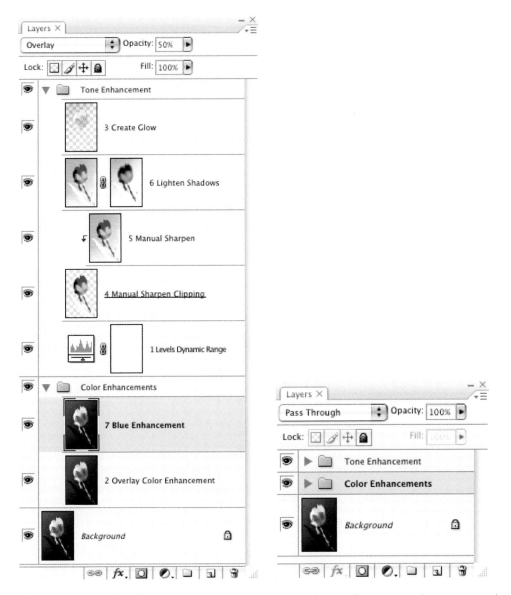

FIG 2.6   The toggle to the left of the folder allows you to expand view of the layers in the group. These two screen shots represent exactly the same image.

📖 Layer Groups were known as layer Sets in Photoshop 7. They are essentially identical features.

You can both create a layer group from existing layers, or create a group and add the layers as you go. At any time you can show/hide the content of the groups, duplicate and move them like any other layer (even between images), and they can be nested up to 5 deep. A little practice with them will get you familiar with how they work. Again, the goal of this exercise is just to experience groups, not to change the image in any way. Do this exercise continuing from the point where we left off in the previous exercise (Figure 2.7):

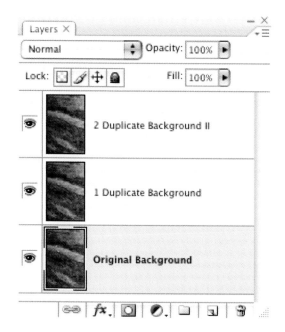

FIG 2.7 The layers palette from the previous exercise should look like this.

📖 Try It Now

1. Highlight the two upper layers (2 Duplicate Background II and 1 Duplicate Background). To highlight one layer at a time on PC hold down the Ctrl key and click the layers in the layers palette; on Mac hold down the Command key and click the layers in the layers palette. You can also highlight multiple consecutive layers

at once by clicking the upper layer to highlight it, and then Shift-clicking the lower (or vice-versa).

📖 Highlighting layers one-at-a-time is useful for selecting layers that are not consecutive.

2. Choose New Group From Layers from the layers palette menu. This will open the New Group from Layers dialog that will allow you to rename the group. Accept the default group name (Group 1) by clicking OK.
3. Click-and-drag the Group 1 group to the Create a New Group button at the bottom of the layers palette. When you release, this will immediately create a new group containing the old group. If you toggle the view for the old group (Group 1), you will see the originally grouped layers inside Group 1, inside Group 2 (see Figure 2.8).

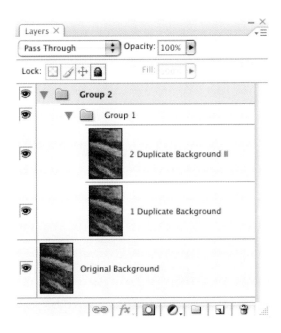

FIG 2.8 Photoshop creates a group from the contents dragged to the Create a New Group button.

4. Now drag Group 1 to the Create a New Layer button. This will duplicate Group 1 as Group 1 Copy, and it will remain inside Group 2 (see Figure 2.9).

FIG 2.9 Using Create a New Layer with layer groups simply duplicates the grouping just as it would duplicate a layer.

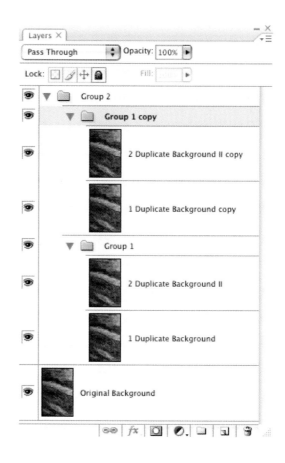

5. Click-and-drag Group 1 Copy over Group 1. As you drag the cursor, note when Group 1 highlights (see Figure 2.10) and release the mouse button. This will move Group 1 Copy inside Group 1.

Layers in any group remain fully editable. The advantage is that the groups can be collapsed so there is less to search through, and groups can be organized so you can quickly find what you need. If you find all this naming by 'Group' a little confusing, please see the previous exercise, and exercise your right to rename the groups as you please. Perhaps this illustrates the benefit of naming layers as you go as well.

Again, leave this image open and available for use with the next exercise.

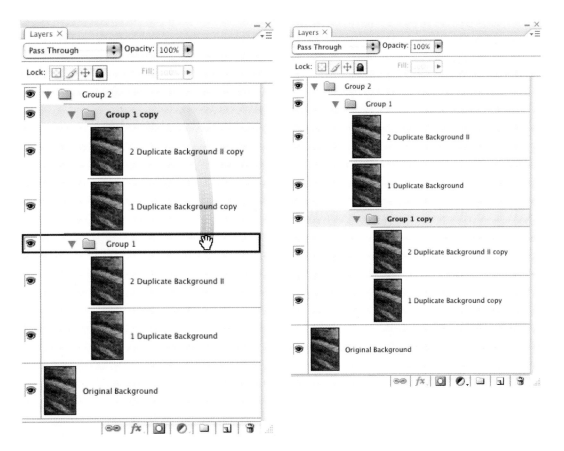

FIG 2.10 Groups can be moved like layers as well and inserted into other groups.

📖 Be aware that the order of how you create and stack layers sometimes matters to the result. Moving layers around in the stack willy-nilly just to accomplish a neat grouping may have an effect on the image result. Always view the image on screen while moving layers to be sure the layer movement doesn't affect the image result!

Merging Layers

There are reasons to create layers, and there are reasons to delete and combine them. Combining layers in Photoshop is referred to as merging. Merging combines the content of two or more layers into a single layer. This saves on file size and simplifies the organization of the layers.

Smart Objects

New to Photoshop CS2, Smart Objects are similar to Groups in function but the content is handled in quite a different way. You can merge layers into a Smart Object similar to the way you create a layer group (see the Convert to Smart Object command on the layers palette menu), and the resulting Smart Object acts like a merged layer. The kicker is, the contents in the layer are not actually merged: it is stored in a separate PSB image. You can still access the content and make changes. To edit the content, you double-click the Smart Object layer and the content of the object will open as another image. You can then save the object as a PSB (Photoshop Object) and use the objects in other images.

Smart Objects can be really handy if there is some type of layer grouping that you use in different images. For example, say in your exploration of layers you hit on a combination of adjustment layers that seems to you to correct every image you took in a photo session. You could create a smart object from the layers, save it, and then incorporate it into all of the other images from the session. Other more probable uses are developing templates for snapshots. For example, say you were elected to shoot your son or daughter's team pictures. You might make a frame like a baseball, softball, or soccer sports card, and then import it to the individual team player shots like a template.

To create a Smart Object, highlight the layers you want to group (on Windows hold down the Ctrl key and click the layers in the layers palette; on Mac hold down the Command key and click the layers in the layers palette), then choose Group Into New Smart Object from the layers palette menu.

Layers can be merged from various groupings: linked layers, grouped layers, visible layers, active (highlighted) groupings and simple pairs can all be merged. Usually you will want to merge layers that do the same thing but somehow end up separate, or you will want to merge layers which you otherwise really don't have a good reason to keep separate. Lets use the image from the last example starting from where we left off.

📖 Try It Now

1. With the Group 1 Copy layer active, choose Merge Group from the Layers menu. This is the same as pressing Command+E / Ctrl+E. The content of the group will be merged into a single layer named Group 1 Copy.

   📖 By active I mean to click on the layer so that it is highlighted in the layers palette. An active layer is the 'live' layer in your image, or the layer you are currently working on. Often problems that occur in applying changes happen because the wrong layer is active. Your first place to check when a change doesn't behave as you expect should be to look at which layer you have active and be sure it is the layer you really want to work on.

2. Click on the 1 Duplicate Background layer in the layers palette to make it the active layer, then choose Merge Down from the Layers menu. You will notice that the menu item you are choosing is in exactly the same place as Merge Group was in step 1. The merge commands are named with context sensitivity, and the names will change according to the actions that are available. Note that the resulting layer from the merge is Group 1 Copy, as per the lower layer in the merge.

3. Undo the changes from the last step by pressing Command+Z / Ctrl+Z (you can also step back in the History or choose Undo from the Edit menu). This will restore the 1 Duplicate Background layer.

4. With the 1 Duplicate Background layer active, hold down the Shift key and click the Group 1 Copy layer. Both the 1 Duplicate Background and the Group 1 Copy layer should appear highlighted (see Figure 2.11).

5. Again, choose Merge Layers from the layers menu as in step 2. Note that the resulting layer is named 1 Duplicate Background, as per the upper layer in the merge. If you compare steps 2

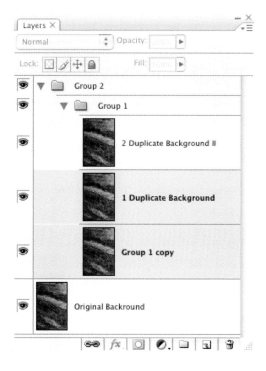

FIG 2.11 Highlighted layers (in blue) are both currently active.

and 5, the dominant name changes depending on how you merge layers.

6. Choose Flatten Image from the Layers menu. This is the ultimate merge. The entire contents of the image will be merged as a Background layer (whether or not one existed in the image previously).

📖 While it is all well and good to merge these layers and groups to see how they react, it is important to remember that you are performing permanent adjustments that will prevent you from further editing of individual layers that are merged.

7. Choose the Type tool, set a color and font (size and style) and click on the image to make a new type layer. Make the font large and bold – a little over-sized as it will come in handy later (the next exercise). Type in your copyright (e.g., Copyright © 2007 Richard Lynch). For an 'appropriate color' use a light color on a dark image or a dark color on a light image.

8. Press Command+E / Ctrl+E.

9. Choose the Move tool (press V) and move the copyright into position.

Wait…can't do that? How about just deleting the copyright. But you can't do that either. Perhaps that drives home the idea. You had superfluous layers in the image before – just duplicates of what was there. You could create more and merge and it didn't make a difference, and actually it was better that you ended up removing them. However, when you have your copyright, you'll want to be able to move it around and maybe shut off the view for it or remove it for some purposes. If you merge it with another layer, the content becomes permanently affixed. You want to keep all distinct changes separate so you have the opportunity to move or delete them when necessary.

Just so you know you aren't too far up a creek without a paddle:

10. Press Command+Z / Ctrl+Z
11. Move the copyright where it belongs using the move tool (press the V key)

Undo (step 10) to get back to two layers (background and type layers) so you can edit the image the way you want without having to start all over.

Navigating Layers

There are ways to move layers in the layers palette and navigate in the layers palette using just keystrokes. Some of the more common ones you might use are the following:

Purpose	Mac Shortcut	Windows Shortcut
Move an active layer up in the layer stack	Command+]	Ctrl+]
Move an active layer down in the layer stack	Command+[	Ctrl+[
Move an active layer to the top of the layer stack (or layer group)	Command+Shift+]	Ctrl+Shift+]
Move an active layer to the bottom of the layer stack(or layer group)	Command+Shift+[	Ctrl+Shift+[
Select the next layer up in the layer stack	Option+]	Alt+]
Select the next layer down in the layer stack	Option+[	Alt+[
Select the next layer up in the layer stack (keeping the current layer(s) selected)	Option+Shift+]	Alt+Shift+]
Select the next layer down in the layer stack (keeping the current layer(s) selected)	Option+Shift+[	Alt+Shift+[
Select the top layer in the layer stack	Option+.	Alt+.
Select the bottom layer in the layer stack	Option+,	Alt+,

Clipping Layers

Probably one of my favorite layer types (and not everyone will share this preference) is the clipping layer. It is really just an easy way to target changes so they affect the content of one particular layer. That is, say you have an object that you have separated into a layer above the Background. You would like to make a change to the object, but not the Background. While there are several potential solutions, clipping layers offer the opportunity to target an adjustment only to that layer.

The implications are slightly more broad reaching than simply being an alternative to masking. You can use clipping layers as masks, and again, as organizational tools for your corrections. The best way to see them work is through example, so let's see what they do in a simple exercise. Continue with the same image you were using in the previous exercise.

📖 Try It Now

1. Duplicate the Background layer in the previous exercise, and name it 2 Inverted Background.
2. Press Command+Shift+] / Ctrl+Shift+] to move the 2 Inverted Background layer to the top of the stack (Command+] / Ctrl+] would work just as well in this case, but I chose the other command as it is specifically designated to move the layer to the top of the stack).
3. Press Command+Option+G / Alt+Ctrl+G to create a clipping group from the Copyright type layer and the 2 Inverted Background layer.

   📖 Earlier versions of Photoshop (and Elements) use the simpler Command+G / Ctrl+G for creating a clipping group, but that shortcut is assigned to Groups as of Photoshop CS3.

4. Press Command+I / Ctrl+I to invert the content of the layer. The copyright should appear as reversed/negative against the background. Your layers should look like Figure 2.12.
5. Choose the Move tool and be sure the preference for Auto-select is unchecked. The pull down menu next to auto select should be set to Layer. Click on the Copyright layer to make it active and move the text around while watching the appearance of the image. The type layer acts like a canvas for the inverted layer content.

FIG 2.12 After step 4, there should be three layers as pictured here.

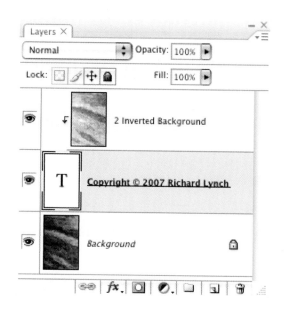

You can go much further with this by stacking multiple corrections in the clipping group. Each will act on the content of the bottom layer in the group in order of the stack. Hold on to that image one more time to continue into the next exercise…

Linked Layers

One final potential organizational tool is layer linking. It is really somewhat subservient to other types of layer organization (like groups). Linking allows you to make layers behave as a unit, whether consecutive or not (unlike Groups). This can be handy for moving layers both up and down in the layer stack and in unison on the layer plain.

📖 Try It Now

1. With the Copyright type layer still active, hold the Shift key and click the 2 Inverted Background layer in the layers palette. This will highlight both layers.
2. Click the Link Layers button (looks like a chain) at the bottom left of the layers palette. A linking icon will appear to the right of both layers indicating that they are linked.
3. Click on the Copyright type layer so that it is the only one active.
4. Choose the Move tool and move the type layer around while watching the appearance of the image. You should notice that, unlike the previous result, the type will not change color as it

moves. That is because the layer it is linked to is moving with it. All layers in a linked grouping will move at the same time.

5. Choose Select Linked Layers from the Layers palette menu. This will select all layers linked to the currently active layer (in this case, just the one above, but as many as you would otherwise want to link). This offers an option for quickly selecting a stack of linked layers – handy if you need to adjust their position in the layer stack.

6. Close the image without saving. Closing the image without saving will stop you from saving over your original.

Summary

While we have done nothing glamorous here as far as exercises for image editing, we have begun to explore some of the more serious basic functionality of layer creation and organization. With what you have learned here you should begin to see some possibilities for organizing your layers in three types of groups (Groups, Clipping Groups and Linking), and should begin to see the flexibility of adjusting content in the layer stack. Coupled with layer naming, you have all the tools you need to keep your layers in order and sensible as a record of your corrections. We will look at examples throughout the book that reinforce these basic exercises in real-world editing situations and applications, starting with the very next chapter.

CHAPTER 3

Ham

Object and Image Area Isolation in Layers

One of the fundamental values of working in layers is the ability to isolate image areas for change. This gives you the freedom to correct image areas independently, and revisit those changes as part of image development and workflow. Once you begin to use layers to isolate changes, you can make adjustments, and then fine-tune adjustments in ways that are impossible using selection alone.

Layers allow you to isolate changes in many different ways. In fact, the bulk of this book is dedicated to describing how different layer features enable change in images. This chapter looks at the simplest concepts behind isolating change, including the purpose and use of adjustment layers, and the idea of isolating objects and areas within images in the simplest form. As we go, we'll look at several key concepts for image correction that apply to just about any image you will work with to form the core of your correction workflow. This includes adjusting dynamic range, color correction and color balance as initial application of layers in your images.

Isolating Correction in Adjustment Layers

Adjustment layers are based on correction functions, but instead of directly applying the adjustments to the image, adjustment settings are retained in a separate layer that you can re-adjust later, temporarily hide or even remove at any point in the processing. The point again is that the correction or change remains distinct within the layer stack and never directly changes the original image pixel information.

One of the first steps that I suggest in working with any image is making a general Levels correction. The correction helps make the most of the dynamic range (brightness from white to black) and helps establish color balance that can bring out richness in image color. The technique of Levels correction applies to the whole image, but on occasion may apply to isolated image elements as well. In this case, the Levels correction is a useful way to demonstrate a simple application of adjustment layers. This correction works on just about any image, and sometimes really works wonders.

First, let's outline the process, and then look specifically at how to make the adjustment using the controls on the Levels dialog.

📖 Try It Now

Applying Levels for Color Correction
1. Open the image you want to correct.
2. Choose Layer>New Adjustment Layer>Levels. This opens the New Layer dialog box.
3. When the New Layer dialog appears, leave the defaults for now and click the OK button. This will accept the settings, creates a new Levels adjustment layer and opens the Levels dialog.
4. Select Red from the Channel drop-down list. This reveals the histogram for the red component.
5. Make a Levels correction for the component. Do this correction by evaluating the histogram and moving the sliders.

📖 We'll look at exactly how to make this correction by moving the sliders in a moment. See 'Detailing the Levels Slider Changes'.

6. Repeat step 5 for the green component. Do this by selecting Green from the Channel drop-down list and making the levels change.
7. Repeat step 5 for the blue component. Do this by selecting Blue from the Channel drop-down list and making the change.
8. Make a tone adjustment to the image midtones. To do this, choose RGB from the Channels drop list and adjustment with the middle (gray) slider to brighten (left) or darken (right) the image.
9. Accept the changes in the Levels dialog by clicking OK. This closes the dialog box.

This levels correction can work wonders on an image, and it is useful in almost any image. The changes compensate for exposure and lighting conditions and improve color balance and the dynamic range of images, without a lot of complicated measurement. The results are non-destructive as the correction is made in layers. The following section outlines the details of how to make the levels change.

Detailing the Levels Slider Changes

Making the Levels slider adjustments is a fairly simple process, once you have an outline for what to do. The histogram on the Levels dialog will become your visual guide to all you need to know to make the basic adjustment. Additional changes can be made that reflect user preferences once you get used to using the tool.

The characteristic to look for in Levels histograms is shortened tonal range. Shortened tonal range is represented by a histogram that does not have information (or so little consistent information that it is more likely image noise than detail) across the entire range of the graph, with a gap at either the light end (right, highlights) or dark end (left, shadows) of the graph or both. A shortened tonal range in any of the channel components indicates that the light source was not full spectrum.

Levels is an extraordinary tool for making adjustments in this situation. All you do to correct a shortened range is move the sliders (black/shadow and white/highlight) to maximize the range of each component. The right, white slider is moved to the left to a position where the graph shows anything more than image noise; this will make whites brighter. The left, black slider, is moved to the

Light's Fingerprint

When the exposure is captured, the camera captures a fingerprint of the lighting for the scene. Natural lighting at sunset or sunrise, where lighting tends to color objects with warmer tones of yellow and red, is an example of light creating an effect in a scene. But taking that further, if your light is pure red, everything in the room will only reflect the red light, and everything (with any red in it to reflect) will appear red. Objects with no red at all will appear black.

Objects in a scene reflect the quality and color of the available light. If the light isn't completely neutral, lacks full spectrum (full colors of the rainbow), and/or tends to favor a particular color, the scene reflects the quality of the light. As the scene can only reflect colors in the original light source(s), a capture serves as a reliable fingerprint of the general qualities of the lighting in the scene.

This fingerprint is a valuable clue to detecting the correct color for your image. If you can sample the fingerprint and correct for the deficiency of the light, you can correct image color.

Image Histograms, found by looking at the Histograms, or by looking at the Levels dialog, are exactly what you need to evaluate the quality of the light, and the fingerprint it has left on the scene. A histogram (see Figures 3.1–3.3) shows a definitive mapping of exactly how the lighting fingerprint reacts with the objects in the scene. By examining light's fingerprint as a clue, we can easily determine how to correct image color.

The idea of light leaving a fingerprint is something I talk about to teach the idea behind the theory. If you talk with other people about 'light's fingerprint,' there is a good chance they will have no idea what you are talking about.

right, again to a position where significant information is displayed in the graph; this will make shadows darker. See the examples in Figures 3.1–3.3 for the Red, Green and Blue channels.

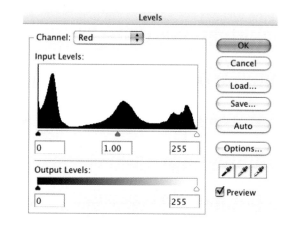

FIG 3.1 The Red histogram shows a full range from black to white, and needs no adjustment.

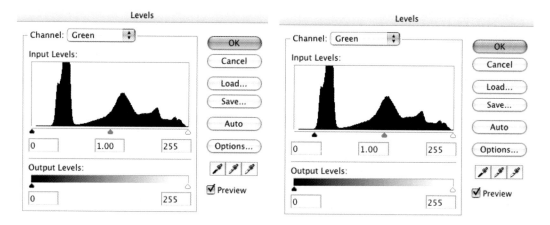

FIG 3.2 The Green channel shows a tail to the left, or shadow portion, of the green spectrum. In this case move the black (left, input) slider to the right to compensate and clip the tail as shown.

After setting the sliders, you commit your changes by clicking OK on the Levels dialog. The tails and anything outside the range of the black and white sliders are cut off, and the image information

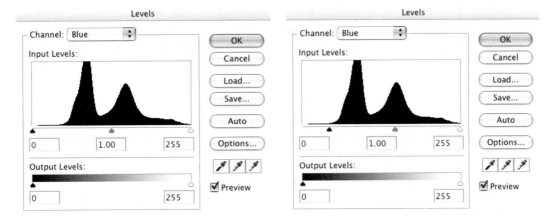

FIG 3.3 The Blue channel also shows a tail to the left, or shadow portion, of the spectrum. In this case move the black (left, input) slider to the right to compensate as shown.

will be re-distributed over the tonal range. The new range of the graph is extended as in Figure 3.4.

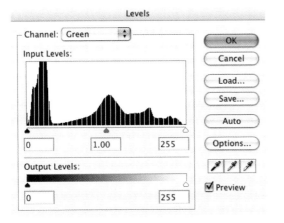

FIG 3.4 The image information is re-distributed evenly after levels changes are accepted so that the color range is broadened.

This Levels change is one you can often make almost strictly by looking at the appearance of the histogram and adjusting it accordingly – without looking at the image, just as we have done here. If you toggle the Show/Hide icon for the layer on the layers palette, the change in the image should appear to improve image dynamics, contrast and color.

📖 A Levels adjustment will not always work well with images that have inherent color casts (sunsets) or where color filters have been used to achieve color shifting effects, as it will tend to counteract desired color shifts.

Tails on the histogram usually represent image noise rather than image detail, which is why you can generally you cut an entire tail. However, sometimes you will crop none, some, or all of a tail, depending on the image, desired color shift and the length of the tail. Usually you cut less of a very long tail. After making the levels adjustment for each of the channels, evaluate the change by eye, on screen (preferably on a calibrated monitor!). If changes seem extreme, you can mediate them using the Levels layer opacity. Lowering the Opacity will reduce the intensity of the correction – something that could not be done if the Levels were applied directly to the layer content.

Even more advanced adjustments can be made with Levels using the center, gray sliders for each channel. Moving these sliders allows you to adjust midtone color balance. However using a separate correction for Color Balance will give more control, and a better overall result. We will look at Color Balance later as we get more specific with corrections.

With all that in mind, the point of this section was to look at how isolated corrections and adjustment layers can be useful. If you open the sample1.psd image from the CD (or you can use another image that has not already been color corrected), you can run through a levels correction using an adjustment layer.

📖 Try It Now

1. Run through a standard Levels correction described in 'Applying Levels for Color Correction' above, but don't bother adjusting midtones.
2. Change the Opacity of the Levels 1 layer to 50%.
3. Duplicate the Levels 1 layer and name the duplicate Levels 2. This is a really simple example of something adjustment layers allow you to do: compare two results. Toggle the view for the Levels 1 layer off and on, and that will allow you to see the difference between applying the Levels change at 50% or 100%. But the next steps are truly unique to adjustment layers.

4. Delete the Levels 2 layer by dragging it to the Delete Layer button at the bottom of the palette.
5 Change the Opacity of the Levels 1 layer back to 100%.
6. Double-click the Levels thumbnail. The Levels dialog will open.
7. Adjust the midtone RGB slider to brighten or darken the image, then close the dialog by clicking OK.

So what happened here that is so unique? You just opened the Levels dialog a second time. You made adjustments, or at least considered them, and then accepted the changes. This is unique because if you applied the levels correction directly to the background without using an adjustment layer, you'd have had to undo the change and start over. That is the advantage of adjustment layers in a nutshell: you can make repeated changes to your adjustments without starting over. Even in this simple exercise, it saves several steps, in a more complicated correction, you can multiply the savings exponentially.

Keep that image handy; either save a version with the Levels correction or leave it open for the next exercise. Now lets look at how layering can be an advantage in isolating objects.

Isolating Image Objects

Isolating image elements is simply using layers to isolate objects or image areas into separate layers so the objects can be controlled separately. The basic idea of isolating objects in your image is as easy, conceptually, as making a selection of an image area and then copying and pasting that image area to its own layer. The ability to create the isolation and executing it in a controlled way can give you ultimate control over image composition.

To complete basic isolation of an object, you will use any one of the selection tools – or a combination of them – to create a selection. Once the selection is created, you can copy the content of your selection to the clipboard (press Command+C/Ctrl+C [Mac/PC]), then paste it back into the image (press Command+V/Ctrl+V). Photoshop will automatically make a layer and insert the content from the clipboard. Other methods, such as Command+J/Ctrl+J (New Layer Via Copy) or Command+Shift+J/Ctrl+Shift+J (New Layer Via Cut), will also work to create the new layer from the selected area. The method of getting the selected area isolated onto its own layer is less important than getting the area into a layer on its own.

With the object isolated, you will be able to more easily target changes to that area directly, using additional isolation layers, or using later techniques we will explore such as clipping groups or other masking. Isolating a single element in an image is relatively simple, and it can open the door to many other image changes. Sometimes it will be desirable to take apart an image into a variety of smaller components for the sake of correction and/or composition adjustment. While it may seem that taking apart an image object by object can be a pain, it can also sometimes lead to better corrections, and more flexibility with the end result.

For example, Figure 3.5 shows a still life of some pears shot on the spur of the moment. There were probably about 20 images in the series, and admittedly it didn't seem any of them represented what was desired – as sometimes happens. It seemed the result could be altered by making some changes to the composition.

FIG 3.5 The original shot of some pears on an old crate. It seems too crowded, and begs experimentation.

To make the desired changes the image was broken down into several components to handle separately: the background, the foreground wood, the wood plateau, the two pears to the right and the pear to the left. Ultimately the pear to the left was eliminated by the change, giving the image a bit more starkness. Color was borrowed from the pear that went missing, and stems were borrowed from other images. The breakdown of steps to re-create the image and the resulting layers is shown in Figures 3.6 and 3.7.

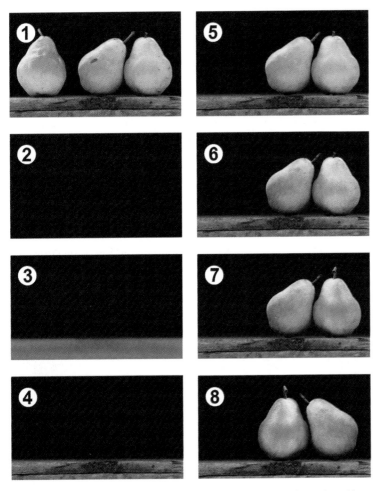

FIG 3.6 (1) The original, (2) a new background, (3) fabricated wood top, (4) copied wood face (with repairs), (5) two pairs isolated, (6) pear pair enhanced, (7) pear pair recolored and (8) two pears flipped and moved.

You will rarely go to such lengths as rebuilding an image to get the result you want, but you may see a key here in getting what you need, and an advantage provided by layers. The separation of objects goes one step further than merely selecting the object and copy/pasting to its own layer. Once the object is isolated, you put yourself in position to have ultimate control of the composition. See the result in Figure 3.8.

One key point about making such adjustments: there is a difference between photography and shooting a picture. In your photography, you can remove an object from a scene by just

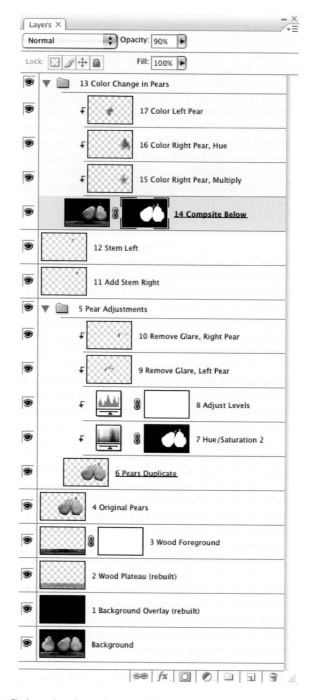

FIG 3.7 The layers show the numbered steps taken to make the adjustments – some of these being more advanced techniques with clipping and masking that we will look at in the following chapters.

FIG 3.8 The final result is cropped, color corrected, patched and re-organized using the power of layers.

moving it out of the camera's view. When you isolate an object in Photoshop layers, the layer from which you plucked the object either still contains the object, or has a hole where it was. The background doesn't magically re-appear when the object is removed. In the case of the example, the background is mostly pretty simple, and it can be repaired by re-creating it. Making the repair to patch the hole left behind can be more difficult as the complexity of the background increases. But to build some confidence in the strategy, lets look at how it applies to the sample image continuing from the point where you left off in the last exercise.

📖 Try It Now

1. Choose the Polygon Lasso by pressing L and Shift+L to scroll the Lasso tools, or choose the Polygon Lasso from the toolbar. Change the settings on the Options bar to Feather 0 Pixels, and check Anti-alias.

    📖 Feather and Anti-alias are both means of softening the edge of the selection, and do not usually need to be used together. Softening the selection either way will tend to blend edges of selections with the surrounding area rather than making hard, noticeable edges.

2. Open the image window so you have some room around the edge of the image to apply the tool (Figure 3.9).

69

FIG 3.9 Use the window controller at the lower right of the window to click and drag the window larger, or zoom out from the image using the zoom tool and Option+click / Alt+click on the image.

3. Make a selection of the wood facing. To do this click outside of the image to the left, then move the cursor and click right at the top of the facing at the edge of the image. Continue moving and clicking across the top of the facing, following the contour of the wood. When you reach the right side of the image, click outside the image, then outside the lower right corner of the image, then outside the lower left corner and then on the starting point to complete the selection (see Figure 3.10).

FIG 3.10 Going outside the boundaries of the image with a selection tool (as shown here) will make sure you select tightly to the edge of the image.

4. Activate the Background by clicking it in the layers palette, then Copy and Paste to create a new layer with the wood facing. Name the new layer: 2 Wood Facing.
5. Activate the Background layer again. Create a new layer and fill with black (Edit>Fill Set Content to Black). Call the new layer Black Background.
6. Shut off the view for the Black Background layer so you can see the pears.
7. Select the Polygon Lasso tool, and use it to follow the contour of the two pears to the right of the image, using short segments between clicks (see Figure 3.11). You can use other selection tools if you feel more comfortable. The goal is to isolate the pears. Technically you will not have to make an incredibly tight selection around the part of the pears that is over the black, but try to make the selection as tight as possible.

FIG 3.11 Using short segments with the Polygon Lasso can make a selection that is rather smooth, and fine for the purpose of this exercise.

8. Activate the Background layer, Copy and then Paste. This will create a new layer with the pair of pears. Name the new layer: 4 Isolated Pears.
9. Move the 4 Isolated Pears layer above the 2 Wood Facing layer in the layer stack, and turn on the view for the Black Background layer. The layer stack should look like Figure 3.12.

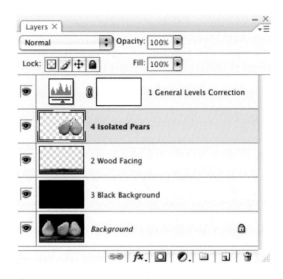

FIG 3.12 In a few quick steps the components of this image are isolated into separate layers.

This simple example isolates the pair of pears, and gives you the freedom to move them in the image and change the composition. Using the move tool, try placing the pears in a different position, or even flip the pears horizontally (Edit>Transform>Flip Horizontal). You'll want to either keep this image open or save it to continue with the exercise in the next section.

The basics of re-creating the pear image required isolating each of the image areas and/or replacement of those areas with suitable substitutes. The additional effort of re-creating the image proves more fruitful than trying to do something like stamp out the pear on the left with the Clone Stamp. It would be painstaking to fill in the area behind the pears using the Clone Stamp and make associated repairs look right. Inevitably it would look uneven, blotchy, and repaired. Re-creating the entire black background from scratch does several things, including providing the opportunity to remove any distracting imperfections from the black background.

Of course this replacement is not perfect. We could build back in the wood platform, and add noise to the background to make it appear more like the original. In the pear example in Figures 3.6–3.8, I used quite a few different types of layers, some which will not be apparent by the screenshot of the layers palette alone. Some of the layer changes employ Modes, which we will look at later in Chapter 5, and more than one includes a mask or clipping group, which we will look at in Chapter 4. As these techniques are covered in layer chapters, it isn't appropriate to cover them here, but we will look at similar examples in chapters to come.

Adding Layers for a Change

Layers can be added to an image that act like adjustment layers because they serve to make changes in the image, but actually are also similar to isolation layers. Objects are added to separate layers, either from scratch (using Paintbrush, Clone Stamp or Healing tools) or as image areas (copied from other images, or even cloned from elements in the same image). The objects are added to layers to give freedom in adjusting, positioning, repairing and replacing objects, as well as offering flexibility in masking and positioning in front of or behind other image elements in the layer stack.

Additions for change in the example are represented by layers such as the Remove Glare layers. For these adjustments, new layers were created, and then repairs were stamped over select areas of the pears using a combination of the Clone Stamp and Healing tools. Pear stems were borrowed from different shots in this same series of images so the stems would reflect the same or very similar lighting qualities. Color adjustments were added by sampling color from the pear that was removed and painting it back over the existing pears using different layer modes (which, again, we'll discuss in Chapter 5).

The most obvious use for this type of 'added change' layer is in repairing damage, or in patching plain ol' ugly areas of an object or area. You could do this directly to objects without adding layers, but keeping the changes separate in layers again offers opportunities that you will not have with direct, permanent application of image changes.

Simple Layer Repair Example

If you still shoot film, have tried to convert old photos to digital, or if you have ever had a dirty sensor or lens, you will be no stranger to correcting minor imperfections in your images that come in the way of dust and debris. Digital shooters may not see as much dust as they see other minor imperfections in their images like litter, crumbs, etc. You can often make quick work of dust and minor debris corrections by applying the Clone Stamp or Healing tool directly to an image background. However, applying these corrections to a blank layer offers much more flexibility. Once you are sure the correction is the way you want it, you can commit the change by merging the layers, or just leave them in separate layers. The advantage here is that if you muff up part or all of the correction, you still have the opportunity to fix it. You also have the opportunity to use tools in combination with one another such as using both the Clone Stamp and Healing tool for a correction.

The pear in this example has some obvious imperfections that needed to be taken care of. Of course, you can do this before taking the image apart into separate objects. One large dent in the middle of the three pears needed some fixing. This is taken care of with simple layered repair.

📖 Try It Now

1. Continuing from the previous exercise, create a new layer above the 4 Isolated Pears and call it 5 Clone Stamp.
2. Create a new layer above the 5 Clone Stamp layer and call it 6 Healing.
3. Shut off the view for the 1 General Levels Correction layer, leaving the layer visible may affect cloning corrections.
4. Activate the Clone Stamp layer by clicking on it in the layers palette. Choose the Clone Stamp and set the options to Sample All Layers – if you don't, it will not stamp to a blank layer. Apply the tool to make a correction of the damaged areas.

   📖 To apply the Clone Stamp, note the color and shape of the damage, and try to find a spot in the image that will make a good replacement. Set the brush size to just slightly larger than the width of the problem area, and use 50–80% hardness (leaving a soft edge to blend corrections). Usually I set the tool to Aligned (check the box) which keeps alignment between the brush and sample point. Sample the area you will be using to replace the damage by holding down the Option/Alt key and clicking on the area. Move the brush over the damage and apply. It is best to apply in short bursts, and it is a good idea to resample from different areas to avoid obvious patterning, and to blend in texture, contour and detail from multiple directions. Doing so will help create unique corrections of the areas.

5. Activate the Healing layer by clicking on it in the layers palette, and then choose the Healing tool. Set the brush and Options like

you do for the Clone Stamp, but make the brush 100% hard – the nature of the tool blends in the application. Make a sample and apply the tool to make a second correction over areas corrected with the Clone Stamp to blend in the corrections.

The resulting layers and image can be seen in Figures 3.13 and 3.14.

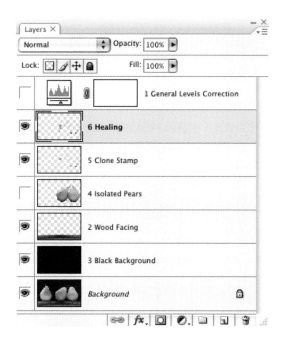

FIG 3.13 The layers palette shows the separate correction layers for Clone Stamp and Healing.

FIG 3.14 In a few quick steps the corrections for this image are isolated into separate layers.

Applying the Healing tool directly to a problem can lead to similar results, but it has been my experience that applying the Clone Stamp first to neutralize the ugliest part of the damage and then applying the Healing tool will yield better results (less noticeable edges) more consistently.

The most difficult parts of this correction will be the damage near the edges of the pears – where the pears meet the black of the background. The problem will be that the Healing tool will try to do too much: it will pull in some of the black background as part of the repair that it tries to make. There are several things you can do to eliminate this problem:

- Use only the Clone Stamp in those areas near edges.
- Make a selection around the area you want to correct to exclude the black from the background.
- Make a selection around the area you want to correct including the replacement area, then isolate that on its own layer via Copy/Paste (see Figure 3.15), and shut off other layers.

FIG 3.15 A distinct advantage of using Healing with layers is that you can limit what gets sampled for use in the correction.

Following these techniques you can make freehand corrections to this image infinite different ways, each equally as convincing. Check your handiwork by toggling the view for the correction layers. You may want to group them so you can toggle the view as a group. This will let you compare before and after, and should you want to flip the pears horizontally, you can flip the whole group (see Figure 3.16).

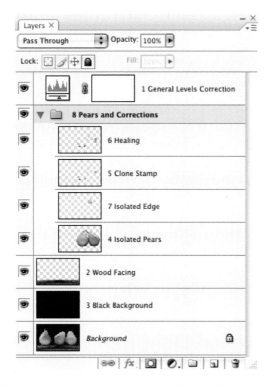

FIG 3.16 This shows the final layer set for this set of examples, including the Isolated Edge layer and grouping.

The Art of Color Balance

While levels are excellent tools for normalizing color, they may not always produce the most pleasing color if you use them only to extend the dynamic range. A tweak to color balance will often do quite a lot to enhance your image's color.

The idea of the Color Balance function is to allow you to shift the balance between opposing colors: cyan balances against red, green against magenta and blue against yellow. These adjustments can be made using separate ranges: highlights, midtones and shadows. Working through a Color Balance correction by gaging the changes on screen can often clear up muddy appearances by balancing color casts caused by lighting conditions. The Color Balance dialog box is a friendly, easy way to make these changes. Rather than trying to calculate a result, you'll work with Color Balance interactively. The goal is to achieve more vibrant, balanced color.

📖 Try It Now

1. Open the Vanishing Point.psd on the CD. You'll also find this image in the Samples folder in the Adobe Photoshop CS3 program folder and on the installation CD in with the Sample images.
2. Treat this as a new image and do a Levels correction as described earlier in this chapter. You won't be able to do to much, but you'll see a small change in the image.
3. Open Color Balance by choosing Color Balance from the Adjustment Layers sub menu (Layer>New Adjustment Layer> Color Balance).
4. Start with the Midtones (under the Tone Balance panel), and slide the Cyan/Red slider between −50 and +50, watching the effect on the image. Narrow down the range that looks best by swinging the slider in smaller ranges until the best position is achieved based on the screen preview. The 'best' position is where the color seems most balanced against the extremes (which you use +50 and −50 to preview).
5. Repeat step 4 for the Magenta/Green slider.
6. Repeat step 4 for the Yellow/Blue slider.
7. Click the Highlights radio button on the Color Balance dialog and repeat steps 4 through 6. This will make adjustment to Color Balance for the Highlights.
8. Click the Shadows radio button on the Color Balance dialog and repeat steps 4 through 6. This will help you make adjustment to Color Balance for the Shadows.
9. Repeat steps 4 through 8. This will allow you to review earlier adjustments in context of the changes you made to the shadow changes.

The steps here might seem an oversimplification, but this is really all you have to do with Color Balance to achieve the desired result. The critical part of this exercise is that you have to be able to trust your monitor, so it will need to be calibrated (and hopefully tested against output as well). Depending on your choices, the Vanishing Point.psd image will show a dramatic difference after Color Balance, even with small movements of the sliders. Changes will influence color, saturation, dynamics and even details in the image. You can see the effect on details usually in the highlights (the back of the dog's head – or if you try to apply a Color Balance change to the pear image, you will see some variation in the specular highlights where the light is reflecting from the source). The color result of a correction on the Vanishing Point.psd appears in the corrections on the CD. You'll want to toggle the view for the Color Balance 1 layer to see the difference before and after the application. Figure 3.17 shows the Color Balance settings used to make the change.

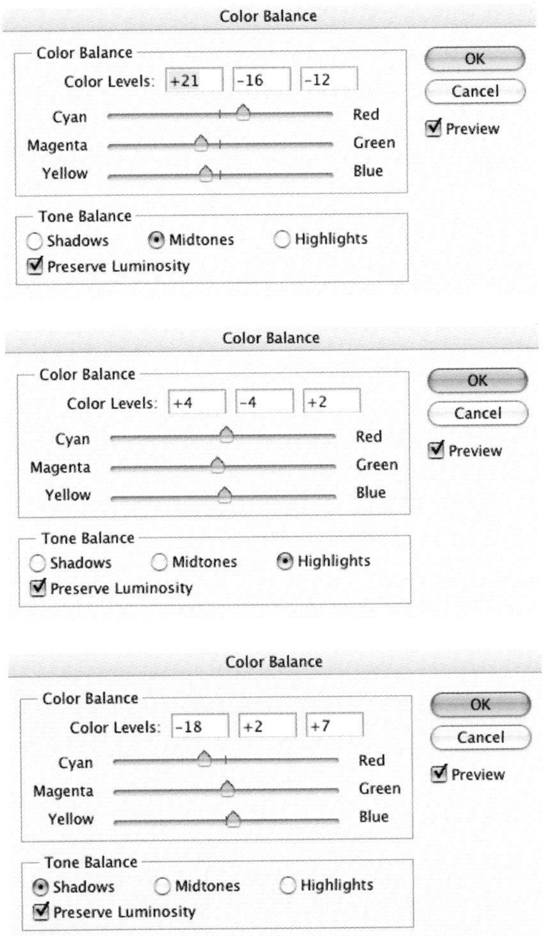

FIG 3.17 Color Balance influences many parts of the appearance of your images. When it is corrected for this image, the scene will appear to gain some depth of color.

Summary

In this chapter we have begun to use layers to actually make a difference in image appearance, first with an isolated Levels correction, then with isolating objects in the image for control of the composition, and then for making isolated corrections.

79

The Levels correction and Cloning/Healing corrections are techniques you can use on virtually all your images. Object isolation may not be something you will do every day, but the basic concept of isolation is something you may use all the time – actually we used a variation at the very end of the section on Healing corrections by isolating the edge area.

Thinking about your images and your corrections as made up of separate, layered corrections is the key concept that should be coming across here. Layers offer opportunities for isolated correction that pose advantages while making the change and have additional advantages once the correction has been created in terms of potential adjustment.

Changes to this image need not be limited to the corrections shown in this chapter, and other corrections can certainly be considered. Think about what you would like to see in this image, and imagine how that requirement might be solved with additional layers, or those you have already created. Attempting to make some or all of those additional changes is good practice with layers.

A valuable thing to do with the information in this chapter is to begin applying the changes to your own images. Choose one or more of your images and test out selective enhancements using layers. You don't have to do everything from this chapter to every image, but you should make an attempt to try out everything to see how the techniques might apply to your corrections:

- Start with making a Levels Adjustment Layer to correct image color.
- Attempt to isolate an image area by selection, copy and paste.
- Adjust the position of an object if you are really daring.
- Locate some image area(s) that you want to improve with simple cloning corrections, and create new layers to help you incorporate change. Then stamp out and heal problem areas.
- Fine tune with Color Balance.

Keep in mind that working with additional images can be exercises without a real goal of achieving improvement in the image: it is enough at this point to perform the techniques as exercises or practice. Do, however, make serious corrections if they are warranted in your images to exercise the true value of layers.

CHAPTER 4

Mushrooms

Masking: Enhanced
Area Isolation

In the previous chapter we looked at layers as a means of isolating image corrections so you can target change. This covered the idea of applying corrections on separate layers, using adjustment layers, and isolating image objects. This chapter looks at some similar types of isolation using layers and masking as a means of creating flexibility with the way you handle layers.

A big deal is often made about masking and the power it provides. Masking, put simply, is blocking off areas of an image from view. This is different than erasing areas of the layers, as erasing is permanent removal; using masks is really hiding pixels rather than removing them. One of the most basic types of masking is something we did in the exercise at the end of Chapter 1. In that exercise we used a duplicate of the Background layer to hide mask the Drop Shadow layer (see Figure 4.1).

FIG 4.1 The simplest type of masking with layers is using the content of an upper layer to hide the content of the lower – the content of the lower layer is still there, but it is hidden from view.

More sophisticated means of masking are comparable to the simple masking we explored in the exercise, they just do it with more finesse. All types of masking share the same concept: masking acts to block image content from view without removing it or destroying it like erasing might.

Expanding on Process

We have advanced in the chapters from discovering where functions are, to applying functions just for the joy of seeing them work, then to seeing how they work to achieve a purpose. In this chapter, we'll advance even further by exploring functions as part of the layers workflow working with the image in Figure 4.2.

Looking back at our outline for correction (Chapter 2), it is a good idea to start corrections by evaluating the image. A developed hit list of corrections you intend to make, roughly conforming to our previous outline, might look like this for the image in Figure 4.2:

1. Clean up pollen and dust specks.
2. Reduce the significant digital noise.
3. Enhance natural color and tone.
4. Add soft focus to go with the flow of the image.
5. Sharpen and enhance contrast.
6. Add color enhancements (paint in color).

Though the image is not a terribly good capture, when all is said and done, this image will have gone through enhancement to bring out what is lurking there. The result will be something like Figure 4.3, remarkably similar to the original capture.

The image may seem to need a lot of corrections, but the results will be worth the effort and it will offer the opportunity to learn

FIG 4.2 Even though this image initially appears to be sub-standard, there is potential in the soft lighting and gentle tones, and several interesting possibilities to enhance.

FIG 4.3 Following the corrections list, this image takes a dramatic turn for the better.

how to apply more layer techniques. We'll look at masking as it applies to layer transparency, layer clipping, Adjustment layers, and proper layer masks. We'll use layer masking to paint in effects, affect image sharpness selectively, and change image color selectively. Let's take each step in our hit list in order and explore corrections for this image fully to help you see application of layers in process.

Clean Up

There are some obvious detail problems in this image that can be immediately wiped out, like the obvious dust speck and several smaller areas where pollen has been scattered. You will want to clean these areas up using the Clone Stamp and Healing layer techniques discussed in the previous chapter. You can probably get everything done here with one or the other of these tools, but you can set up the two-layer technique if you want.

📖 Try It Now

1. Open the Sample2.psd on the CD.
2. Create a new layer and call it 1 Spot Adjustments. Choose the Healing or Clone Stamp tool and make corrections for the obvious problems. If you use both the Clone Stamp and Healing tools, consider creating separate layers for each and name them appropriately so you can better blend the applications.

If you need more detail or to review the techniques, please see the exercise in the previous chapter. When you have finished the cloning/healing, save the image so you can come back to it as we continue working through the hit list. One of the new techniques we'll explore thoroughly here is reducing image noise.

Reducing Image Noise

There are several ways to reduce noise in your images, few of them are probably obvious beyond the Reduce Noise filter. One of the key factors to keep in mind when addressing noise is that noise is just the opposite of blur. You can see this in a quick exercise.

📖 Try It Now

1. Open a new blank image (choose File>New). Be sure the image is Red, Green and Blue (RGB) and 1000 × 1000 pixels. After choosing your settings for the new file, click OK. For settings see Figure 4.4.

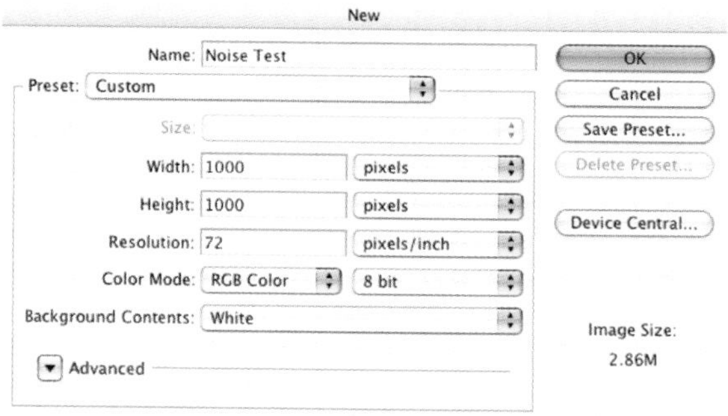

FIG 4.4 The New Image dialog settings.

2. When the image opens, fill with 50% gray. Use the Fill function (Edit>Fill), and select 50% Gray from the Use drop list. Leave the Blend Mode at Normal and the Opacity at 100% (see Figure 4.5). Click OK.

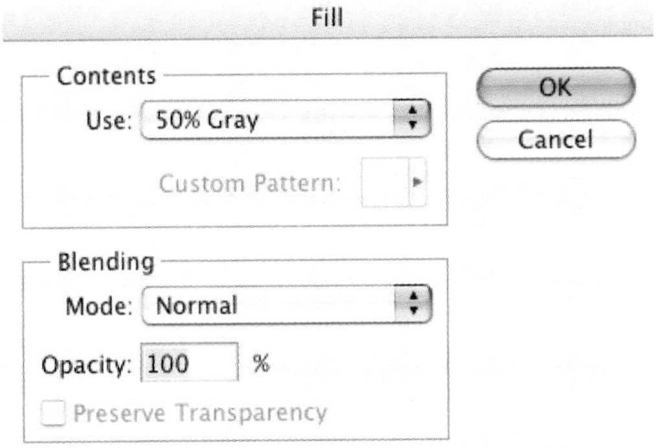

FIG 4.5 The Fill dialog settings.

3. After the fill, apply some noise to your image with the Add Noise filter (Filter>Noise>Add Noise). When the Add Noise dialog opens, make the Amount 10%, and the Distribution Uniform. Leave the Monochrome box unchecked. When you have completed the settings (see Figure 4.6), click OK on the dialog. Your image will fill with noise.

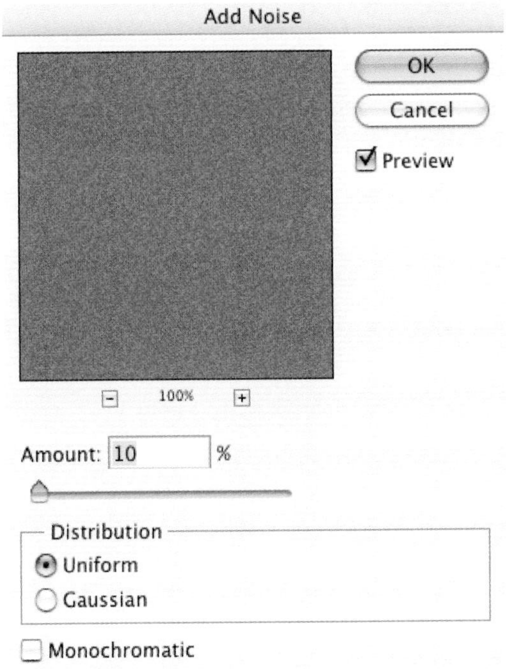

FIG 4.6 The Add Noise filter dialog settings.

85

4. Now open the Gaussian Blur filter (Filter>Blur>Gaussian Blur). Set the Radius for the filter to 25 pixels and click OK. This will mediate all the noise you added in step 3, and you'll be back to flat gray, eliminating the noise (Figure 4.7).

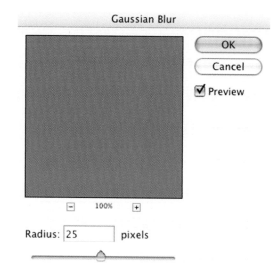

FIG 4.7 The Gaussian Blur filter dialog settings.

Hopefully you see from the quick example that you can obliterate noise with blur. However, applying blur to everything in your image will lead to a blurry image. You'll obliterate detail as well as the noise. Often you'll need to be selective about just what to blur. There are many ways we could go about this, and we'll look at a method that allows us to explore noise reduction while maintaining the advantage of layers by continuing work on the sample2.psd you saved earlier in this chapter after making the initial cloning/healing corrections.

☐ Try It Now

1. Create a new layer above the Healing/Clone Stamp layers, call it Manual Masking, and number it accordingly. This exercise assumes you have used one layer for healing/cloning, so it will be named '2 Manual Masking'. This layer will be the canvas for defining the mask you will create in the following steps.
2. Choose the Brush tool and press D to set the default colors (the foreground will be black). Be sure the brush you have selected

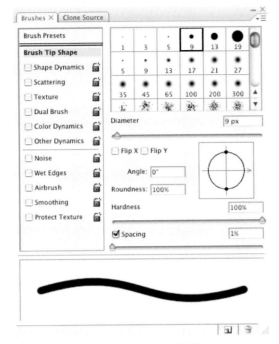

FIG 4.8 Uncheck the boxes under Brush Presets to shut off all brush dynamics.

is round, 100% hard, 100% Opaque and turn off all brush dynamics (see Figure 4.8). Try to use a larger brush 20–30 pixels in diameter. Either use the Brush Preset Picker on the Options bar when the tool is selected, or the Brush palette (Window> Brushes). This brush will be used to outline the mask you are creating.

3. Begin applying the brush to the image to outline the petals (see Figure 4.9). You want to get pretty tight to the petals to create a solid outline. Most of your movement will be freehand, but using short line segments can often be easier to control. To create line segments, hold down the shift key and click between points to draw a straight line between clicks. Complete the outline (see Figure 4.10).

📖 Brush size can be changed with keyboard shortcuts. Increase brush size with the] key, and decrease brush size with the [key.

FIG 4.9 Use the larger brush to define the general outline, then come back and fill in the smaller areas using a smaller brush.

FIG 4.10 Complete the circuit around the petals.

4. Choose the Magic Wand tool, set the Tolerance to 10, check the Anti-alias box, check the contiguous box and click on the flowers. Sample All Layers should be unchecked and the 2 Manual Masking layer should be active. This will select the area inside the black outline you created.

5. Expand the selection (Select>Modify>Expand) by half the diameter of the brush selected for step 2 (e.g., 10 pixels if you used a 20 pixel brush). This will push the selection out over the outline you created.

6. Invert the selection (Command+Shift+I / Ctrl+Shift+I [Mac / PC]) then Fill with black. This will invert the selection so it is over everything but the flower petals and will fill the area around the flowers completely with black (see Figure 4.11). Deselect by pressing Command+D / Ctrl+D.

FIG 4.11   Once filled with black, the flowers are visibly isolated and we can use this as a selection and mask for additional changes.

Composite Layers

Composite layers are useful in certain circumstances to either provide a point to freeze your changes as a solid stopping point to continue working from, or to provide image information that is otherwise not available. What they do is take a freeze frame of whatever you have visible in the image at the time you capture the composite.

To capture the composite, make sure the image shows the layers you want to be in the composite (you may need to toggle layer views), then create a new layer and press Command+Option+Shift+E/ Crtl+Alt+Shift+E. Pressing these keys will stamp the visible content to the new layer. Usually you will want to rename the new layer with an appropriate name!

Sometimes you will capture the composite of the entire image with all of the layers on in order to have a point to move forward cleanly from after making a lot of changes. Other times, such as in this example, there are specific layers to take a snapshot of. Because a mode was applied to the Dupe Manual Mask layer, it only appears desaturated because of the calculation the layer performs: there is no layer that actually has the desaturated content. Making a composite allows you to re-group the image information in one place and commit it to tangible pixels. When you have gathered

7. Duplicate the 2 Manual Masking layer and rename it. I called it 3 Dupe Manual Masking Blurred and Desaturate. You will use this layer to make additional refinements to the mask.

8. Change the mode of the 3 Dupe Manual Masking Blurred and Desaturate layer to Color and apply a Gaussian blur to soften the edge (I used 3.5 pixels). The change in the mode will desaturate the area under the mask; blurring will soften the edges and assure the changes based on this mask will blend in at the edges of the petals.

9. Shut off the view for the 2 Manual Masking layer, be sure the 3 Dupe Manual Masking layer is active, capture the composite Command+Option+Shift+E / Ctrl+Alt+Shift+E. This will reveal the content under the 2 Manual Masking layer, and then create a new layer with the current visible saturated and desaturated content collected. Name the new layer 4 Composite.

10. Hold down the Command / Ctrl key and click on the layer thumbnail for the 3 Dupe Manual Mask layer. This will load the solid part of the layer as a selection.

11. Activate the 4 Composite layer, and duplicate the selected area to a new layer. Command+J / Ctrl+J will do the trick. Name the new layer 5 Copied Masked Area from Composite. This will isolate just the desaturated area of the image into its own layer.

12. Duplicate the 5 Copied Masked Area layer, and name it 6 Duplicate of Copied Masked Area.

13. Group the 6 Duplicate of Copied Masked Area layer with the 5 Copied Masked Area layer by pressing Command+ Option+G/ Ctrl+Alt+G. This makes a clipping group from the layers. Apply a Gaussian Blur of 6 pixels to the 6 Duplicate of Copied Masked Area layer, then apply Add Noise at 2% using Gaussian distribution. Your layers should look like Figure 4.12. The blurring will soften the area around the flowers, mitigating the noise, and the Add Noise application will help rough up the texture of the area again so it is a better fit to the rest of the image.

Steps 1 through 6 create the template you will need to isolate the area to change in the later steps. Once the base mask is created, it can be adjusted and applied. Making the clipping group assures that the blur will be contained to the original masking shape,

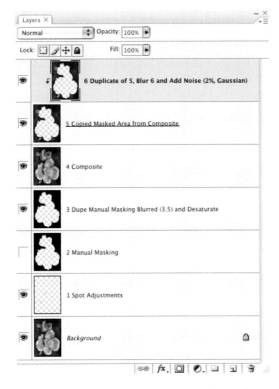

image information in a composite, blurring will affect the desaturated masked area directly; and in isolation from the rest of the image.

Remember this compositing technique as another means of organizing content in layers! It is frequently a handy technique.

FIG 4.12 Some layers are becoming extraneous to the result at this point, but provide valuable clues as to how the result was achieved.

rather than allowing the blurred edges to bleed into the petals. Applying blur softens the noise, and adding noise back roughs up the blurred image area so it doesn't seem unnaturally smooth. The result should show a slightly softer peripheral area with greatly reduced noise (see Figure 4.13).

The main concept to keep in mind here is that Blur and Noise filters can work well together in reducing the appearance of noise in your images and maintaining a realistic appearance. A secondary concept is isolating the image area(s) that you want to affect. Here we used manual masking techniques, selection and clipping layers to achieve isolated effects.

Again, you will want to retain this image so we can continue making corrections. Now let's look at enhancing natural color.

FIG 4.13 Masking and blurring helped reduce noise without compromising important detail.

Enhancing Natural Color and Tone

After taking quite a while to examine some options with noise, we'll step back to a hopefully more familiar area of Levels corrections. You want to apply a Levels correction as an Adjustment layer masked to the flowers to be sure you are making the most of color and tone as they were captured and to do some balancing for the color and light. As you have already made the mask, applying it is easy. A second part to this color enhancement will be using Hue/Saturation to emphasize and control colors in the image.

📖 Try It Now

1. Command+click / Ctrl+click the 3 Dupe Manual Masking layer icon to load the layer as a selection again. Invert the selection. The inverted selection targets the flower.

2. Choose Layer>New Adjustment Layer>Levels from the program menus, when the New Layer dialog appears, name the layer 7 Levels Correction for Flowers and click OK. The Levels layer will be created with a mask that targets the flowers using the selection loaded in step 1. Make your best effort in the levels correction (consulting the instructions from the previous chapter if you need to).

3. Choose the Eyedropper tool (press I), and set the Sample Size option on the Options bar to 5 by 5 Average. The settings for the Eyedropper affect samples we will be making in later steps on the Hue/Saturation dialog.

📖 Setting the Sample Size for the Eyedropper affects the way sampling tools behave on other tool dialogs.

4. Command+click / Ctrl+click the 3 Dupe Manual Masking layer again to load the layer as a selection. Invert the selection (Select>Inverse). This selects the flowers again.

5. Choose Layer>New Adjustment Layer>Hue/Saturation. Move the Saturation slider to +10. This creates a Hue/Saturation adjustment layer targeted to the flowers and saturates the colors that already exist in the flower.

6. Choose Magenta from the Edit drop list on the Hue/Saturation dialog. We are going to work a little more with the petal color in a particular color range, and this is the first step in narrowing the range.

7. Click in the image over the pink area of the petals. Then click the Add to Sample eyedropper on the Hue/Saturation dialog. This tool will adopt settings you chose in step 3, and allow you to expand on the color range selected in step 6. Click-and-drag the sampler across one of the flower petals (see Figure 4.14). This will select the color range for the petals.

8. Drag the Saturation slider to the right until the pink area of the image is just about to burst with color. I chose +20 for Saturation and +3 for Hue. We will be softening the look a bit so making the color strong is OK as it will be mediated.

📖 The latter Hue setting was merely a preference, but checking a range of hues by moving the Hue slider should tell you how successful your range selection was for the petal color.

FIG 4.14 The initial click sets the standard range, the click-and-drag samples a range of color to add to the initial sample.

This Hue/Saturation technique can be used in a variety of combinations of masking and color range selections, making it a very versatile tool. You might, for example, consider making a change to the center of the flower by choosing another color to edit on the Hue/Saturation screen, creating another range using the sampling tools, and making an adjustment. You may need to combine this with additional masking to achieve the result you are looking for (Figure 4.15). For example, if you set the color range and make a hue adjustment, and it changes other parts that you don't want it to, you can easily block the changes by adjusting the mask.

Masking in this case allows you to make a change, and then localize the change to the area you want corrected. This is just a small hint as to the enormous power of masking. Hold on to that image, there is more to come as we work on soft-focus effects.

FIG 4.15 Because there is a lot of yellow in the eye of the flower, it is virtually impossible to isolate the change by a color range selection alone. Adding masking to the Hue/Saturation can easily limit the change to just the center of the flower.

Add Soft Focus

While there are certainly parts of this image that are in focus, the very shallow depth of field and lighting make the nature of this image a little soft. I find it is usually better to go with the flow, and not try to force a softer image to pretend to be tack sharp. There are ways to make this image look sharper, and we'll look at that a bit later. Enhancing the soft focus may be the more natural and helpful in making this particular image look its best.

Soft-focus effects are achieved photographically by scattering light. You can use soft-focus filters and soft-focus lenses to achieve the effect, and a similar effect can be had by using a UV filter and smearing the outer edge with Vaseline while leaving the center of the lens clear. The latter may seem like quite a sloppy solution, but the reasoning is all the same: disburse some of the light passing into the lens and diffuse it.

To have light you have to have brightness. That is, darker parts of your image will tend to have less light to disburse, and lighter parts will have more. The logical solution for creating soft-focus effects would be to make a selection of image content based on brightness and then copy that to its own layer and blur and that is exactly right. You might follow this up using layer opacity to control the effect, and perhaps layer modes to refine the effect you want.

That is the general idea, although it may be a slight bit oversimplified (technically, you probably want to make this adjustment separately for each component of light, RGB). Following this logic, we can look at a slightly more advanced and satisfying result for this image. Remember that we have already blurred the background, and maybe we want to contain further blurring and effects. We can do that by compounding masks.

📖 Try It Now

1. Create a composite layer at the top of the layer stack and name it 10 Composite Color Enhancements (see Figure 4.16).

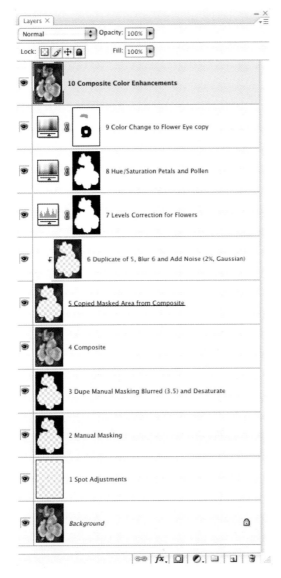

FIG 4.16 Using one layer for the spot corrections early on and adding the color change for the eye of the flower, there are currently 10 layers in this image including the new composite. You may have fewer or more layers depending on the choices you made in processing.

2. Once again, load the mask we made for the flowers as a selection. You can do this in a variety of different ways, but – as we haven't done it quite this way – hold down the Command /

Ctrl key and click on the mask for the Levels or Hue/Saturation layers created in the previous section.

3. Copy the content of the 10 Composite layer to a new layer using the selection you just loaded. Copy and Paste will work, as will Command+J / Ctrl+J. Name the new layer 11 Copied Composite Using Blurred Manual Mask, or similar name.

4. Blur the content of the 11 Copied Composite layer using Gaussian Blur and a radius of 30 pixels. This will turn the image to a horrible blurry mess – however, this is not the immediate goal.

5. Open the Channels palette (Window>Channels). This shows a display of the RGB information for the image at a glance (See Figure 4.17).

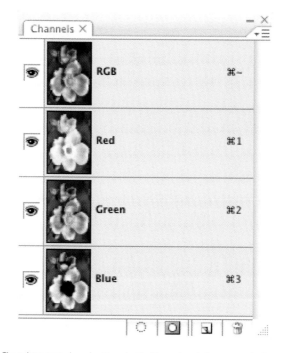

FIG 4.17 The palette controls and options for the Channels palette are very similar to the Layers palette but Channels are quite a different animal, representing the RGB light components of the current image composite.

6. Hold down the Command / Ctrl key and click the thumbnail for the Green channel in the Channels palette to load it as a selection.

📖 Green is at the center of the visible spectrum and as such shares similarities to what we might expect to see as a luminous conversion to black and white, so that is why it is being used. Other channels could be an option as could Luminosity, which is a component of LAB mode. We'll look at Luminosity advantages later in this book.

7. On the Layers palette (you can close the Channels palette if you want), be sure the 11 Copied Composite layer is active, and then click the Add Layer Mask button at the bottom of the Layers palette. This will create a mask for the layer using the Green component. This will block the soft-focus effect in darker portions of the image.

8. Lower the opacity of the 11 Copied Composite layer to 50%. This will allow you to see through the blurring even more.

9. Duplicate the 11 Copied Composite layer and change the mode to Softlight, then name the layer 12 Duplicated Copied Composite. This added layer will enhance the soft focus effect.

The last few steps in the procedure here both lower the effect of the blur by masking and use of opacity, then increase the contrast to compensate for some of the dynamics lost in the blur (Softlight mode). You can further control this effect by making adjustments to the layers you added using Opacity or Modes, increasing/decreasing the amount of blur, or changing the masking (e.g., for variations you could use the Red channel for the mask instead of the Green, or load the mask before making the blur).

This image has come quite a way already, but there is still a ways to go. Be sure to save it off at this point so you can continue with the corrections in the next section. Try toggling the views on and off for the 11 Copied Composite and 12 Duplicate Copied Composite layers just to see the difference before and after the soft-focus addition. You can also compare before and after for the whole process (see the Before and After sidebar).

Before and After
There are several different ways to compare before and after. Here are three different ways:

1. Toggle off the views for all other layers than the Background layer. To do this, you can click-and-drag the cursor over the Layer Visibility Indicators in the layers palette.

2. Use the History palette to toggle between the original and current state of the image by clicking the appropriate states. Click the snapshot at the top of the palette to return to the original state, and the last item in the History to return to the current state (see **Figure 4.18**).

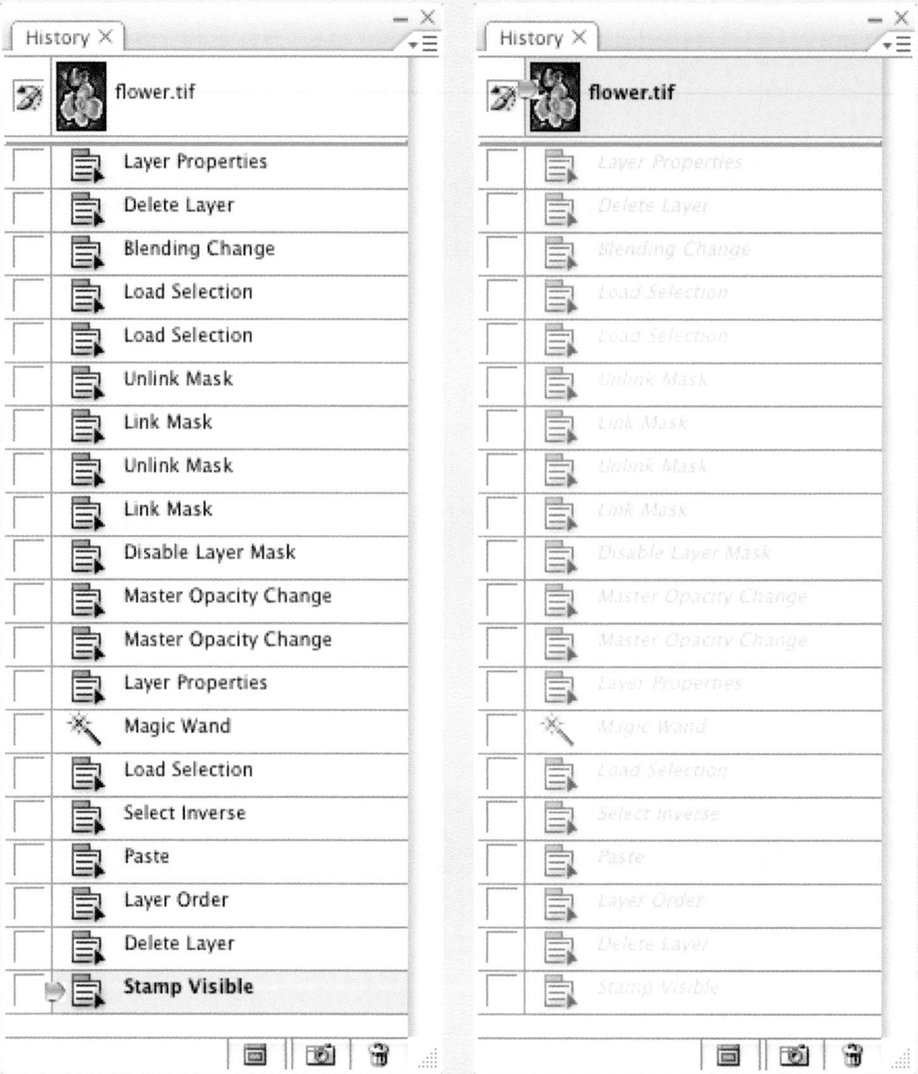

FIG 4.18 The History palette only retains as many states as you have entered in the preferences, but it does maintain the initial state of the image as well. Toggle between the initial state and the last one on the list to see before and after.

3. Duplicate the Background layer and drag the duplicate to the top of the layer stack. Name it Before, and toggle the view as needed.

Any of these methods will work, depending on how you like to work and how you use layers, some methods may prove convenient at different times.

Color Enhancements

Color enhancements for this example image come in two types: enhancement of natural color as we looked at earlier in this chapter, and enhancement by addition which we'll look at here. In this image, adding some muted color to the additional objects in the scene like the stems and buds in the background will make them seem less distant, and more a part of the image, while giving the image a little more dynamics overall. We'll take a look at this color adjustment and how to do it with layers by painting in color enhancements.

📖 Try It Now

1. Create a new layer at the top of the layer stack and call it 13 Green.
2. Choose the paintbrush tool and a small soft brush, then double-click the foreground color swatch on the tool bar and choose a green (I chose RGB: 15, 120, 20). Lower the opacity of the brush to 50%. A 50% brush opacity will layer color as you apply it, yielding density changes that may prove pleasing in the final result.
3. Paint on the 13 Green layer over the areas of the image that you think should be green. I painted over the buds and stems to the left. Don't worry about the coverage being 100% or whether it is completely even – in fact you may not want it to be (see the comments after the exercise).
4. Apply a Gaussian Blur to the layer, just a few pixels (5 or so). This will smooth out and blend in the color.
5. Set the layer to Color mode and adjust the Opacity until it seems pleasing.
6. Add a Hue/Saturation layer as a clipping layer grouped with the 13 Green layer and try variations on the color (adjusting Saturation and Hue sliders) to see if there is a shade you like better.

Add color to additional areas of the image if you wish like the petals, or consider layering color. For example, in this image I used yellow to create some highlights, blue complements may have worked as well. Add a new layer for each of these colors so you can control opacity and blur separately. In fact you may want to add color in layers, using several layers for individual colors to allow varying opacity, blur and modes.

You may also want to experiment using multiple layers, layer modes and brushes. For example, I often use the Fade control and other brush dynamics for size to taper brush strokes and apply other randomizing brush effects. While the layers themselves are acting as masks by locating color to those spots where the brushes are applied, layer masks can be added in addition to confine application areas. There is a lot of room for creative application and we can't possibly cover it all, but we will look at it again in several other exercises as we go.

Sharpen and Enhance Contrast

Sharpening an image is sometimes understood as an action or application of filters done to magically make an image appear to be more in focus. That is not entirely the way it goes. Sharpening is meant to enhance edge contrast and detail that already exist in an image. This means enhancing the sharpness that is already in the image. If an image is utterly out of focus, soft and blurry, then there are no strong edges, nothing to sharpen, and applying some means of sharpening may actually end up making the image worse – depending on how the sharpening is applied and at what strength. The goal of sharpening is not really to snap an out-of-focus image into sharpness.

Sharpening will do several things very well. It will:

• enhance the appearance of sharpness already in an image to make it appear even sharper,
• it can enhance edges in images that are going to print to help counteract dot gain (where ink bleeds into the paper and softens images),
• enhance existing contrast.

On the negative side, sharpening can also:

• cause edges to exhibit haloing, where edge contrast is enhanced too much and appears to create a glow around edges (see Figure 4.19);
• cause image damage by blowing out highlight detail (making color run to absolute white) or blocking up shadow detail (making color run to absolute black).

The upshot is that sharpening can do just as much harm as good if you use it incorrectly. We'll look at best practices for using the Unsharp Mask, and how to use it for both enhancing sharpness and enhancing image contrast. Later we'll look at a much different

FIG 4.19 When images are oversharpened, they may display noticeable haloing on hard edges that appears as an unnatural glow. In this case, with rather extreme settings, a dark halo appears around the flower petals, the edges of the petals blow out, noise is enhanced and detail lost.

means of sharpening by combining several techniques that we have already looked at.

The basic application of the Unsharp Mask attempts to enhance the apparent sharpness of an image. This can work wonders in some images that are already reasonably sharp, and can work well with fine detail like fur. Continue working with the image we've been using throughout this chapter.

📖 **Try It Now**

1. Create a new layer at the top of the layer stack, call it 14 Unsharp Mask.
2. Copy the visible content to the layer by pressing Command+Option+Shift+E / Ctrl+Alt+Shift+E. The unsharp mask will need to be applied directly to the image content.

Unsharp Mask

The Unsharp Mask filter causes a lot of confusion because of its name. It seems incongruous that a filter called 'unsharp' is used for sharpening image.

The name unsharp comes from darkroom practice. A blurred, inverted copy of a negative was sandwiched with the original to create an edge mask. During exposure in the darkroom, that 'unsharp mask' was used to enhance edge separation, increasing the apparent sharpness of the results.

The Unsharp Mask filter attempts to mimic the results of this type of masking using a digital calculation.

An Alternative to Layer Masking

There is an alternative to applying a layer mask that yields identical results, but can sometimes come in handy: using a clipping layer instead of a mask. Try using clipping groups instead of standard layer masks:

1. Activate the Unsharp Mask layer by clicking on it in the layers palette.
2. Create a new layer by clicking the Create New Layer button on the layers palette. Call it Unsharp Mask Masking.
3. Press Command+[/ Ctrl+[to move the new layer below the sharpening layer.
4. Activate the Unsharp Mask layer again by clicking it in the layers palette and press Command+Shift+G / Ctrl+Shift+G (this was Command+G / Ctrl+G for Photoshop CS or earlier). This creates a clipping group from the Unsharp Mask and Unsharp Mask Masking layer.
5. Choose the paintbrush tool, your brush and apply it to the Unsharp Mask Masking layer to reveal the sharpened contents of the Unsharp Mask layer.

With this type of masking it is the solidity of the lower layer (rather than the tone of the mask) which controls what can be seen.

3. Open the Unsharp Mask filter (Filter>Sharpen>Unsharp Mask).
4. In the dialog, set the Amount to between 50% and 100%, the radius to between 1 and 3 pixels and the threshold to 0.

📖 Higher amount and higher Radius will affect more pixels more intensely. The settings noted here work with most images (4–8 megapixels). Use higher Radius and Amount settings for larger images.

5. Click OK.

Depending on your settings and how you have handled the image thus far, sharpening may have given you pleasing, somewhat pleasing, or sorta ornery results. The fact is that very little of this image will need sharpening, and because of the nature of the image and added noise, you may actually experience unpleasant enhancement of noise. Sharpening does not play favorites, it enhances everything in the image.

Your choices are to use the same measures we've been looking at throughout this chapter to control the result: use masking or opacity. Here it may be best to mask the change to the parts of the image that benefit most: the eye of the flower.

📖 Try It Now

1. Be sure the 14 Unsharp Mask layer is active, and click the Add Layer Mask button at the bottom of the Layers palette. This will add a mask to the layer.
2. Fill the mask with black. You can do this by using the Paint Bucket tool with black as the foreground color, or choose Fill from the Edit menu and use Black as the Content.
3. Choose the brush tool and a medium-soft brush, change the foreground to white (press D with the mask thumbnail active), and paint over areas you would like to selectively sharpen (in following the exercise that would be over the eye of the flower). Painting white into the mask reveals those areas.

Another means of applying Unsharp Mask is using a smaller Amount (10–30%) and broader Radius (50–100 pixels). This will enhance the local contrast in your image. This can often work well with images that seem a little flat, but can still be abused and may lead to trouble. There are other techniques that we will look at in later chapters using layer modes that will also enhance local contrast.

📖 Local contrast is part of how objects and colors play against one another. Enhancing local contrast is not as radical as flatly enhancing contrast in an image as it depends on object and color proximity.

Additional Manual Sharpening

One thing you will be able to do here (for practice, fun, learning and if you have the time) is to try and sharpen up the edge of some of the petals which seem soft. Much of this is an artistic decision, but one that relies on a simple idea: lack of sharpness is apparent where edges are blurry. Fix the edges and you improve the sharpness of the image.

A manual way to enhance edges and create sharpness where it seems to be lacking is to paint in new edges using our Clone Stamp and Healing layers.

📖 Try It Now

1. Create a new layer at the top of the layer stack and call it 15 New Edges. This will be used to hold your new adjustments.
2. Choose the Clone Stamp, and a brush that is relatively hard – relative to the image. For this image I set the brush hardness to 80% and chose a brush of 45 pixels without brush dynamics (uncheck other dynamics options in the Brushes palette).

📖 An absolutely hard brush will make an absolutely hard new edge, a softer brush will make a softer edge; 80% seems to work well with this image because it enhances the look of the edge without seeming impossibly sharp in comparison.

3. Sample from another portion of the petal, and then use that sampled to stamp a new edge in the areas where you want the petal to be sharper (see Figure 4.20).

FIG 4.20 Applying the Clone Stamp allows you to make a new harder edge that seems to have more focus, and applying Healing next to that allows you to seamlessly blend in the new edge.

4. Create a new layer for the Healing tool and blend in the new edge by applying Healing to the area between the new edge and the petal. This brush can be about the same as the one chosen for the Clone Stamp but should be 100% hard.

Figure 4.20 shows the technique described in steps 3 and 4 and the immediate result of the edge creation. Continue to build and blend. You can do this right on the same Clone Stamp and Healing layers. See the before and after in Figure 4.21.

FIG 4.21 Applying the Clone Stamp allows you to make a new harder edge that seems to have more focus, and applying Healing next to that allows you to seamlessly blend in the new edge.

Summary

Throughout this rather rambling exercise you have looked at many implementations of layers and masking and the type of separation and application advantages they provide in a real world situation. Six desired adjustments have led to a plethora of changes, and 19 layers in my sample image (see Figure 4.22). The resulting layers can be perused if you open the Sample2_complete.psd image on the CD.

FIG 4.22 Layer stack may differ from the one shown here depending on the steps you have chosen to include throughout this chapter and how you chose to handle them, but the results should be similar.

Throughout this chapter, we have looked with some depth at a variety of ways masking is applied in images. The basic concept is indeed 'masking hides' but it can hide and reveal and becomes a particularly powerful tool when used in combination with layers for the purpose of corrections.

What can be a mask?

- *Layer content*: It masks what is below in the layer stack.
- *A clipping group*: It masks what is grouped above based on layer content.
- *Layer Opacity*: This will allow you to mask the intensity of how an upper layer supersedes content below in the layer stack.
- *Layer Mode*: This will allow you to vary the means by which how an upper layer combines with layers below (we'll look at this in more depth later), effectively masking change.
- *Selection*: It masks changes so they are applied to the selected area only.

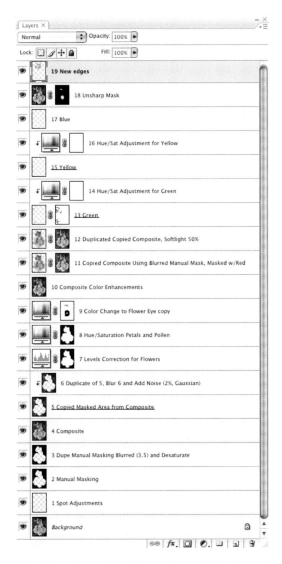

FIG 4.22 (Continued) Depending on what choices you have made (e.g., how you handled cloning changes and color additions) you may have more or fewer layers than shown here.

- *Layer masks*: They mask the portions of the layer they are associated with. Black hides, white reveals, gray hides as a percentage gray or as a semi-transparent mask.
- *Adjustment layer settings*: These can target a color or tonal range.
- *Channels*: These store layer masks and selections, but can become masks themselves.

And there are more advanced masking options left to dig into, like Blend If. The real challenge is to take some of what you have learned about masking in layers and apply it to your own images.

It isn't so important to remember the various means of masking or even the terms. What is important is that masking is a layer property, and you can use it instead of erasing image details, or instead of applying changes directly. Either erasing or applying directly end up permanently obliterating, which is directly opposed to the advantages of non-destructive editing as we intend to explore it in this book. In short, use masks, not the eraser.

Keep in mind that the corrections list you develop for each photo drives your layer creation and the steps you take in making adjustments to your images. Creating the list of what to correct takes a disciplined eye. Some image needs will be obvious, and others may be found as you work through corrections. For now, if you start making those lists in your mind and on paper every time you look at an image, you will begin to see your workflow layout before you like a map. Hopefully with layers you can make all the topographical lines fit together without much trouble. Think about what you are doing with each step, and help yourself with later adjustments by letting layers define the order of changes in the image.

If you get stuck at any time and have questions, visit http://www.photoshopcs.com!

CHAPTER 5

Applying Layer Effects

Somewhere just beyond isolating objects into their own layers and more advanced blending lies the genus of layer-based effects. Effects encompass a broad range of enhancements and adjustments from solid color fills and stroked outlines, to drop shadows and bevels, to combinations of these that create more complex layer styles. Application can be wild effects (often used with type, see Figure 5.1) to more moderate doses that add separation between image objects and subtle image enhancement.

FIG 5.1   A fairly simple application of standard styles can radically change the appearance of type.

It is useful to know what Styles and Effects are, where to find them, how to apply them and how they act. Further utility comes from methods for using and controlling these effects using multiple layers, Fill and Opacity controls, Global Settings and considering application of manual effects – which leads nicely into other topics of correction.

Styles are akin to filters in that you can waste hours and hours applying and adjusting them, then undoing and applying again. It can become addictive when doing creative projects. However, there is a practical side to styles, and we'll look at an overview of effects in this chapter from a standpoint of practical application in image enhancement and touch on the implication for broader creative effects.

The Basics of Effects and Styles

The difference between Styles and Effects is that Effects are the separate functions that can be applied to a layer, and a Style is a preset for any Effect or combination of Effects. There are 10 total effects (Table 5.1).

TABLE 5.1 The basics of Effects and Styles.

	Drop Shadow	Adds a shadow on the outer perimeter of the layer content. Affects only the content in layers below the current layer content.
	Inner Shadow	Adds a shadow inside the perimeter of the layer content. Affects only the content of the current layer.
	Outer Glow	Adds a glow around the content of the layer where it is applied. Affects only the content below the current layer.

TABLE 5.1 (Continued)

	Inner Glow	Adds a glow inside the content of the layer where it is applied. Affects only the content in the current layer.
	Bevel and Emboss	Adds highlights and shadows to a layer to affect a raised (Up) or lowered (Down) appearance. Can be used in several modes, including Outer Bevel (applied to the outer perimeter affecting only layers below), Inner Bevel (applied to the inner perimeter affecting only the current layer), Emboss (applied as both Inner and Outer bevels), Pillow Emboss (applied as Inner Bevel Up and Outer Bevel Down) or Stroke Emboss (applied to Strokes effects only).
	Satin	Applies shading to the inner perimeter of the layer. Supposed to give a satin look.
	Color	Fills the layer content with a color. Affects only the current layer.
	Gradient	Fills the layer content with a gradient. Affects only the current layer.
	Pattern Overlay	Fills the layer content with a pattern. Affects only the current layer.
	Stroke	Strokes the outline of the current layer content using color, a gradient or a pattern.

Photoshop has a set number of Effects (see the list of Effects), and comes with a few canned/prefabricated Styles that you can apply just by choosing an effect from a menu. Styles can be created and saved, or you can download them from the Internet or buy collections and load them to apply at will. These canned styles work well usually for more creative applications, and far less frequently for enhancements. The list of Styles currently loaded can be found on the Styles palette.

📖 Try It Now

1. Open the Sample3.psd image on the CD.
2. Click on the Wild Type Effectz layer in the layers palette if it is not already active.
3. Choose Styles from the Windows menu to open the Styles palette (see Figure 5.2).

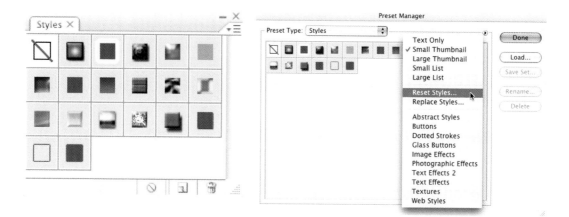

FIG 5.2   The Styles palette shown here has the default Styles. To return to the defaults, choose Preset Manager from the Styles Palette menu, and Reset Styles from the Preset Manager menu

4. Locate the Style named Chrome Satin, and apply it by clicking the thumbnail.

📖 To find Style names, roll your cursor over the styles one-at-a-time. You can also view the names of the styles in the palette by choosing Text, Small List or Large List from the Styles palette menu. Text is text only; Small List and Large List are text and thumbnail preview combinations.

Really that is all there is to applying a style: locate and click. However, there is a little more to working with the styles as we'll see. In the following steps we'll add another Effect to the existing Style.

5. Choose Inner Glow from the Add a Layer Style menu located either at the bottom of the Layers palette, or off the Layers menu (Layer>Layer Styles>Inner Glow). This will open the Layer Style dialog (see Figure 5.3).

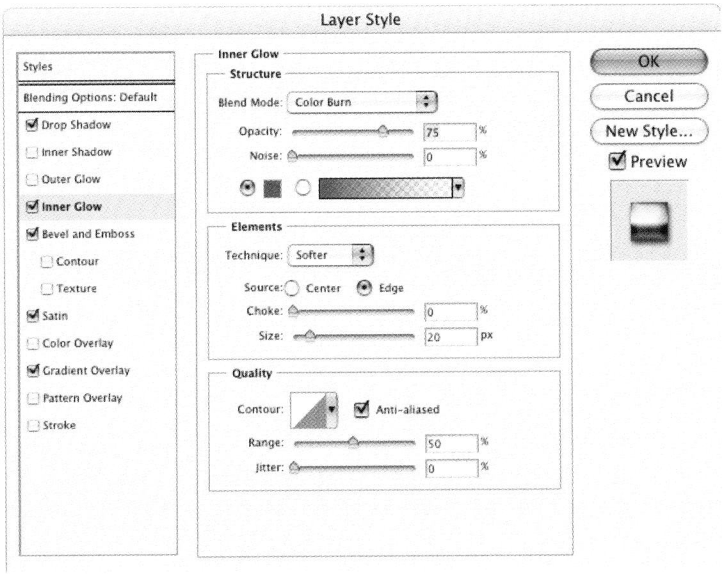

FIG 5.3 The Inner Glow Style to the left of the Layer Style dialog will be checked and highlighted. The Inner Glow options will be displayed at the center of the screen.

6. Change the Blend Mode to Color Burn, and change the color to Red (RGB: 255, 0, 0). This will intensify and burn in the red at the edge of the letters. To change the color to Red, click the Set Color of Glow swatch in the Structure panel and choose the color in the Color Picker that appears.

You can experiment with other settings, but at this point you have replicated the results from Figure 5.1. To see how each of the Effects is contributing to the result of the Style you have applied, uncheck the box next to the Effect at left to toggle the view. To adjust the settings for any of the Effects, just click the name of the Effect to reveal the options, and change them as desired. For example, if you change the Gradient Overlay from –90° to 180°, you will get a much different effect (see Figure 5.4).

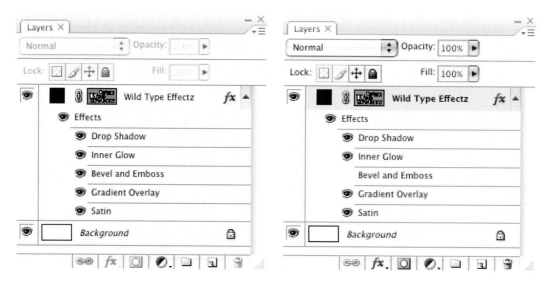

FIG 5.4 Changing the options for any of the Effects will change the result for the Style accordingly.

Separate effects within the style can be managed with a click from the Layers palette, just like they were separate layers. In the layers palette, each effect within the style applied to your layer has a visibility toggle (see Figure 5.5) that you can use to shut off the view for individual effects, or the whole grouping of effects

FIG 5.5 Just click the visibility toggles on individual effects to manage them from the layers palette.

(for the latter use the Effects visibility toggle for the layer). Shut off the Bevel and note the difference in the effect on the image. You can toggle the effect to see, but in the end, leave the visibility for that particular effect off.

This hardly scratches the surface of what styles can do, and hopefully from the fact that you made a small change in one parameter and completely remade the style suggests something about the potential for variety. Be careful with the amount of time you devote to playing around with these and experimenting and set a limit before hand, or you can lose hours of what would otherwise be productive work time correcting images.

Don't close this file; you'll need it in a moment.

📖 I personally find styles most useful for storing favored settings. For example, I occasionally use a bevel effect that is sets both the Highlight and Shadow to black and multiply in combination with the Inner Shadow effect. I like the opportunity the combination gives me to tune the beveling effect. Storing that as a style allows me to apply it with a click. Likewise, you may find half a dozen or so practical settings for reuse, but Styles are more often a creative tool than a correction tool.

Saving Styles

If you hit on a Style that you want to save and perhaps use in the future, you can save the style. Not only that you can save style libraries that you create for specific purposes, or to help you manage styles that you find handy. Say, for example, you like the effect created for the type in **Figure 5.4** in the previous section. You can save the effects as a style and store it for future use.

📖 Try It Now

1. Double-click the Effect item in the layers palette under the layer for the image you were just working on (see **Figure 5.6**). This will open the Layer Style palette.
2. Click the New Style button at the right of the Layer Style palette. This will open the New Style dialog.

FIG 5.6 Double-click right on the item named Effect directly below the layer where the Style that you want to save is applied.

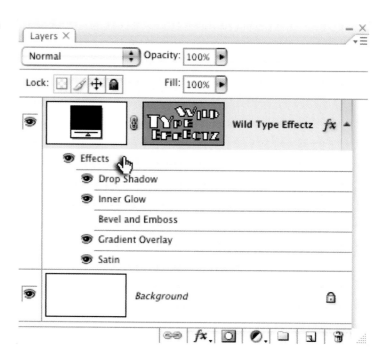

3. Name the new style by something that you will recognize, and click OK (see Figure 5.7). Options at the bottom of the New Style dialog allow you to save blending options (Opacity, Blend If, Channel targeting) as well as the effects. We'll look more at blending options in Chapter 7.

FIG 5.7 Naming the Style may be the most difficult part of this exercise. Try to make the name clarify what the effect does, and feel free to name parameters/effects used.

Now that you have stored the style, you can access it from the Styles menu any time you need to.

📖 Try It Now

1. With the previous image still open, click directly on the Effects item and drag it to the trash at the bottom of the Layers palette. This will remove the effect from the image.

2. Open the Styles palette and click on the Effect you saved in the last segment of the exercise (you should be able to locate it by name). This click will apply the style to your image.

Take a look at the Layers palette. You will notice that if you completed the preceding exercise steps, that the view for the Bevel is included in the saved Style, but that its visibility is off. In other words, the style is stored exactly as it was when you saved it.

Managing Styles

You can download styles from the Internet and load them into Photoshop to have ready-made styles at your disposal. It is easy to build a library of thousands of freebees by downloading them from the Internet and loading them into Photoshop. But keep in mind that all styles are not created equal. Some designers with experience really know what they are doing and how to have a style render with quality, and do very useful things. Don't just download everything in sight, or you will have a huge library that you can't filter through for practical application.

I've included a styles set on the CD put together by my good friend and Photoshop Styles/Effects master, Al Ward (see his website: http://www.actionfx.com). You can use this set to practice loading styles, and to see the kind of effect that good styles can produce.

📖 Try It Now

1. Open Photoshop and insert the CD from The Adobe Photoshop Layers book into your CD-ROM.
2. Open the Preset Manager for Styles. You can do this by choosing Preset Manager from the Edit menu and choosing Styles from the Preset Type list, or by choosing Preset Manager on the Styles palette menu. If you use the Style palette menu, the Styles will be pre-selected.
3. Click the Load button on the Preset Manager screen. This will open a Load dialog (much like a standard Open dialog).
4. Locate the CD in the Load dialog, and then click the ActionFx. com-Styles-00001.asl file in the Styles folder, and then click the Load button on the Load dialog. The styles will populate in the Preset Manager screen.

5. Close the Preset Manager by clicking Done. The styles will be loaded on the Styles palette. You can use them with a click.

Beside the Load option described, you also have the option to load by replacing the current Styles, which will remove the current styles before loading the library that you pick. To return to the default library of preset styles, choose Reset Styles.

Periodically you may want to save your Styles set as a library so you can use it with some flexibility. Depending on how you like to work, you may save several libraries to group your styles, or a single library with your most used effects. Saving will allow you to return to set should you inadvertently delete them or replace them. To save a Style library, just choose Save Styles from the Styles palette menu. When the Save dialog appears (see Figure 5.8), name the file (leave the .asl extension on the file name), and you can save it anywhere you'd like.

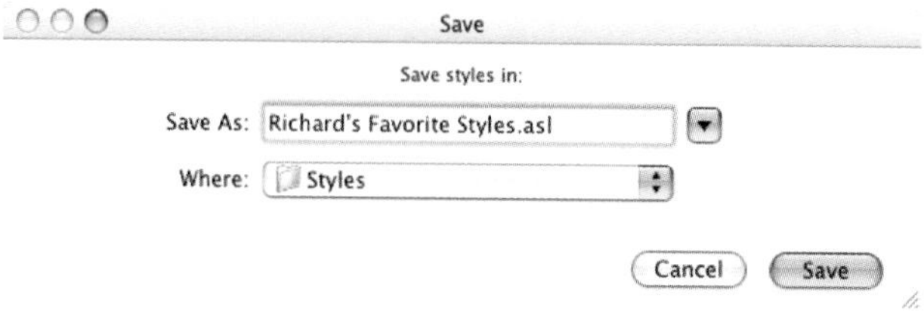

FIG 5.8 It may be best to save to a folder that gets backed up periodically, or to the Photoshop Styles folder inside the Presets folder in the program directory/folder.

Manual Effects

Although layer styles are handy for quick application of effects, there are built-in limitations to them. You are not limited to creating effects by using the layer styles. You can create effects manually so long as you understand how to create them. In fact, making your effects manually can offer a measure of flexibility that you simply can't get from applying the canned effects, with more potential for variations.

📖 Try It Now

1. Open the sample3.psd again from the CD. We'll want to start from scratch here with the original image.
2. Click on the Background layer to activate it in the Layers palette if it isn't active already.

3. Create a new layer and name it Drop Shadow.
4. Hold down the Command/Ctrl key and click on the vector mask thumbnail for the Wild Type Effectz layer. This will load the vector mask as a selection (see Figure 5.9).

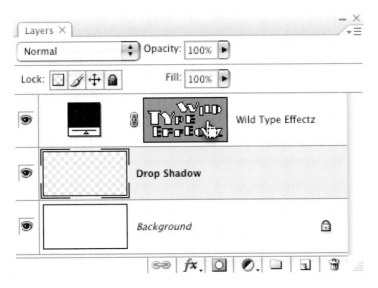

FIG 5.9 Holding down the Command/Ctrl key and clicking the vector mask will load the mask as a selection.

5. Fill the selection with Red (RGB: 255, 0, 0). You can do this by setting the foreground color and then using the Paint Bucket tool or with the Fill function (Edit>Fill) with the color set to Foreground. The selection will fill in the active Drop Shadow layer.
6. Deselect (press Command+D/Ctrl+D).
7. Apply a Gaussian Blur of 5 pixels. This will soften the edge of the color added in step 5.
8. Change the Opacity of the Drop Shadow layer to 75%. This will lighten the drop shadow.
9. Offset the content of the Drop Shadow layer down and to the right. To do this choose the Move tool (press V) hold down the Shift key and press the down arrow on the keyboard and then the right arrow. You can use the Offset function if you want (Filter>Other>Offset). The result should look something like Figure 5.10. This offset will simulate the angle between the object (in this case type) and the light source.

FIG 5.10 The reddish drop shadow is one of the simplest effects to create manually.

📖 Holding the Shift key when using the arrows on your keyboard will move the content on the active layer ten pixels at a time rather than one.

All other effects can be created in a similar fashion using layers. For example, you can do inner shadows and glows by clicking the Wild Type Effectz layer in step 2, making a clipping group with the new layer created in step 3 and inverting the selection in step 4.

The real advantage to making effects manually is that the effects are actual pixels rather than virtual ones so you can treat the effects more like an editable part of the image. If you want you can apply layer styles to the layers where you have created the effects. You also have freedom of movement and adjustment without having to visit the Layer Styles dialog. We'll look at making custom adjustment near the end of the chapter.

You can see from the nine steps above used to create a drop shadow that it probably is not worth the trouble if you can get a similar effect with a one-click layer style. However, there are ways to simplify creating manual effects, and we'll look at those next.

Automated Manual Effects Tools
On the CD you will find a file named Layer Actions.atn, which is a set of actions that will create several layer-based effects with a click. The actions are time-savers because they will run through a series of steps that have been pre-recorded. For example, the steps above for creating the drop shadow have been recorded for the Drop Shadow/Glow action, and you can replay it with a single-click and some minimal user input. First you'll need to load the actions.

Loading Actions

We will load actions several times throughout the book to simplify lengthy procedures and provide tools for completing repetitive tasks, like making manual drop shadows. Come back to these steps if you need a refresher on loading actions later.

a. Open the Actions palette by choosing Actions from the Window menu, or press Option+F9/Alt+F9.

b. Choose Load Actions from the Actions palette menu.

c. When the Load dialog appears, locate the CD for the book, and the Actions folder. Choose Layer_Effects.atn and then click the Load button. The actions will populate in the Actions palette. The actions should appear like **Figure 5.11**.

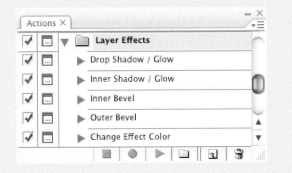

FIG 5.11 You may have other actions in your actions palette, but Layer Effects will load as an action set, containing Drop Shadow/Glow, Inner Shadow/Glow, Inner Bevel, Outer Bevel and Change Effect Color.

📖 Try It Now

1. Start with Sample3.psd. Either open it fresh from the CD, or revert the file to the original image state by clicking the thumbnail in the image history.
2. Load the Layer_Effects.atn action into the Photoshop Actions palette. You will only have to load the actions once.
3. Set the foreground color to Red (RGB: 255, 0, 0). This color will be used by the action to define the color of the effect.
4. Activate the Wild Type Effectz layer by clicking it in the layers palette.
5. Run the Drop Shadow/Glow action. To do this, click the Drop Shadow/Glow action in the Layer Effects set on the Actions

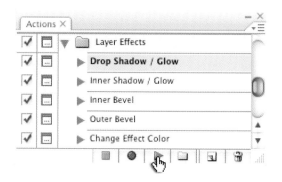

FIG 5.12 Click the Play button at the bottom of the Actions palette to play the active selection.

palette, then click the Play button at the bottom of the Actions palette (see Figure 5.12).

6. Follow the instructions as they appear on screen. Use the default Offset (+10, +10) and change the Gaussian Blur radius to 5 pixels to match the results of the previous exercise. This will create a drop shadow that falls to the lower right.

Now that the actions are loaded, the process is several steps easier. In the case of applying a bevel, it is many steps easier. But the true glory of knowing how to apply layer effects manually is not just in being able to apply a simple drop shadow or bevel to some isolated type. Benefits come in as flexibility in placement and control as well as in options you gain for applying layer styles in combination with manual effects, or even applying the styles to the effects themselves. Part of what distinguishes manual effects from layer styles, as you will have a difficult time applying compound effects if you use only Layer Styles. We'll look at a more complicated example in the next section that combines Layer Styles, manual effects and even masking.

Close this image without saving before proceeding.

Combining Manual Effects and Styles

In keeping with the layer mentality, it is sometimes best to apply effects to separate layers rather than all at once as a single style on a single layer. However, there are times when layer Styles do everything you need them to, and times when you will want to use both manual and canned effects to orchestrate your results.

Say, for example, you want to create an effect on your type where it looks like the type is transparent. That is, the effects that appear in the background will be seen through the type. You could try reducing the opacity of the layer, but what you'll find is that it reduces the opacity of the effect as well. Combining style and effect application in various ways will help get the desired results.

In this example we will build an effect using a combination of layer styles and draw on everything we have touched on in this chapter.

📖 Try It Now

1. Open the Sample3.psd image from the CD.
2. Click the Wild Type Effectz layer in the layers palette to activate it.
3. Apply the type effect saved earlier in this chapter by clicking it in the Styles palette. The text shows it saved as Wild Type Effect in Figure 5.7, but you may have used another name. The result for the image and Layers palette should look like Figure 5.13.

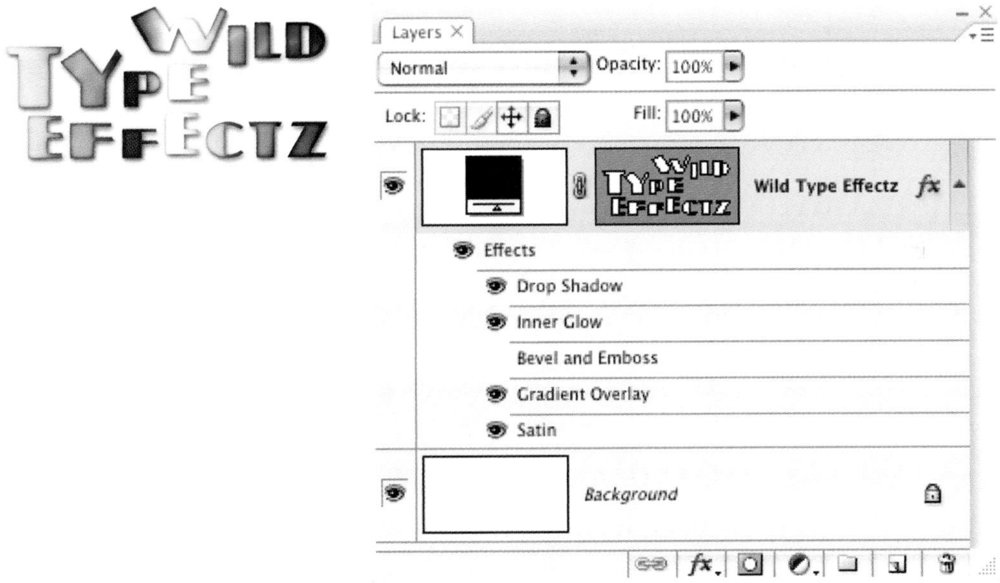

FIG 5.13 After applying the saved style, the image should display the properties inherited from the stored Style.

4. Drag Bevel and Emboss, Gradient Overlay and Drop Shadow to the trash on the layers palette. This should leave you only with Inner Glow and Satin effects, as in Figure 5.14. This removes those effects from the style as it is applied in the image.

125

FIG 5.14 After removing the effects, the image will visibly revert to what it looked like when it was opened, but two effects are still being applied — you just can't see them because of the black color of the layer.

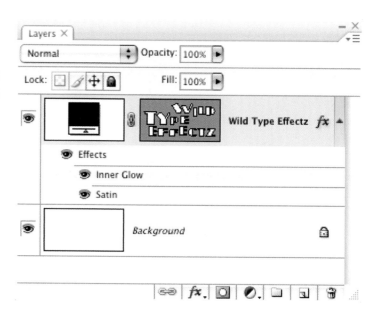

5. Choose Color Overlay from the Add a Layer Style menu at the bottom of the Layers palette. This will open the Layer Styles with Color Overlay selected.
6. Double-click the Set Color of Overlay swatch to the right of the Blend Mode drop list, and set the color in the Color Overlay to RGB: 110, 170, 240 in the Color Picker when it appears (Figure 5.15).

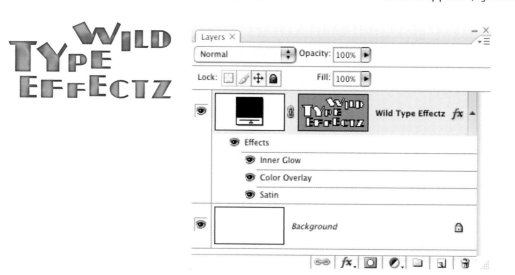

FIG 5.15 The color suggested was sampled from the 'I' in Wild in the image after step 3. You should now see the results of all three effects: Inner Glow, Color Overlay and Satin.

📖 The remaining effects make specific results in the image. The Satin will leave a slight sheen on the letters. The Color Overlay provides the base color. The Inner Glow provides the reddened edges.

7. Change the Foreground color to Black (RGB: 0, 0, 0). This will be used in applying a manual drop shadow.
8. Apply a manual drop shadow using the Drop Shadow / Glow action provided with the Layer Effects action set loaded earlier in this chapter. Use an Offset of +20, +20 and a Gaussian Blur of 10 (the default blur) (Figure 5.16).

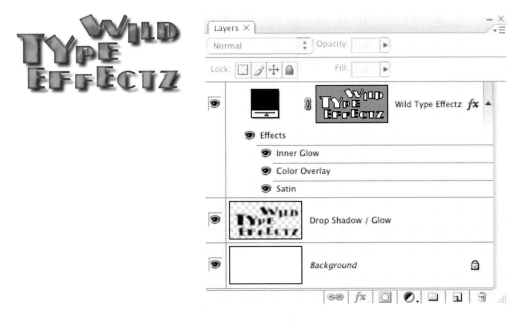

FIG 5.16   The result at this point shows a plain drop shadow in blue, as if the type object were very much opaque.

9. Copy the Layer Style applied to the Wild Type Effectz layer. To do this on PC/Windows, right-click on the Effects item under the Wild Type Effects layer and choose Copy Layer Style from the menu that appears. On Macintosh, hold down the Control key on the keyboard and click the Effects item, then choose Copy Layer Style from the menu that appears.
10. Paste the Layer Style copied in the previous step to the Drop Shadow/Glow layer. To do this, activate the Drop Shadow/

Glow layer, and follow the instructions in step 9, but choose Paste Layer Style. Alternatively you can choose Paste Layer Style from the Layer menu (Layer>Layer Style>Paste Layer Style). Pasting the style applies it to the layer.

11. Shut off the visibility toggle for the Satin effect for the Drop Shadow / Glow layer, and lower the Opacity to 70%. This will remove the Satin's sheen from the drop shadow and fade the drop shadow a bit. At this point the results should look like Figure 5.17.

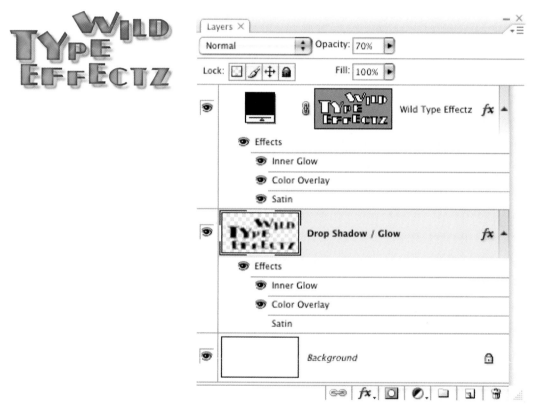

FIG 5.17 Copying the layer Style from one layer to another makes sure the settings are similar between the drop shadow and the original object. Only appropriate effects should apply, so the Satin is turned off as the drop shadow will not reflect the sheen. However, the type still is not acting translucent.

12. Duplicate the Drop Shadow/Glow layer, rename the layer Translucence and move it to the top of the layer stack. This layer will be used to make the letters seem translucent.

13. Load the Wild Type Effectz vector mask as a selection. To do this hold down the Command/Ctrl key and click on the vector

mask thumbnail in the layers palette. This will be used to mask the translucent effect to the letters only.

14. With the Translucence layer still active, click the Add Layer Mask button at the bottom of the layers palette. This will use the selection you just loaded to define the mask and target the Translucence layer to the type only.

15. Lower the opacity of the Translucence layer to account for the opacity of the type object. The more you lower the opacity, the more opaque the type will appear (Figure 5.18).

FIG 5.18 Setting the Translucence layer to 35% Opacity makes the letters about 50% transparent (half the original 70% opacity of the drop shadow).

Vector Masks

Vector masks are similar to layer masks but are controlled with vector content. Vectors are used in the Sample images in this chapter to define the content of the type layers. This is done for several reasons: the most prominent of which is that not everyone will have the type face that I used (Plug-NickelBlack). If you don't have the type face and I left the type layer as it was, Photoshop would choose a substitute. I converted the type to vectors using Convert to Shape (Layer> Type>Convert to Shape). This command will make perfectly defined type shapes. Though the result can no longer be edited as type, it does have the advantage that it can be infinitely scaled.

Part of what makes vector components in your images distinct is that vectors are not resolution dependent. Vectors act more to corral pixels than define them absolutely. You will more often find vectors are used for logos and illustration rather than image correction (though some like to use the pen tool to help define selections). The advantage to defining illustration elements as vectors lies in the ability to infinitely scale them: if you design a vector logo, it will look its best on a business card or billboard, and won't develop the fuzzy edges you would get with pixel-based design.

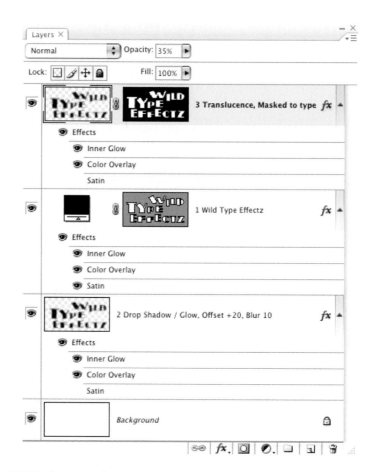

FIG 5.19 Comments and numbering help round out the layer advantage.

At this point we have successfully combined manual effects and layer styles in a way that would likely be more difficult and more time consuming using either alone. Check your results against the sample4.psd file included on the CD.

The layer styles do the bulk of the work in this example by simplifying the application and making the result more consistent, but without the help of the manual drop shadow the result becomes more difficult to achieve, as well as less flexible. As with most results in Photoshop it is not a single tool or application that provides the best results, but combinations.

To finish off the example to conform with the technique of using Layers for organization, you may want to add numbers to the layers so that you know what order they were created in. You may also want to add some notes as to settings used for the offset and blur. With these final additions, the layers palette would look like Figure 5.19.

Summary

Later Styles and Effects are layer-specific tools that carry with them a plethora of possibilities. The effects are the tools, but the real catalyst here is layers. Layers are the means by which layer effects and Styles can be assimilated and propagated in images for corrective and creative purposes. They are also the means of creating new sources to which additional effects and styles can be applied to (such as the shape for the drop shadow, and mechanism for creating translucence).

In the seemingly simple examples in this chapter, we have used vector and layer masks, manual and layer-based styles and effects, visibility toggles, opacity and modes. The results achieved are not so much an application of any one item as an orchestration of various functions and capabilities that culminate in the result. This is the *modus operandi* for much of Photoshop correction: results are born in the application of tools in unison. Layer styles are a powerful tool in their own right, but will likely often work best with layer modes. One of the hardest things to envision using layers may be what Layer Modes achieve. We look at them in the next chapter.

Layer Styles can help do many things, from adding a creative frame to an image in varying complexity, to creating text effects, to driving some image enhancements. Things that come to mind as practical corrections are simple exercises in separation where you add a drop shadow or glow to burn or dodge an edge around an isolated object, or where beveling or embossing may actually help enhance contour.

Creative application of styles on the other hand opens endless possibility. Though they may not technically be 'styles' in that they cannot be defined by the set number of layer 'effects', we see examples of applying 'styles' throughout this book in various examples, akin to the manual styles we looked at in this chapter. These effects include everything from simple dodge and burn, and application of techniques for soft focus (like those we looked at in Chapter 4), to more elaborate calculations such as manual sharpening techniques, and beyond. Many of these techniques could just as easily be relegated to standard calculations and

Fill vs. Opacity

Fill and Opacity may cause some confusion if you apply them casually to layers and try to determine the difference in using one over the other. Let's try the following to make the difference more clear. Open the Sample3.psd image one more time. Click the Wild Type Effectz to activate it, and choose Outer Glow from the Add a Layer Style menu at the bottom of the layers palette. When the layer Style dialog appears, change the Blend Mode to Normal (or perhaps Dissolve), the Size to 100 pixels, and the color to Red (RGB: 255, 0, 0), then click OK.

Go to the Opacity for the layer on the layers palette and swing the slider from 100% to 0% and back again to 100%. The whole content of the image will fade and return. Now try the same thing with Fill (leaving Opacity at 100%). Only the actual content of the layer will fade and return, the effect remains the same.

Opacity affects the entire layer, and Fill affects the content of the layer only – not the styles that have been applied.

effects (but they are just not defined as such because they are not in the standard Effects grouping).

One of the key concepts for looking at layers in this chapter is the concept of orchestrating layers to achieve a result. It is not often practical or desirable to try and achieve a result in your images all at once with one application of one tool, or even one application of one layer or one effect. Most effects and results can be achieved in more than one way. In the examples in this chapter it took only a few layers to achieve the translucence effect, but the example is steeped in the broader vision you will need to use layers effectively. As we have seen, the background and lower layers are a stage to build from. Older layers in the image can be borrowed from, reused, and generated to varying results. Envisioning the result is the key to success, and layer styles are just another building block to help form results.

Please visit http://www.photoshopcs.com for more information and resources for Photoshop styles.

CHAPTER 6

Onion

Exploring Layer Modes

ayer Modes are an enigma. They are located in a drop list at the top of the layers palette in a very prominent spot, which suggests they are one of the most important tools in the layers palette. The modes have names, but few people really understand how to work with them or what they do from the name alone, unless they read about changing a mode in a tutorial.

Many times people don't stray from the Normal mode as the rest is mostly a mystery. Other episodes of layer mode use will find people applying modes by trial and error: they experiment till they see something that they like, and either keep the result or try another mode. This kind of hit-or-miss application is fine, and can produce pleasant surprises but it will gobble up huge amounts of your imaging 'play' time. There is, however, a better approach to applying layer modes: actually knowing what they do and when they can be helpful.

In this chapter, we'll look at a general overview of layer modes, what they are, how to apply them and what they can accomplish. We'll look at ways that you can use layer modes every day for image enhancements and improvements using layer modes to target your corrections.

Layer Mode Behavior

Blending modes can be a creative or practical tool for combining and enhancing images and layer content. However, as the misunderstood half-sister of Styles and Filters, modes proffer little more to most users than a means for experimentation. Like winery visitors lining up at the tasting bar after a tour, users swish and sample anything that gets poured in a glass, hoping something will stand out to their palette. Here too, experimentation can be fun, but better understanding can turn fruitless experimentation into selective choice.

Modes, put simply, are a means of blending the content of two or more layers. It can help to start thinking of modes as a means of turning layers into image calculators. When a layer is set to a particular mode, the content of the layer acts in that mode on the content of the visible layers below it in the layer stack. The visible result is a direct correlation to a cold calculation built into the mode. Most layer modes are not really useful for everyday correction, but some are, and when they are useful, they are very powerful tools. The whole problem in making calculations work for you is deciding what to do – and what mode you'll want to use to accomplish the result. Using modes is dependent on knowing how they act.

Though it is often what users look for, flat descriptions of the numeric calculations may be the least helpful means of really understanding what a mode accomplishes. It is often difficult even for the mathematically inclined to envision how a calculation applies as a result. Descriptions of the effect may be slightly more helpful, but not entirely intuitive. A combination of description and a simple example may be most helpful, and that is what we will look at here to start you thinking about how to employ modes.

Figure 6.1 shows two simple layers that will be used as the source images for comparing how the modes behave when applied to tone. You can find these layers in the Sample5.psd file on the CD, already stacked in layers in an image if you want to play along.

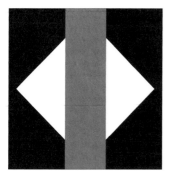

FIG 6.1 There is more to modes than evaluating how black, white and gray combine, but simplicity can be a valuable teacher. This should reveal how tone and even color channels will behave in a particular mode.

Figure 6.2 shows two layers that can be used to evaluate how modes behave when applied to color and tone. You can find these set up in the Sample6.psd file on the CD.

FIG 6.2 These color swatches pit one color rainbow against another to show color behavior. It is perhaps prettier as a result exploring the full harmonics, but harder to intuit.

To test the modes, all we will be doing is changing mode of the upper layer in the test file (and when applicable, opacity) to see the effect modes have on what we see on screen. Simply open one or both of the sample images, activate the Upper Layer/Calculation Layer, and choose a mode from the Mode drop list. This will apply the mode, and hopefully give you some visual sense of what happens when layers are applied with different modes, then we'll look at some more concrete examples as to how this applies to images.

   📖 All descriptions listed here assume the upper layer is opaque (layers set to 100% Opacity with pixel solidity), unless opacity is otherwise mentioned. The name of the mode is followed by the previews and description, which includes practical uses for the modes. This is not meant to define limitations; there may be many creative uses for any particular mode that go beyond the simple descriptions.

Normal

FIG 6.3 Straightforward application of layer content where the upper layer covers everything below. Used most frequently of all modes.

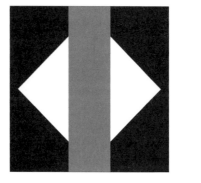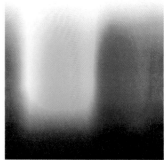

Normal mode is a plain overlay of content in the upper layer. The result takes on the color/tone of the pixels in the upper layer. This is the default mode of layers, and is probably by far the most often used (Figure 6.3).

Dissolve

FIG 6.4 Shown here at 50% Opacity. Creates a dithering effect. Used infrequently in corrections/enhancements.

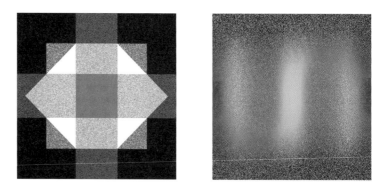

The result is the color/tone of the pixels in either the upper layer or the lower layer, determined on a pixel by pixel basis according to the opacity of the layer. The upper layer is dithered according to the Opacity percentage and solidity of the layer content: the Opacity percentage dictates the percentage of pixels in the layer that will display. The greater the opacity, the more pixels display. At 100% opacity, 100% of the pixels in the upper layer display; at 50% opacity, 50% of the pixels in the upper layer display. Pixels are hidden in a randomized or dithered effect. May be best for specialized uses for web graphics and other dithered effects (Figure 6.4).

Darken

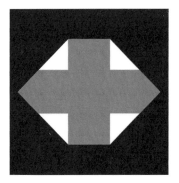

FIG 6.5 Nothing becomes darker than either of the 2 pixels occupying a space. Used occasionally in corrections/enhancements.

Chooses the darkest color value in each channel comparing the upper layer and the layer(s) (Figure 6.5). No portion of the image gets lighter. For example, in an RGB image, if the upper layer pixel is RGB 255, 170, 33, and the lower layer pixel is RGB 45, 165, 44, the result in Darken mode is the lower of any of these numbers for each channel, or RGB 45, 165, 33. The result will never get darker than existing values. Used as a means of darkening content where the application cannot exceed lightening beyond the colors being applied.

Multiply

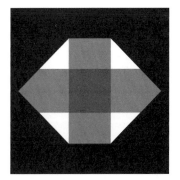

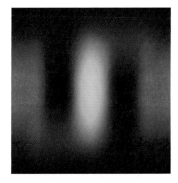

FIG 6.6 Each pixel darkens, equal to or darker than pixels occupying the space. Used frequently in corrections/enhancements.

Darkens the result by darkening the lower layer based on the darkness of the upper layer. Any tone darker than white in the Multiply layer darkens the appearance of content (Figure 6.6). Successive applications of layers in Multiply mode will produce a continually darker result, and will get darker than existing values.

No portion of the image can get lighter. Often used with effects like drop shadows and beveling. Useful in layer-based color separation for RGB and CMYK (Chapter 8).

Color Burn

FIG 6.7 Each pixel darkens, equal to or darker than pixels occupying the space based on the difference between pixel colors. Used infrequently in corrections/ enhancements.

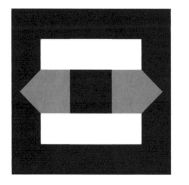

Burns in (darkens) the color of the lower layer with the upper layer, darkening the result. Tends to burn in or enrich color density. No portion of the image gets lighter. The greater the difference between the applied pixel colors and the content (Figure 6.7), the greater the percentage of change. Used for special effects and some color enhancement.

Linear Burn

FIG 6.8 Each pixel darkens, equal to or darker than pixels occupying the space. A linear application of darkening. Used infrequently in corrections/ enhancements

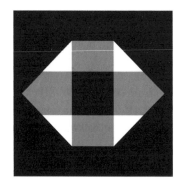

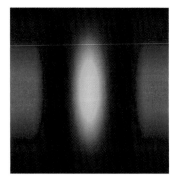

Similar to Multiply but more extreme and linear in application. No portion of the image can get lighter (Figure 6.8). Used in calculations, like layer-based channel mixing (see Chapter 8).

Darker Color

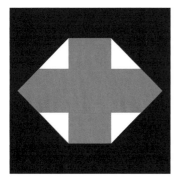 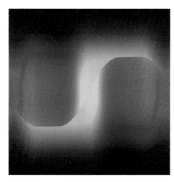

FIG 6.9 Chooses the darker of two colors for pixels occupying a space. Used infrequently in corrections/ enhancements.

New in CS3. Chooses the darker of two colors in comparing pixels in the upper layer to pixels (Figure 6.9). No color in the image can get lighter.

Lighten

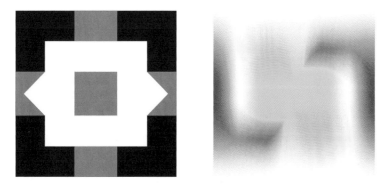

FIG 6.10 Nothing can become lighter than either of the RGB values of the two pixels occupying a space in the layer stack. Used occasionally in corrections/ enhancements.

Chooses the lightest color value in each channel comparing the upper layer and the layer(s) (Figure 6.10). No portion of the image gets darker. For example, in an RGB image, if the upper layer pixel is RGB 255, 170, 33, and the lower layer pixel is RGB 45, 165, 44, the result is the greater of any of these numbers or RGB 255, 170, 44. Used as a means of lightening underlying content, where the application cannot exceed lightening beyond the colors being applied.

Screen

FIG 6.11 FIG 6.11 Each pixel lightens, equal to or lighter than pixels occupying the space in the layer stack. Used frequently in corrections/enhancements.

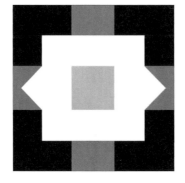 

Brightens the result by lightening the lower layer based on the lightness of the upper layer. Any tone lighter than black in the upper layer lightens the appearance of the content (Figure 6.11). Successive applications of layers in Screen mode will produce a continually lighter result, and will get lighter than existing values. No portion of the image can get darker. Often used with effects like glows and beveling. Useful in layer-based color separation for RGB and CMYK (Chapter 8).

Color Dodge

FIG 6.12 Each pixel lightens, equal to or lighter than pixels occupying the space based on the difference between pixel colors. Used infrequently in corrections/enhancements.

Dodges (lightens) the color of the underlying layer with the upper layer, lightening the result. Tends to desaturate and wash out color. No portion of the image gets darker. The greater the difference between the applied pixel colors and the content (Figure 6.12), the greater the percentage of change. Used for special effects and some color enhancement.

Linear Dodge

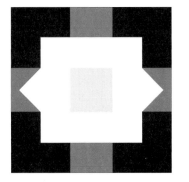 

FIG 6.13   Each pixel lightens, equal to or lighter than pixels occupying the space. A linear application of brightening. Used infrequently in corrections/enhancements.

Similar to Screen but more extreme and linear in application. No portion of the image can get darker (Figure 6.13). Used in calculations, like layer-based channel mixing (see Chapter 8).

Lighter Color

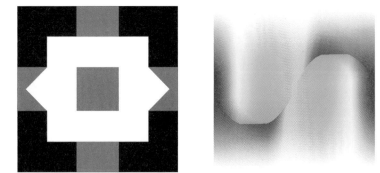

FIG 6.14   Chooses the lighter of two colors for pixels occupying a space in the layer stack. Used infrequently in corrections/enhancements.

New in CS3. Chooses the lighter of two colors in comparing pixels the upper layer to pixels (Figure 6.14). No color in the image can get darker.

Overlay

FIG 6.15 Used in many places in the book for layer-based correction/enhancement. Used frequently in corrections/enhancements.

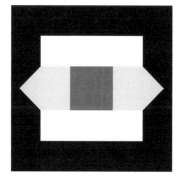 

FIG 6.15 Used in many places in the book for layer-based correction/enhancement. Used frequently in corrections/enhancements.

Multiplies (darkens) the dark colors (1–49% brightness) and screens (lightens) the light colors (51–99% brightness) in the lower layer based on the content of the upper layer. This enhances contrast with like content (if you make a composite at the top of the layer stack and set to Overlay), and lowers contrast in inverted content (if you make a composite at the top of the layer stack, invert it and set to Overlay). If the applied tone is lighter than 50% gray, the result lightens; if darker than 50% gray, it darkens. Colors at the center of the light and dark range (quartertones at 75% and 25% gray) are effected more than the range extremes (0%, 100% or 50% gray). Useful for manual sharpening effects (looked at later in this chapter). Also useful for intensifying color and contrast (Figure 6.15).

Soft Light

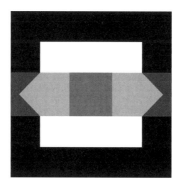 

FIG 6.16 Used in some places in the book for layer-based correction/enhancement. Used occasionally in corrections/enhancements.

Multiplies (darkens) the dark colors (1–49% brightness) and screens (lightens) the light colors (51–100% brightness) in lower layers based on the content of the upper layer. Similar to Overlay but not as strong. If the applied color is light, the pixel lightens; if dark, it darkens. Useful in some special effects (soft focus) and intensifying color and contrast (Figure 6.16).

Hard Light

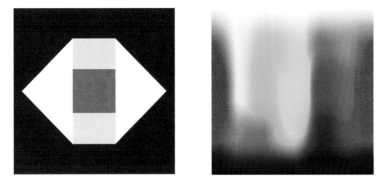

FIG 6.17 Used infrequently in corrections/enhancements.

Multiplies (darkens) the dark colors (0–49% brightness) and screens (lightens) the light colors (51–100% brightness) in the lower layers based on the content of the upper layer. Similar to Soft Light and Overlay but more linear. Useful in some special effects and intensifying color and contrast (Figure 6.17).

Vivid Light

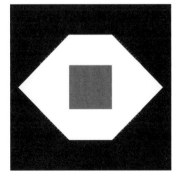

FIG 6.18 Used infrequently in corrections/enhancements.

Similar to Color Burn when the pixel in the upper layer is darker than 50% gray; similar to Color Dodge when the pixel in the upper layer is lighter than 50% gray (Figure 6.18).

Linear Light

FIG 6.19 Used infrequently in corrections/enhancements.

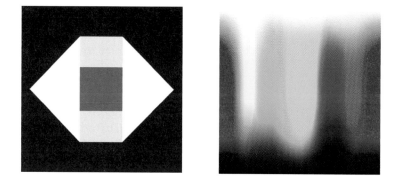

Similar to Linear Burn when the color in the upper layer is darker than 50% gray; similar to Linear Dodge when color in the upper layer is lighter than 50% gray (Figure 6.19).

Pin Light

FIG 6.20 Used rarely in corrections/enhancements.

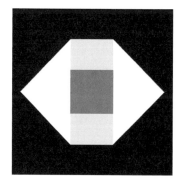

Similar to Multiply when the upper layer is darker than 50% gray; similar to Screen when the upper layer is lighter than 50% gray (Figure 6.20).

Hard Mix

FIG 6.21 Used rarely in corrections/enhancements.

Adds a limited color palette effect to the Vivid Light effect. It will posterize the result to appear as one of eight primary colors: white, red, green, blue, cyan magenta, yellow or black (Figure 6.21).

Difference

FIG 6.22 Used occasionally for comparing layer content.

Shows the result of calculating the difference between pixel values. A large difference yields a bright result; a small difference yields a dark result (no difference yields black). Useful in image evaluations to show/measure differences between corrections, and some special effects (Figure 6.22).

Exclusion

FIG 6.23 Used rarely in corrections/enhancements.

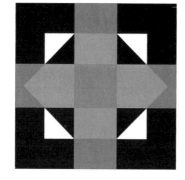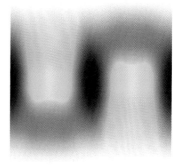

Uses the darkness of the upper layer to mask the Difference effect (see Difference). If the upper layer pixel is dark, there is little change as the result; if the upper layer pixel is black, there is no change. The lighter the pixel in the upper layer, the more intense the potential Difference effect. Mostly used for special effects (Figure 6.23).

Hue

FIG 6.24 Used occasionally in corrections/enhancements to adjust hue.

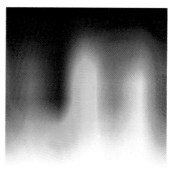

Changes the Hue of the pixels in the lower layers based on the upper layer while leaving the Saturation and Luminosity unchanged. Used for color adjustment (Figure 6.24).

Saturation

FIG 6.25 Used occasionally in corrections/enhancements to enhance saturation or desaturate.

Changes the Saturation of the pixels in the lower layers based on the upper layer while leaving the Hue and Luminosity unchanged. Used for color adjustment (Figure 6.25).

Color

 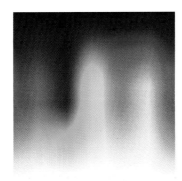

FIG 6.26 Used frequently in corrections/enhancements to adjust or apply and even remove color.

Changes the Hue and Saturation of the pixels in the lower layers based on the upper layer while leaving the Luminosity unchanged. Used for color adjustment and layer-based Luminosity and Color separations (later in this chapter) (Figure 6.26).

Luminosity

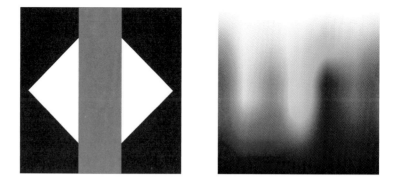

FIG 6.27 Used frequently in corrections/enhancements to adjust tone independently of color.

Changes the Luminosity of the pixels in the lower layers based on the upper layer while leaving the Saturation and Hue unchanged. Used for tone adjustment and layer-based Luminosity and Color separations (later in this chapter) (Figure 6.27).

You can use these pages as a reference. The captions suggest the modes you are likely to use most frequently and with the most success. However, just to highlight them here, these modes are:

- Normal
- Multiply
- Screen
- Overlay
- Soft light
- Color
- Luminosity
- Difference
- Darken
- Lighten.

The reason for dependence on this subset is that the other modes are most often just variations of these, and the result you get might be better controlled with Opacity or duplicating layers with these modes, rather than reaching for a less predictable or more complex mode.

Let's take a look at some practical applications of layer modes to see how you might employ them to accomplish some useful results, starting with separating color and tone.

Separating Color and Tone

In our discussion of isolating objects, image areas and using masking, we concentrated on simple isolation based on shape. A whole different realm of isolation can be explored in isolating by color or tone. Layer modes can help make this possible.

One of the easiest results you can easily digest in working with layer modes is applying Color and Luminosity. With these two modes you can isolate the content of a layer so it affects only tone, or only color. You can also use this same functionality to isolate content based on those modes. Separation is accomplished quickly with simple layer-based calculations and application of layer modes.

📖 Try It Now

1. Open any image. Or you can use the Sample7.psd image provided on the CD (see Figure 6.28).

FIG 6.28   A version of the cover shot for this book will provide plenty of color and tone for exploring the Luminosity and Color separations.

2. Flatten the image if it is not flattened already (choose Flatten Image from the Layers menu). Flattened images will have a Background layer only.
3. Duplicate the Background layer and name the duplicate 1 Source.
4. Create a new layer above the 1 Source layer, and name it 2 Grayscale.
5. Fill the Grayscale layer with 50% gray (choose Edit>Fill then set the Content Use selector to 50% gray).

6. Change the 2 Grayscale layer to Color mode. Your layer palette should look like Figure 6.29, and the image will become a grayscale representation of the image as the gray 'color' is being applied to lower layers.

FIG 6.29 Applying gray as a color desaturates the image. The result is a display of the luminosity of the image — a representation of the image based on tone. You could possibly use this separated component to adjust the image.

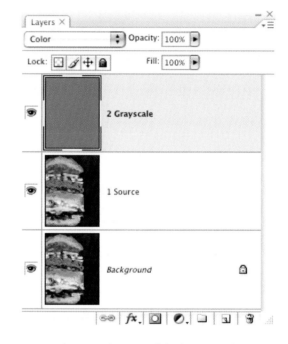

7. Create a new layer at the top of the layer stack and call it 3 Luminosity.
8. Press Command+Options+Shift+E / Ctrl+Alt+Shift+E to stamp the visible image to the new layer. This commits the grayscale change to the new layer.
9. Set the layer mode to Luminosity. This completes separation of the Luminosity component. Shut off the layer view for the 3 Luminosity (see Figure 6.30 for the layer set up).

You now have the luminosity separated from the color and you can isolate tone changes by toggling on the visibility of the 3 Luminosity layer and applying changes to it. To isolate the color, continue with the steps where you left off.

10. Activate the 2 Grayscale layer by clicking it in the layers palette. Change the Mode to Normal (the image will appear to be flat gray again), then press Command+ [/ Ctrl+ [to move the 2 Grayscale layer below the 1 Source layer. The image will become color again (Figure 6.31).

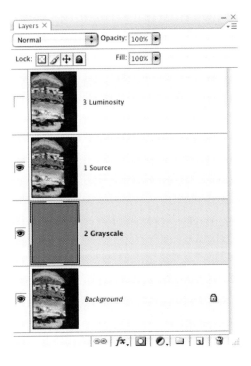

FIG 6.31 Invert the order of the source and grayscale layers to prepare for the next steps

11. Change the 1 Source layer mode to Color. What you will see is the color separated from tone (Figure 6.32).

FIG 6.32 Color isolated from tone appears over a neutral tone background.

12. Create a new layer above the 1 Source layer and name it 4 Color.
13. Press Command+Options+Shift+E / Ctrl+Alt+Shift+E to stamp the visible image to the new layer.
14. Change the mode of the 4 Color layer to Color.
15. Shut off the view for the Background, 1 Source and 2 Grayscale layers, and turn on the 3 Luminosity layer. Only the 4 Color and 3 Luminosity layers will be visible (see Figure 6.33).

All that has happened here is that you are using layer Modes to allow you a different view of your image. When you isolate the view for luminosity using layer mode, you capture a snapshot of that in a composite layer – and then do the same for color. Viewing the newly isolated components alone shows that they simply represent the image in a different form. The new Color and Luminosity layers contain extracted tone and color content from the original image. Because the modes target color and tone separately, you now have control over color and tone components separately. This can be a great advantage in situations where the color is right but the tone is wrong, or vice versa. Apply color correction to the Color layer (e.g., you might apply a Hue Saturation adjustment that would be isolated to the color), and tone corrections to the Luminosity layer (you might apply a Levels correction to extend the dynamic range of the tone independent from the color).

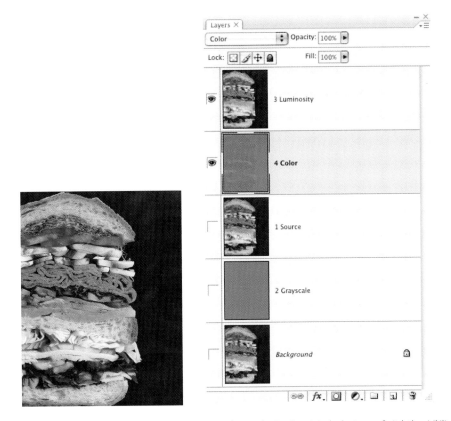

FIG 6.33 The Color and Luminosity components in the image can combine to display the original color image. Switch the visibility toggle off for either to view the companion component alone.

📖 This calculation for separation of color and tone will work with any RGB image. Open any image and try out the steps, then apply isolated color and tone changes to see how it works.

Here we've used layer modes to extract separate components for color and tone. But this is just the beginning of color-based separation and isolation of image components. We'll look at more color separation in Chapter 8, and there we will apply more modes. Now let's look at layer modes used specifically for correction.

Sharpening Calculation

Calculations have many creative and interesting uses, most of which are not immediately obvious. One of the first really useful layer calculations I devised was creating a manual unsharp masking effect. Unsharp masking was a darkroom process before it was ever a Photoshop or Elements filter. The photographer developing in the darkroom would sandwich a blurred film negative copy of the image with the original to enhance contrast in exposure of image edges. The blur would target image edges, and the result after the application would be a sharper look to the image. It was the mask used to create the effect that was 'unsharp'.

The layer-based application of unsharp mask that follows is a little different but it is a viable digital alternative that builds on the same concept. We'll borrow a little of what we learned in the last exercise to isolate our corrections to the image tone.

📖 Try It Now

1. Open a flattened image to which you'd like to apply an unsharp mask calculation, or open the image and flatten it. An interesting image to use with this technique is Sample8.psd (shown in Figure 6.34).
2. Duplicate the Background layer and name the new layer 1 Unsharp Mask.
3. Duplicate the 1 Unsharp Mask layer and name the new layer 2 Color. Change the layer mode of the 2 Color layer to Color. At this point the Background, 1 Unsharp Mask and 2 Color layers all have the same content.

📖 The role that the 2 duplicated layers play in the image dramatically changes with their change in Mode. Changing the mode of the Color layer makes the Color layer a color lock: the positioning at the top of the layer stack with the original color information allows tone to change below without changing the original color. Though an actual separation of the color has not been completed, the change to mode effectively separates the content and effect.

4. Activate the 1 Unsharp Mask layer by clicking on its thumbnail in the layers palette. Change the Mode to Overlay, the Opacity to 50% and then Invert (press Command+I / Ctrl+I). This layer acts as the blurred negative.

FIG 6.34 This unusual vegetable has shading that renders a strong difference when using this technique.

5. Blur the 1 Unsharp Mask layer using Gaussian Blur. The size of the blur will depend on the resolution of the image and the amount of detail. The more detailed the image, the less blur; the higher the resolution, the greater the blur. Start with 15 pixels for a 3 $\times$ 5 image at 300 ppi; use more pixels in the radius for larger images. You can view the changes as you move the slider.

The result of these steps (see Figure 6.35) is a sophisticated mask based on the content of your image. It is not a mask in the traditional sense that you have not made a visible selection with

FIG 6.35 Note the changes to the brightness at the right/shadow side of the parsnip and the brightness of the tendrils. This change is because of the local contrast enhancement brought about by the application of the blurred layer in Overlay mode.

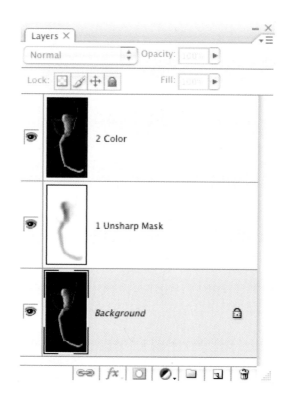

selection tools, however the technique of blurring and setting the mode (Overlay) effectively makes the content self-masking to target the effect. This is a more complicated result than what you achieved with the 2 Color layer, but that can be considered a mask as well: masking image color.

The Unsharp Mask layer you have created ends up working much like the sandwiched negative in the darkroom process, in pretty much the opposite way that the Unsharp Mask filter does: reducing image contrast in the quartertones to pull details from shadows and highlights. Unsharp Mask pushes dark areas darker and light areas lighter, sometimes leading to a loss of detail (blowing out or blocking up image areas). Because the effect of this manual unsharpening procedure is nearly the opposite of the Unsharp Mask filter, the manual unsharp effect and the Unsharp Mask filter effect can be used together. Because you can use them in tandem, you can greatly intensify image contrast changes and apply more sharpening than can be achieved with the Unsharp Mask filter alone.

One added benefit to the manual version of sharpening is that because of the nature of Overlay mode the result will not tend to blow out (move bright areas of the image to RGB: 0, 0, 0) or block up (move shadow areas of the image to RGB: 255, 255, 255) as the Unsharp Mask filter can easily do. Tones and colors at the extremes (absolute white, absolute black) and middle (50% gray) are less likely to change than the quartertones (75% and 25% gray). This can keep you from harming detail in your image, and will likely not cause the type of halo you can get with the Photoshop filter.

Summary

We have looked at the basics of layer mode as an overview and then jumped into two evolved techniques out of hundreds of variations that can be produced with layer modes. Certainly layer modes are not hard to apply, but hopefully this chapter and these exercises have shown that applying layer modes use is not necessarily best to do based on trial and error. It may take some time to develop confidence in using layer modes, but hopefully the few examples here may start you contemplating mode application rather than simply attempting to arrive at pleasant results by chance. Mode is a means of isolating effects, different than, but similar to the purpose of selection.

Sticking with the preferred list of modes outlined (and exploring the examples in the rest of the book) will help you maintain focus on the modes that will be most effective in your image corrections. Practice the exercises for separating color from tone and applying manual sharpening using your own images to see how the techniques behave. The Modes you are likely to have the most success working into your workflow at first are the simple ones: Normal (default), Multiply (darken), Screen (lighten), Color (lock color or change it) and Luminosity (lock tone or change it). These will become your workhorse tools. Overlay, Lighten and Darken will come into play as you have more experience, and Difference for comparison sake (as we use in the next chapter). Concentrate on what these do, and you add the bulk of what modes will enable for you day in, day out.

Just to reinforce the notion of focus for a moment, note that there are section dividers on the listing of modes (see Figure 6.36). These section dividers are really akin to submenus. The first section applies straight color/tone from the layer, the second section

FIG 6.36 Six sections of the Mode menu reflect distinct submenus.

deals with darkening, the third section has modes that lighten, the fourth mixed conditional calculations, the fifth calculations based on difference between applied and base pixels and the sixth calculations based on color or tone. Understanding the behavior of one of the modes in each of the sections will really yield clues as to what the rest of the modes in that section do – even if they do it very differently. The more complex the mode the less likely you will use it often.

The visual result of applying a layer mode does not actually reside in any one layer – especially if multiple layers are combining to produce a result. You see the result of the calculation on screen. Keep in mind that to bind effects (and to apply additional modes), you may need to use the composite layer technique (create a new layer and merge visible to it with Command+Shift+Option+E / Ctrl+Shift+Alt+E).

While layer Modes are certainly a more advanced way to look at image content, the parade of extraordinary layer powers continues in the next chapter with exploration of advanced blending modes.

If you have any questions about layer modes and their use, be sure to visit the website for this book http://www.photoshopcs.com.

CHAPTER 7

Roast Beef

Advanced Blending with Blend If

Y et another means of combining and targeting content changes can be found lurking in the palette in the Photoshop Layer Styles. We have already looked at some of what the Layer Styles dialog can do when exploring layer styles in Chapter 5. However, Blend If is a more advanced feature on the Layer Styles dialog that offers opportunities separate from masking and clipping that we will definitely want to explore in order to round out the layer experience (Figure 7.1).

Blend If: An Overview

Blend If is very much an overlooked and even mysterious feature to almost any Photoshop user. If you ever tried looking this feature up in manuals and books, you may not have been able to find it. In fact even searching Photoshop Help will not yield a title with Blend If in it (though the feature is referenced by function in 'Specify a

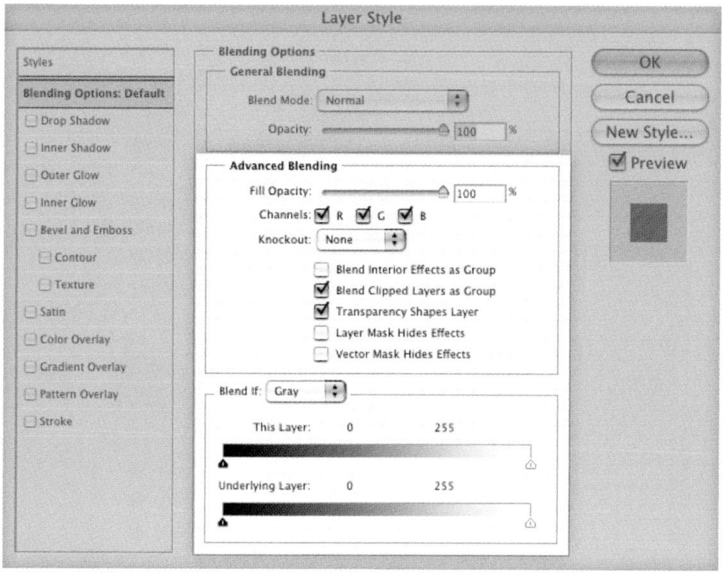

FIG 7.1 The Advanced Blending and Blend If sections of the Layer Styles screen offer additional layer advantages, not often explored by very powerful.

blending mode for a layer or group' and 'Specify a tonal range for blending layers'). While the tool may not be a very popular target for tutorials and documentation, it is an enormously powerful tool that has been part of layers since the very beginning.

What Blend If can do is help you target changes and corrections based on the color or tonal content of a layer. In a way it is like an auto-mask, in that it will mask a layer without you having to actually create a mask or a selection – and these masks can be highly complicated without much work. It will target content of a layer based on a set of sliders (the Blend If sliders on the Layer Styles dialog), and those slider positions. Before we go any further, let's take a look at the basic functionality and how you control it before we really try to look at what it can do.

📖 Try It Now

1. Open a new image 720 × 720 pixels with a white background (see the New Image dialog in **Figure 7.2**).
2. Create a new layer and call it Blend If Test.
3. Press D to set the default colors (black and white).

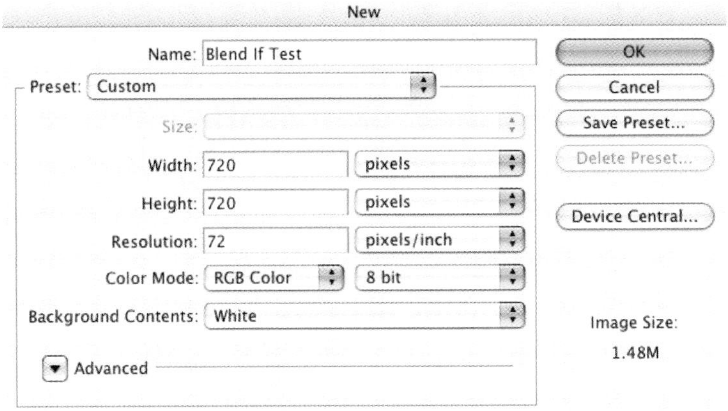

Dialog box content:

New

Name: Blend If Test

Preset: Custom

Size:

Width: 720   pixels

Height: 720   pixels

Resolution: 72   pixels/inch

Color Mode: RGB Color   8 bit

Background Contents: White

Advanced

OK
Cancel
Save Preset...
Delete Preset...

Device Central...

Image Size:
1.48M

FIG 7.2 The suggested sample image should use the settings shown here.

4. Choose the Gradient tool and be sure the Options are set to Linear Gradient, Normal mode, 100% opacity, and uncheck Reverse, Dither and Transparency.
5. Click on the lower left of the image and drag the cursor to the upper right, then release the mouse. The image should fill in a gradient from black to white from the lower left to the upper right.
6. Take a snapshot of the image by clicking the snapshot button at the bottom of the History palette (Windows>History). Leave the name as the default (Snapshot 1). This will make it easy to return to the state of the image before blending is applied and without having to open the Layer Styles dialog to reset.
7. Double-click the Blend If Test layer in the layers palette (anywhere *but* on the thumbnail or over the name). This will open the Layer Styles dialog.
8. Click on the black This Layer slider and drag it to the center of the slider range at 128 (see **Figure 7.3**).

📖 The numbers on the Blend If sliders are measured in levels 0–255. This corresponds to black (0) to white (255) in a grayscale gradient.

The change in position of the slider limits the range of what is visible in the layer (in this case the gradient) so it blends with what is below based on those slider positions. Everything to the left of the black slider and everything to the right of the white slider

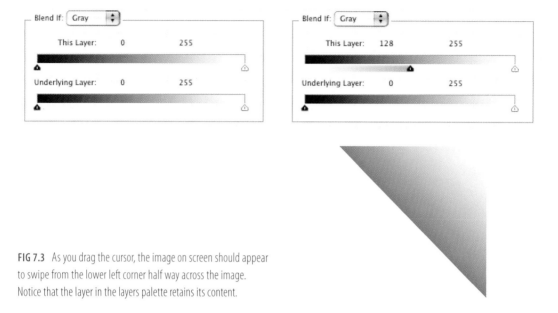

FIG 7.3 As you drag the cursor, the image on screen should appear to swipe from the lower left corner half way across the image. Notice that the layer in the layers palette retains its content.

becomes transparent. If you shut off the visibility toggle for the Background layer you can see the transparency. Continuing from the exercise, try the following slider positions to get a better feel for the way it works:

• Move the black This Layer slider back to 0 and then move the white This Layer slider to 128 (**Figure 7.4**).

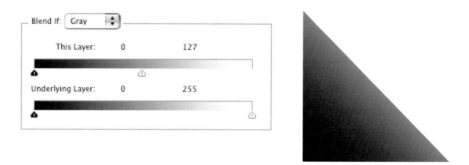

FIG 7.4 The gradient between gray and white will become transparent to see through to the background in the upper right of the image.

• Move the black This Layer slider to 192 and then move the white This Layer slider to 63 (**Figure 7.5**).

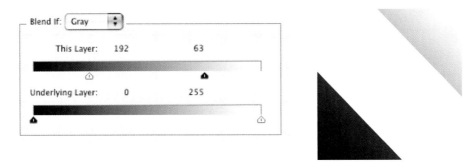

FIG 7.5 The area between the white slider and the black slider become transparent to see through to the background in the middle of the gradient range.

📖 Applying layers with Blend If can occasionally be confounding when using the This Layer slider. *Any changes applied directly to the layer where the Blend If sliders are set may result in unexpected changes in the image.* To test this out, make a Levels adjustment to the Blend If Test layer (Image> Adjustments>Levels). When the dialog opens, swing the center gray slider left and right and watch how the image behaves. Close the Levels dialog without committing the change. Now do the same thing with an adjustment layer by choosing Levels from the Create new Fill or Adjustment Layer menu on the layers palette. This is one more clear case for using adjustment layers instead of direct application of change.

The same concepts hold true for using the Underlying Layer sliders. The main difference is that the content of the current layer will blend based on the content of the layers below, rather than the content of the layer where you apply the blend – layer transparency still effects the current layer. To see the results of using Underlying Layers, do the following:

📖 Try It Now

1. Click Snapshot 1 in the History palette to reset the image and Blend If sliders.
2. Double-click the Background layer and rename it to White Layer.
3. Change the order of the layers in the layer stack by pressing Command+] / Ctrl+].
4. Double-click the White Layer in the layers palette to open the Layer Styles dialog.

5. Click on the black Underlying Layer slider and drag it to the center of the slider range at 128 (see Figure 7.6).

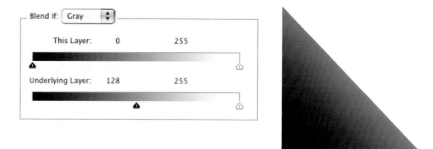

FIG 7.6 The white layer becomes transparent over the darker area of the lower layer so you can see through it to the darker half of the gradient.

6. Move the black Underlying Layer slider back to 0 and then move the white Underlying Layer slider to 128 (Figure 7.7).

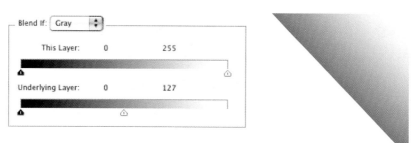

FIG 7.7 The white layer becomes transparent over the brighter area of the lower layer so you can see through it to the lighter half of the gradient.

7. Move the black Underlying Layer slider to 192 and then move the white Underlying Layer slider to 63 (Figure 7.8).

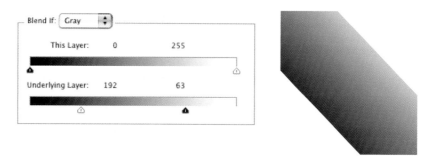

FIG 7.8 The white layer becomes transparent over the mid-tone area of the lower layer so you can see through it to the mid-tone 'half' of the gradient.

These examples are hard-edged application of Blend If in its simplest form. Several other features of Blend If allow partial blending and blending based on color ranges rather than just tone. Partial transparency (the real 'blending' form of Blend If) can be created by splitting the sliders. Color targeting can be done by choosing ranges for the Red, Green and Blue sliders found under the Blend If drop list (see Figure 7.9). Lets look at how to split sliders to have all the basic function in tow:

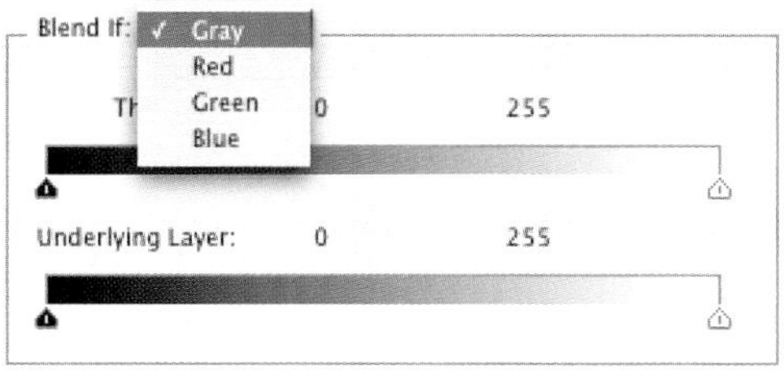

FIG 7.9   Blend If can be adjusted per channel so that blending can be targeted to specific color ranges.

📖 Try It Now

1. Click Snapshot 1 in the History palette to reset the Blend If for the layers and the layer order.
2. Open the Layer Styles for the Blend If Test layer by double-clicking the layer.
3. Move the black This Layer slider so it is at 128 (as in Figure 7.3).
4. Hold down the Option/Alt key [Mac/PC] and click on the left of the black slider and then drag it to 0. The slider will divide into two parts (see Figure 7.10).

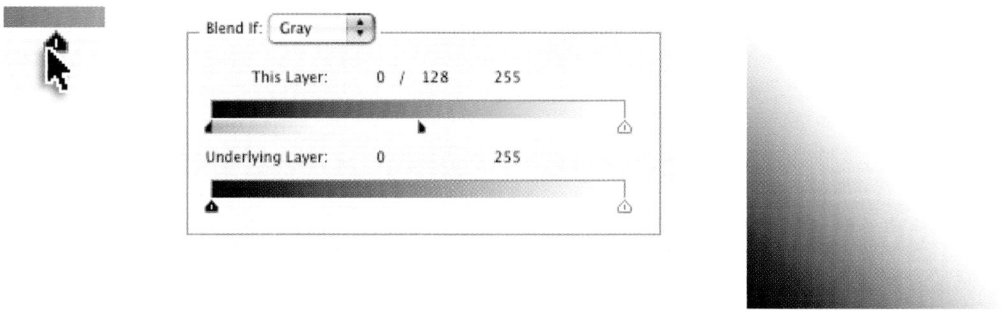

FIG 7.10   Holding the Option / Alt key allows you to split the slider, be sure to click on the side of the slider that is on the side you will be moving toward.

Knockouts

Another feature under Advanced Blending in the Layer Styles palette is Knockout, another seldom-used feature with a specific ability – seldom covered or explored because it is hidden on the Layer Styles dialog. Knockout can behave much like solidity in the base layer of the clipping mask or as a mask, but it does it from the top down rather than below like a clipping layer or as a sidecar for layer masks.

To make a Knockout, try the following using the image from the previous exercise:

1. Click Snapshot 1 to restore the defaults you saved.

2. Double-click the background layer and name it White Base.

3. Choose the Type tool, and be sure you have selected a large type face like Arial Black at 300 points, and change the type color to Red (RGB: 255, 0, 0).

4. Activate the Blend If Test layer, then click on the image and type the word HOLE in all caps. Center the type vertically and horizontally on the image.

5. Shift+click on the Blend If Test layer to highlight both the HOLE layer and the Blend If Test layer.

6. Drag the layers to the Create a New Group button at the bottom of the Layers palette. Leave the default name,

Splitting the slider will blend from 0% to 100% between the split halves. Splitting the sliders allows you to make a softer transition in blends, similar to blurring a mask or feathering a selection. The idea is that you gain control over how blends dissipate, rather than using them as an on/off switch for a particular range. As on/off switches the edges might end up hard and blocky, but by splitting the sliders you can offer better opportunity to control the blend.

Heavier Lifting with Blend If

So, what would you use Blend If for? Really, often for situations that seem otherwise hopelessly complex. For example, say you have taken a shot of a leafless tree in silhouette against a blue sky and you think it might look better with some other sky, some interesting clouds, or against a sunset, etc. It might seem to be a daunting task to make a selection between all those branches. You might try dabbling with the magic wand, but your results will be pretty sketchy. Blend If offers the opportunity to make the replacement without having to make a potentially unnerving and complex mask or selection. You can use measurements from your image to determine a range you want to replace, and then apply appropriate Blend If settings you make directly from the image.

That makes it sound like a miracle cure to use Blend If … and there are occasions where it will produce some amazing results with little effort. On the other hand, getting to do what you want may require combining it with masking or other techniques to achieve a result – like any other tool it is best to think of it as a companion to other functions rather than the lone ranger or some other hired gun. The only way to really get a feel for Blend If is to look at the reality of the way it works, and the advantages it affords first hand.

The shots in **Figure 7.11** were taken on the same day, one in the morning at South Street Seaport in New York City early in the morning facing nearly east, and the other about 400 miles away near Rochester, NY facing west. They have little in common but the day they were taken. However the lighting is close enough that a merge might work – if we have the patience. These images are Sample9.psd and Sample10.psd on the CD.

In the picture of the mast, the rigging is a real problem if you are looking to replace the background. There are many cords crossing the scene, they are different weights, and somewhat different tone. The scene is lighter than the image taken at dusk, and the light wraps a little around the ropes. If it were more of a silhouette this might be easy.

but toggle the arrow to expand the group.

7. Double-click the HOLE layer to open the Layer Styles dialog. Change the Fill to 0% (the type will disappear), then choose Shallow from the Knockout drop list. The type will appear in white having knocked out the base layer in the group (Blend If Test).

8. Change the Knockout to Deep. The word HOLE will knock out to the background. As there is no background in this image, it will knock out to transparent.

Shallow knockouts punch through to the bottom of their group if they are in one; Deep knockouts punch through to the background – or transparency if no background is available in the image.

FIG 7.11 There is no accounting for weather, and you'll often have to make due with what you get. In this case the drab sky can be replaced with the more interesting one taken later in the day.

FIG 7.11 (Continued)

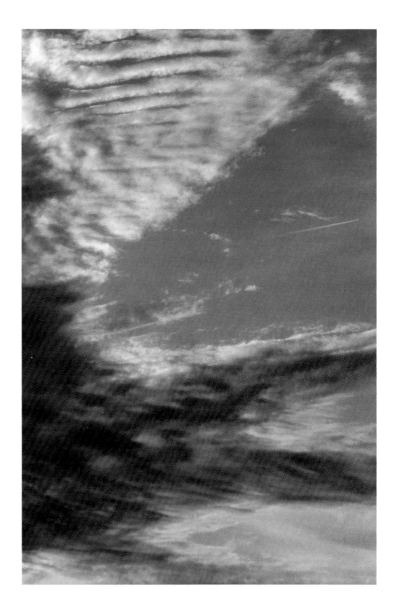

📖 Try It Now

1. Open the Sample9.psd image off the CD. This is the mast from **Figure 7.11**.
2. Double-click the Background layer and rename the layer to Original Mast in the New Layer dialog, then click OK to accept the changes.

3. Open the Sample10.psd image off the CD. This is the sky image from Figure 7.11. Place the images side by side on screen so both are in view.

4. Choose the Move tool, hold down the Shift key and click-and-drag the sky from the Sample10.psd image into the Sample9.psd. Holding the shift key will automatically center the layer you are dragging. Alternatively you can duplicate the layer from Sample10.psd to Sample9.psd using the Duplicate layer command, or even select all, copy and paste. All you are looking to do is to get the two images in the same document. Name the new layer Original Sky.

5. Close the Sample10.psd image, leaving open only the Sample9.psd which should contain the source layers from both sample images.

6. Duplicate the Original Mast layer, name the layer Blend If and move it to the top of the layer stack by pressing Command+] / Ctrl+].

7. Open the Threshold function (Image>Adjustments> Threshold). We will use this to measure the target for the blend. Swing the Threshold slider to the right and left looking for the point where the sky begins to darken in the upper right of the image. Note the number and close Threshold by clicking Cancel so the change is not saved in the image. If you push the slider left you will note the sky never completely becomes all black; if it had this would define a range for the blend and you would have to get the black slider involved (Figure 7.12).

📖 Threshold is a tool that is useful in determining measurements of your image content, and is an unlikely candidate as a tool that you will generally use in corrections themselves – though you might occasionally use it to help create masks. Threshold turns an image into a pure bitmap where pixels are either white or black – there are no grays or colors when the tool is applied.

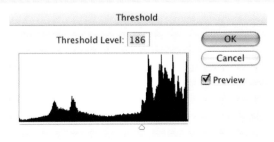

FIG 7.12 At about 186 on the threshold function, the sky at the upper right of the image begins to turn. Your threshold may be somewhat different based on color settings.

FIG 7.12 (Continued)

8. Double-click the Blend If layer to open the Layer Styles dialog. As you want to drop away the lighter portion of the layer to reveal what is beneath, use the white This Layer Blend If slider and move it to the left to the value you measured in step 7. Then split the sliders and give about 20 levels of blending (see Figure 7.13).

At this point the blending of the two images may not be all that you'd hoped … and likely this is where some might give up.

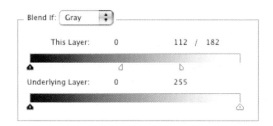

FIG 7.13 After splitting the sliders, visual evaluation suggested a broad blend to try an allow the ropes to transition smoothly, but not so far as to lose rope details.

Sometimes things will look a little worse before they start to look better, and a little more effort can go a long way – combinations of tools and techniques often win the battle. The problem here is the mismatch of the images, and you will want to do something to lighten the sky.

9. Change the opacity of the Original Sky layer to about 50. This will significantly lighten the sky and the ropes will blend better (see Figure 7.14).

FIG 7.14 Lightening the sky brings the two parts of the image closer, but there is still more to do. The image can be color corrected, sharpened and saturated to build back some of the impact that is lost in the compromise.

10. Make a levels correction to the image using a Levels adjustment layer. It should have settings similar to Figure 7.15.

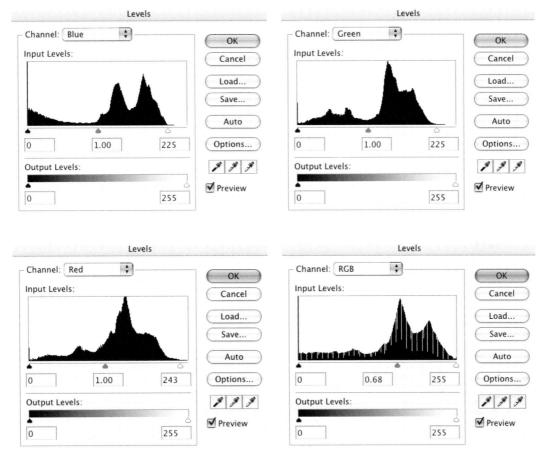

FIG 7.15 A general color correction that we did not do earlier helps bring these two blended images into sync.

11. Next using Color Balance will help you enhance color and create balance between the components that is pleasing (see Figure 7.16).
12. Make a composite at the top of the layer stack and then apply sharpening to enhance contrast (sharpening to enhance contrast uses a broad radius and small amount) (see Figure 7.17).
13. Adjust color with Hue/Saturation to enhance the sky and mast. You may need to do some selective enhancement and create custom ranges to get the best results. Figure 7.18 shows the result and a screen shot of the layers palette.

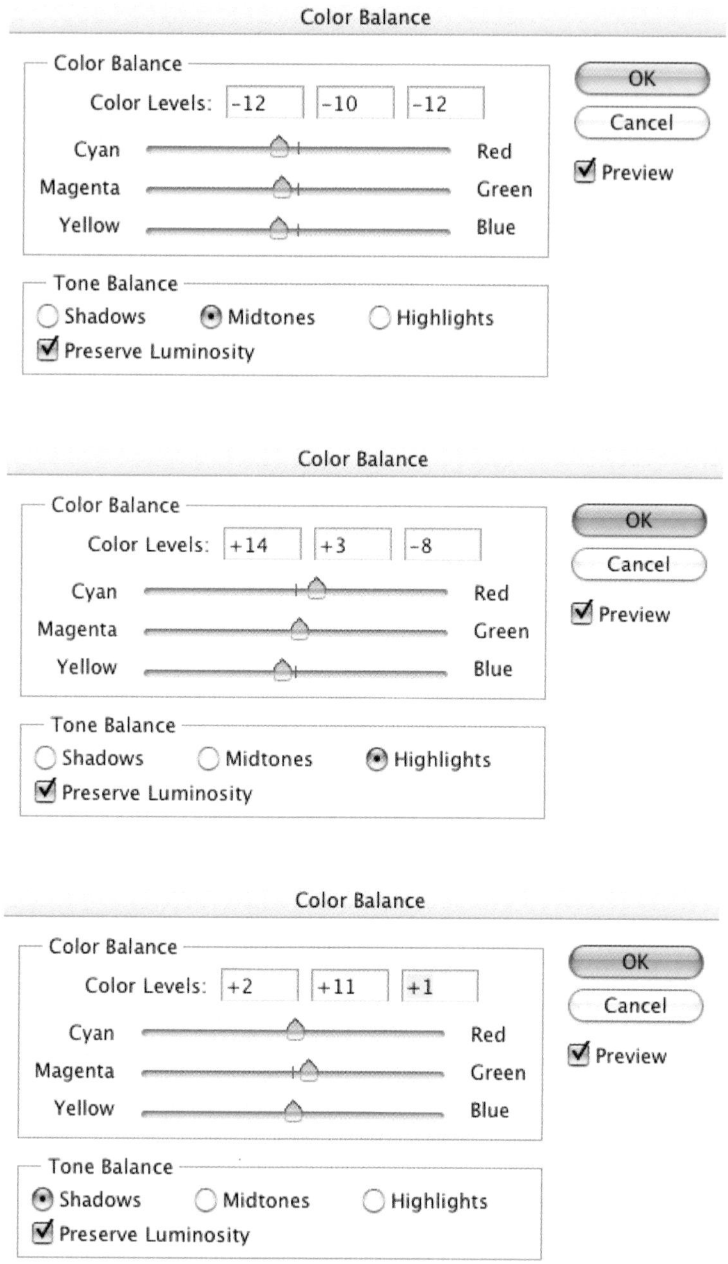

Color Balance

Color Balance

Color Levels: -12 -10 -12

Cyan   Red
Magenta   Green
Yellow   Blue

OK
Cancel
☑ Preview

Tone Balance
○ Shadows   ⦿ Midtones   ○ Highlights
☑ Preserve Luminosity

Color Balance

Color Balance

Color Levels: +14 +3 -8

Cyan   Red
Magenta   Green
Yellow   Blue

OK
Cancel
☑ Preview

Tone Balance
○ Shadows   ○ Midtones   ⦿ Highlights
☑ Preserve Luminosity

Color Balance

Color Balance

Color Levels: +2 +11 +1

Cyan   Red
Magenta   Green
Yellow   Blue

OK
Cancel
☑ Preview

Tone Balance
⦿ Shadows   ○ Midtones   ○ Highlights
☑ Preserve Luminosity

FIG 7.16 Color balance shifts between highlights and shadows, reflecting difference in the lighting and emphasis of the blended images.

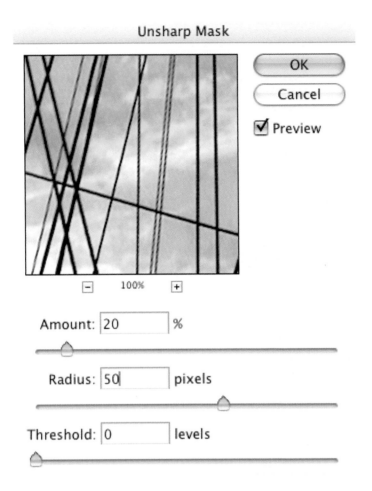

Unsharp Mask

OK

Cancel

☑ Preview

− 100% +

Amount: 20 %

Radius: 50 pixels

Threshold: 0 levels

FIG 7.17 The goal with sharpening is to enhance the contrast in the image without imposing halos.

You can try this same exercise using the Sky layer as the Blend If layer without duplicating the mast layer. That is, instead of making the duplication of the Original Mast layer, just use the Original Sky layer and apply the Blend If function there. The major difference will be that you will use different settings for the blend: instead of using settings for the mast layer that will blend out the sky, you will use settings to blend into the mast image. As it turns out, the opposite settings work just fine (see Figure 7.19).

In either case we are looking to target the range of sky between the rigging in the mast layer. Blend If can accomplish the task because there is enough of a distinct difference between the sky

FIG 7.18 The result becomes somewhat of a mediation between the extremes rather than one image dominating the result.

and the rest of the layer content. Blend If will also likely be useful in situations dealing with compositing HDR (High Dynamic Range) images (images shot with different exposures to achieve HDR). But most often you will use it in tandem with masking and other techniques.

Though Blend If can make precise adjustments to specific areas of an image and is handy for some types of targeting and blending,

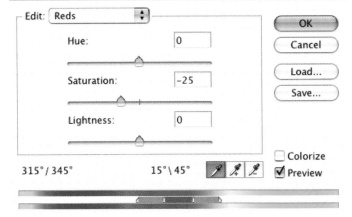

FIG 7.18 (Continued)

it is a little rigid when it comes to adjustment. The drawback becomes more apparent when you get into a situation where you know Blend If would be more useful if you could adjust the results like you can with a layer mask. The secret is in conversion. Let's take a look at Color Masking and transition with Blend If.

Blend If as a Mask

Blend If is a very powerful tool for working in exacting ranges, and with the right technique it can be used for everything from coloring black-and-white images to blending layer content, to

FIG 7.18 (Continued) These layers complete the composite. The key layer using Blend If is 3 Blend If 0,0 / 112,182

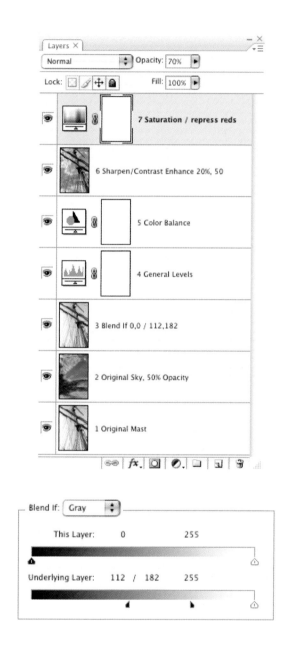

FIG 7.19 The Blend If settings would be reversed if blending the sky into the mast. You want to drop away the portions of the sky layer that correspond to the dark portion of the mast layer.

being used as a substitute for, or in conjunction with, masking. There are, however, at least two glaring problems with Blend If. First, the range is exact, which doesn't leave any allowance for manipulation to fit shapes. If you have an area that isn't exactly within your range, Blend If won't target it precisely. Second Blend If is not entirely intuitive when working with tone, and it is even more difficult to work with to address color ranges. All isn't black and white so the problem of addressing color is inevitable.

The solution is to stick to using Blend If for what it is superior at: making transparency. Because Blend If creates transparency in the current image layer, you can convert that transparency to a clipping mask, a selection or mask by manipulating the results. Once you have converted Blend if to something else, the results can be manipulated. For example, you could create a mask using Blend If sliders to target a range of tones to either keep or throw out (based on slider positions).

1. Duplicate the layer you want to make into a mask and name it Blend Mask.
2. Determine the range of tone you want to use in the layer as a mask using measurement or conceptual ranges (e.g., midtones).
3. Create a new, blank layer below the Blend Mask layer.
4. Activate the Blend Mask layer and set the This Layer range to the range determined in step 2.
5. Merge down, and change the name of the layer to Transparency Mask. This will commit the transparency of the Blend Mask layer to the Transparency Mask layer.

Steps 3 to 5 lock the transparency based on the Blend If range according to the original tone. You can now use the Transparency Mask layer as a clipping group base, shift+click it to load a selection, or load the selection and use it to create a mask. Committing the Blend Mask allows you to make it a physical element so you can make changes in it – either by changing the solidity of the Transparency Mask layer, by altering the selection, or by making adjustments to the mask.

Using this scheme, you can quickly use layer content to convert to custom masks:

- Create a highlight mask based on transparency in the current layer by splitting the black slider to 0 and 255.
- Create a shadow mask by splitting the white slider to 0 and 255.
- Create a mask that targets the lightest half of the image; split the black slider to 128 and 255.
- Create a mask that targets the darkest half of the image; split the white slider to 0 and 128.

You can probably see from this that Blend If can be very effective in targeting tone. If color is isolated as tone (like you can do with

RGB, CMYK or other separation), application areas can be based on specific ranges within a color component. But Blend If can also allow you to convert specific color ranges to masks, with the help of Hue/Saturation.

Creating a Color-Based Mask

The trilobite in **Figure 7.20** would prove to be a very tedious selection to make manually. The general shape along with lumps and bumps could take hours to trace in contour with one of the manual tools. The mixture of light and shadow make any kind of selection based on tone difficult or impossible.

FIG 7.20 This trilobite has many ribs that protrude, making a manual selection cumbersome. Techniques for selection and isolation can be made easier using Blend If techniques.

Using the following combination of tools, it is possible to isolate an area based on color, and then convert that to a selection or mask via Blend If:

☐ Try It Now

1. Open the Sample11.psd.
2. Duplicate the Background layer and name it Source. You need a duplicate because you will be changing the layer content rather than using non-destructive methods.

3. Open Hue/Saturation to apply it directly to the Source layer (Command+U / Ctrl+U). You want to make changes to the layer instead of using an adjustment layer.
4. Choose Blues from the Edit drop list. You choose Blues here because that seems to be the closest range to the area outside the object; had you been looking to change a green or magenta, you should select that range instead.
5. Change the Saturation slider to −100 (see Figure 7.21).

FIG 7.21 This will desaturate the areas that Photoshop considers part of the Blue range.

6. Click the Add to Sample tool on the Hue/Saturation palette. Click in areas of the image using the sampler where there is still color in the background. All areas of blue should desaturate as you click on them (change to gray). Click OK to accept the changes (**Figure 7.22**).

7. Activate the Background by clicking it in the Layers palette, then create a new layer (Command+Option+Shift+N/ Ctrl+Alt+Shift+N) and fill with 50% gray (Shift+F5). Name the new layer Commit 2. Duplicate Commit 2 and name it Commit 1. See **Figure 7.23** for the setup. This layers will be used to commit a series of image changes that create the mask.

FIG 7.22 Clicking and dragging the Add to Sample tool through the background will desaturate the areas you pass over because they will be sampled into the desaturation range.

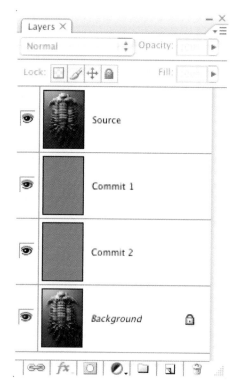

FIG 7.23 The layers should be Source, Commit 1, Commit 2, Background.

8. Change the mode of the Source layer to Color and merge down. This will isolate the color in a color separation.

9. Change the mode of the Commit 1 layer to Difference. This will show the difference between the saturated parts of Commit 1

and the unsaturated 50% gray of Commit 2. Merge down to commit the difference.

10. Change the name of the current layer to Blend Mask. The layers will look like they do in Figure 7.24.

FIG 7.24 The series of mode changes between steps 9 to 11 produce these results and leave you with only the Background and Blend Mask layers.

11. Double-click the Blend Mask layer to open the Layer Style dialog.
12. Under Blend If on the dialog, click the black slider for This Layer and slide it to the right while watching the image. Slide this right only 1 or 2 levels. The black should disappear from sight in the image. Close the Layer Style dialog by clicking OK.
13. Activate the Background. Create a new, blank layer. Name it Transparency Mask.
14. Merge the Blend Mask layer down into the Transparency Mask layer to commit the transparency.
15. Clean up the Transparency mask layer. Clear debris with selection tools and the Delete button, or the Eraser tool. Fill holes in the object by just painting with a paintbrush.
16. Duplicate the Background, name the duplicate Source and move it above the Transparency Mask, then make a clipping group from those layers. Your content will be restored to the original look, but with the difference that you can alter the background without effecting the object (or vice versa). See the layer stack in **Figure 7.25**.

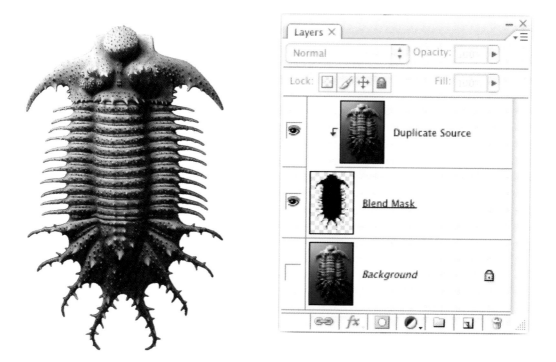

FIG 7.25 Adjust the Transparency Mask layer after committing the transparency using the Paint Brush tool or Eraser to add or remove masking, respectively.

What is happening here is that you manipulate the color to desaturate the image, isolate the desaturated areas with a calculation, and then use Blend If to re-define the visible portion of the layer. By moving the black This Layer slider to the right, the black areas of the layer are eliminated from view (though not yet deleted). Once committed, the exact range of pixels can be manually altered to account for edge blending and other differences that are not guided by strict numeric relationships.

A Color Mask action is provided in the Blend If actions included on the CD. This tool will run through the steps for the Hue/Saturation Blend If as discussed in this section. It also has tools which will do the following Blend If setups:

- Target highlights, full range (set the Underlying Layer black slider to 0 and 255)
- Target highlights, half range (set the Underlying Layer black slider to 128 and 255)
- Target shadows, full range (set the Underlying Layer white slider to 0 and 255)
- Target shadows, half range (set the Underlying Layer black slider to 0 and 128)
- Target midtones, full range (set the Underlying Layer black slider to 0 and 128; set the Underlying Layer white slider to 128 and 255)
- Target midtones, half range (set the Underlying Layer black slider to 63 and 128; set the Underlying Layer white slider to 128 and 192)
- Exclude midtones, full range (set the Underlying Layer black slider to 128 and 255; set the Underlying Layer white slider to 0 and 128)
- Exclude midtones, half range (set the Underlying Layer black slider to 192 and 255; set the Underlying Layer white slider to 0 and 63)
- Reset (set Underlying sliders to 0, 0/255, 255).

These presets can serve a variety of purposes. You may be able to guess at how these will come in handy, but we'll look at specific examples in Chapter 9.

Summary

Blend If provides yet another opportunity to isolate objects: by creating transparency. In this way it can provide a means of blending layers that no other tool will provide, but it also provides alternatives to using other tools like the Magic Wand or color range tools for making selections, masks and creating object isolation based on tone and color.

Keys to success with Blend If lie in using it in conjunction with other tools and techniques. It won't be the magic bullet for problems so much as it will be a masking helper, selection helper, and companion to other masking and selection techniques. Flexibility is offered by the quick Blend If actions and will keep you from having to dig into the Layer Styles every time you want to try something from the Blend If bag of tricks.

We have looked at quite a few layer-based adjustments in the past several chapters. Some are convenient for shape, others for tone, still others for color and some for general calculations. One thing to keep in mind as you move forward from this point is that it is rarely a single method that does everything you need it to if you are hoping for the best outcome. For a given image there will be occasions that I use every one of the techniques and functions mentioned in these chapters, and probably fewer times where I will use one or two. Get familiar with each of these techniques, and add them to your tool belt. If not immediately, work on them one at a time to get familiar with and master each.

One more useful feature is hidden on the Advanced panel of the Layers Styles, and that would be the deceptively simple-looking Red, Green and Blue check boxes. We'll look at the implications these features bring to layer-based separations in the next chapter.

If you have questions about Blend If techniques, please visit: http://www.photoshopcs.com where you can ask questions about techniques in the Layers forums.

CHAPTER 8

Sprouts

Breaking Out Components

I mage components are separations of an image into distinct color or tone parts. We looked at separating an image into brightness (luminosity) and color in Chapter 6, but there are many ways to separate images into other types of components, including color components of light (red, green and blue) and ink (cyan, yellow, magenta and black). Separating images into components can offer advantages in making corrections, creating masks, calculations and other tasks such as converting images to black and white.

Separations also provide essential understanding of how images are comprised, stored and viewed. Being able to work with color components directly as separations is nearly the exclusive reason for Channels – which Adobe has dedicated an entire palette to in Photoshop. When the Photoshop user learns to look at channels as component parts of their images in layers, they gain many times the potential flexibility of looking at channels in a separate palette. Working with components in layers leads to a better understanding of how they fit into images, and how they can be used directly in corrections.

An Historic Interlude

One of my favorite digital lessons is learned from taking a set of black-and-white images created before there was color film and making a color representation of the image. A special case are the photos of one Russian photographer, Sergei Mikhailovich Prokudin-Gorskii.

📖 You can find digitized images in several libraries online:
http://www.cs.cmu.edu/~dellaert/aligned/
http://www.loc.gov/exhibits/empire/

Using a special camera that he designed, Prokudin-Gorskii captured images on glass plates three at a time (it is said in rapid succession, rather than all at once). During the capture, color filters separated red, green and blue color components to different areas of the plate. The result was a single plate with black-and-white representations of the image's core light components (see **Figure 8.1**).

The solution still offered only black-and-white representation of RGB channels, was a bit awkward, and required a customized projector to reproduce the color. But really this first color captures mimic what your digital camera does even today, separating color into Red, Green and Blue light components. About 100 years after they were taken, we can treat Prokudin-Gorskii's images as components of an image and put them back together as color representations using Photoshop.

Working with separations provides some valuable background for what we've already been doing in correcting for different components of light with Levels. It also opens doors to additional techniques for working with color and black-and-white images.

Creating Color from Black and White

The concept of RGB and the idea that an entire world of color can be stored in combinations of three colors really doesn't seem plausible until you see it at work. That is, the 16 million color variations in 8-bit per channel and 35 billion of 16-bit per channel are all produced from capture of red, green and blue core components.

In the following short example, we'll look at putting together a Prokudin-Gorskii image from his original black-and-white captures.

FIG 8.1 A scan of an original Prokudin-Gorskii 'color' plate taken between 1907 and 1915, 20 years before Kodachrome . . . the first color film. Stacked here from the top down are the Blue, Green and Red color components.

📖 Try It Now

1. Open the three Samples12 images off the CD. They are named Sample12-red.psd, Sample12-green.psd and Sample12-blue.psd. Be sure to keep them in order, or your result will not turn out correctly (**Figure 8.2**).

FIG 8.2 The three sample images clockwise from the upper left are the Red, Green and Blue components.

📖 If you'd like an extra challenge, there is a Sample12-RGB.psd on the CD as well. This image has a scan of the complete glass plate. You can work from that if you'd like, but be forewarned that there are issues of alignment and distortion that have mostly been addressed in the cropped version provided.

2. Activate the Sample12-blue.psd image, then press Command+A / Ctrl+A [Mac / PC] to select the entire image, then press Command+C / Ctrl+C to copy. Doing this stores a copy of the image as well as the image dimensions, which helps automate the next step.
3. Create a new image (File>New), name the file Prokudin-Gorskii Composite, as in **Figure 8.3** and be sure to change the Color Mode to RGB Color (it will initially be Grayscale). We will use this new image to assemble a color image from the components in the other three images.

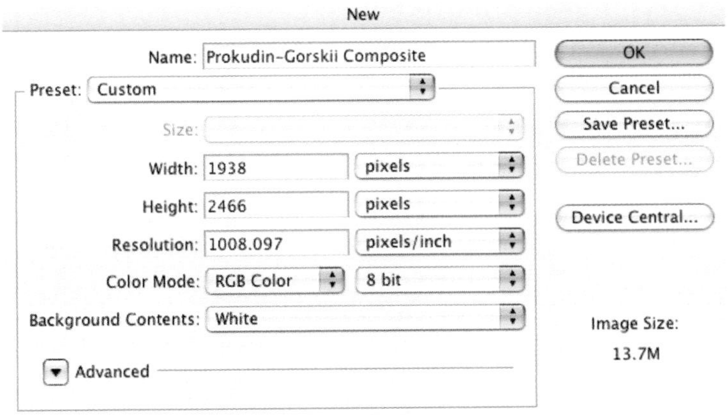

FIG 8.3 Your New screen should look very much like this when opened, as Photoshop will have automatically defined the new image size from the image information on your clipboard.

4. Create a new layer, call it Compositing Screen and fill it with black (Edit>Fill and set the Use content to Black in the drop list). This will act as a projection screen for the image components.
5. Press Command+V / Ctrl+V to paste the content of the clipboard to the image. Name the resulting layer Blue (**Figure 8.4**).
6. Arrange the Prokudin-Gorskii Composite image and the Sample12-green.psd so you can see both on your monitor,

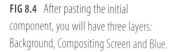
FIG 8.4 After pasting the initial component, you will have three layers: Background, Compositing Screen and Blue.

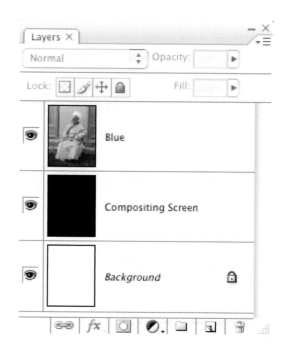

choose the Move tool (press V), hold the Shift key and click-and-drag the Sample12-green image into the Prokudin-Gorskii Composite file. Release the mouse button and then the shift key. Name the new layer in the Composite file Green.

7. Arrange the Prokudin-Gorskii Composite image and the Sample12-red.psd so you can see both on screen, choose the Move tool (press V), hold the Shift key and click-and-drag the Sample12-red image into the Prokudin-Gorskii Composite file. Release the mouse button and then the shift key. Name the new layer in the Composite file Red. The result of all this clicking and dragging should look like **Figure 8.5.**

8. Close the Sample12-red.psd, Sample12-green.psd and Sample12-blue.psd images, leaving only the Prokudin-Gorskii Composite image open.

9. Shut off the views for the Blue and Green layers so you are viewing only the Red layer. It will appear in black and white.

10. Double-click the thumbnail for the Red layer in the layers palette. The Layer Styles palette will open.

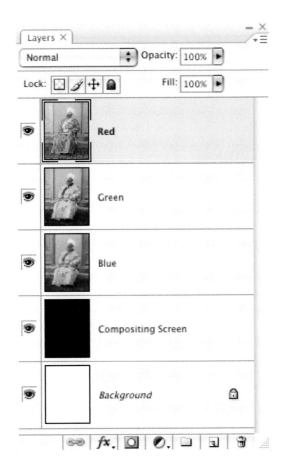

FIG 8.5 The resulting layers from the top down should be Red, Green, Blue, Compositing Screen and Background.

11. Uncheck the Green and Blue checkboxes for Channels under Advanced Blending (see **Figure 8.6**). The image will turn red, showing a view of how the Red light component in the image looks when isolated.

12. Shut off the visibility toggle for the Red layer and toggle the view for the Green layer so it is visible again. The image will appear as a grayscale representation of the Green channel.

13. Double-click the thumbnail for the Green layer in the layers palette for the Prokudin-Gorskii Composite image. The Layer Styles palette will appear.

14. Uncheck the Red and Blue checkboxes for Channels under Advanced Blending. The image will show the Green component channel in green (see **Figure 8.7**).

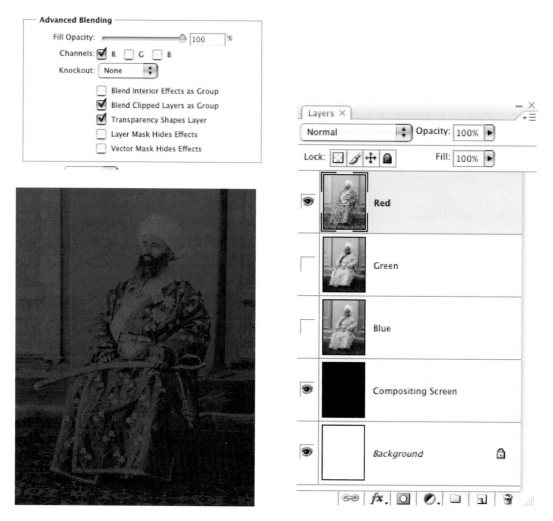

FIG 8.6 Unchecking the checkboxes for Green and Blue make this layer only act on the Red channel. The result is that you see the red light component in red.

15. Shut off the visibility toggle for the Green layer, and toggle the view for the Blue layer so it is visible again. The image will appear as a grayscale representation of the Blue channel.
16. Double-click the thumbnail for the Blue layer in the layers palette for the Prokudin-Gorskii Composite image. The Layer Styles palette will appear.
17. Uncheck the Red and Green checkboxes for Channels under Advanced Blending. As you might expect, the image

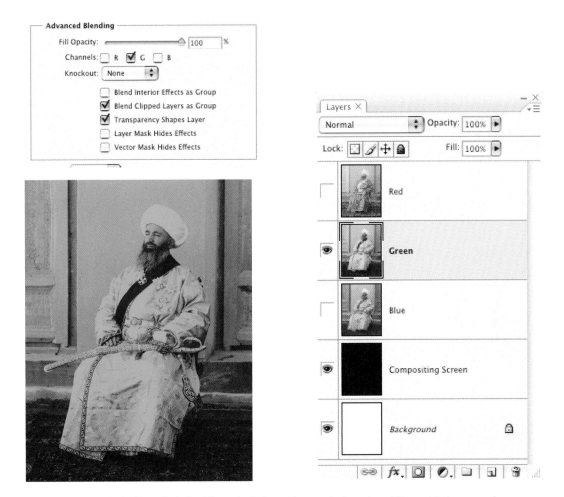

FIG 8.7   Unchecking the checkboxes for Red and Blue make this layer only act on the Green channel. The result is that you see the Green light component in Green.

will show the Blue component of the image in blue
(**Figure 8.8**).

18. Now turn on the visibility toggles for the Green and Red layers.
You will see a full-color composite of the image, though there
is no color at all in any of the layers in the layers palette (see
Figure 8.9).

This is a demonstration of several things from light theory to what
those little checkboxes on the Advanced Blending panel of the
Layer Styles dialog do. Layer Styles targets the content of the layer
to make each act like a specific light component, which projects
on the dark screen. When all three of the light components are

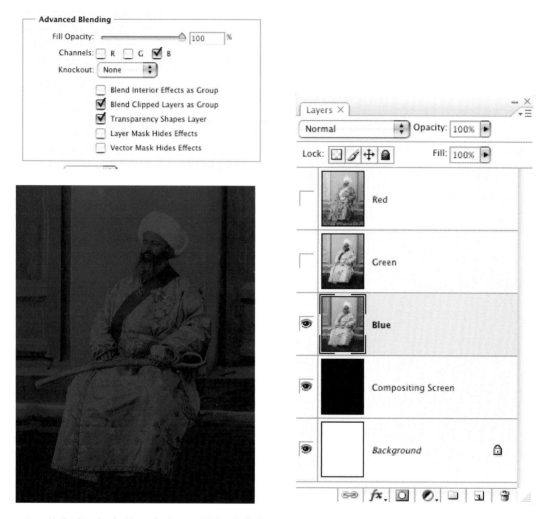

FIG 8.8 Unchecking the checkboxes for Green and Red make this layer only act on the Blue channel. The result is that you see the red light component in Blue.

switched on, the red, green and blue components combine to re-create the color image. This is what your monitor projects, what your camera captures and what Photoshop recreates: red, green and blue components are assembled to make a color image. The example shows that colored light can really be stored by grayscale measurements, and is a sort of demonstration of what Prokudin-Gorskii needed to do to re-create the color he captured: project the filtered images onto a screen. Let's look at this same example in a different way to mix in more light and layer theory continuing on with the same image.

FIG 8.9 The result has some issues as far as needing color correction, dynamic range enhancement and some obvious cleanup, but the fact is that you have just created color from images taken about 100 years ago, 20 years before there was color film.

An Alternative: Creating Filtered Color

Prokudin-Gorskii couldn't just click a checkbox to make his glass plates perform and convert to color. He had to make a more rudimentary effort to filter the red, green and blue light components during projection. Using layer modes, we can mimic filtering the components with color to reproduce color from black and white.

📖 Try It Now

1. Double-click the Red layer in the layers palette in the Prokudin-Gorskii Composite image to open the Layer Styles dialog. Check the Green and Blue boxes, and set the layer mode to screen. This mode treats layer content like light: enhancing brightness only.

2. Double-click the Green layer in the layers palette in the Prokudin-Gorskii Composite image to open the Layer Styles dialog. Check the Red and Blue boxes, and set the layer mode to screen (**Figure 8.10**).

3. Double-click the Blue layer in the layers palette in the Prokudin-Gorskii Composite image to open the Layer Styles dialog. Check the Red and Green boxes, and set the layer mode to screen.

4. Shut off the visibility for the Red and Green layers. Click on the Blue layer to activate it if it is not active already.

FIG 8.10 The layers palette looks no different, but the image at this point will look horribly over-exposed. Keep in mind that sometimes things look worse before they get better.

5. With the Blue layer active, create a new layer (Layer>New>Layer). When the New Layer dialog appears, name the layer Color Blue, change the layer mode to Multiply. This mode acts as a multiplier to darken content below. Check the Group With Previous checkbox. Then click OK.

6. Fill the Color Blue layer with pure Blue (RGB: 0, 0, 255). You can do this by changing the foreground color to blue and clicking in the image with the Paint Bucket tool, or by using the Fill function with the proper foreground or Custom color setting (see **Figure 8.11**).

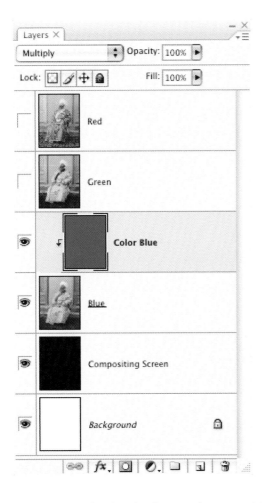

FIG 8.11 The grouped Color Blue layer acts like a filter for blue light as if you were to place a gelatin filter over the Blue content, adding color back to the component.

7. Shut off the visibility for the Blue layer and turn on visibility for the Green layer. Click the Green layer in the layers palette to activate it.

8. Create a new layer (Layer>New>Layer). When the New Layer dialog appears, name the layer Color Green, change the layer mode to Multiply and check the Group With Previous checkbox. Then click OK.

9. Fill the Color Green layer with pure Green (RGB: 0, 255, 0) (see Figure 8.12).

10. Shut off the visibility for the Green layer and turn on the visibility for the Red layer. Click the Red layer in the layers palette to activate it.

11. Create a new layer (Layer>New>Layer). When the New Layer dialog appears, name the layer Color Red, change the

FIG 8.12 The addition of the Color Green layer will cover the green component content with green color, again as if you had applied a gelatin filter.

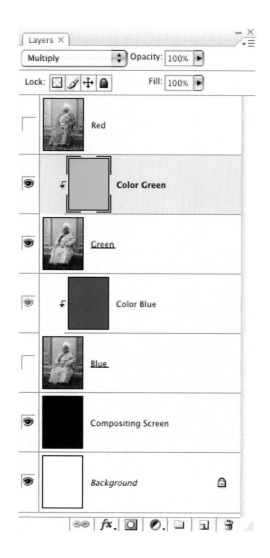

layer mode to Multiply and check the Group With Previous checkbox. Then click OK.

12. Fill the Color Red layer with pure Red (RGB: 255, 0, 0). Your layers should look like **Figure 8.13**.

13. Turn on the visibility for the Green and Blue layers. The image will appear in full color again.

In this scenario, the Color layers act like filters adding color to the grayscale representations using multiply layer mode. Each of the components themselves are then projected like light to the Composite layer by being set to Screen mode.

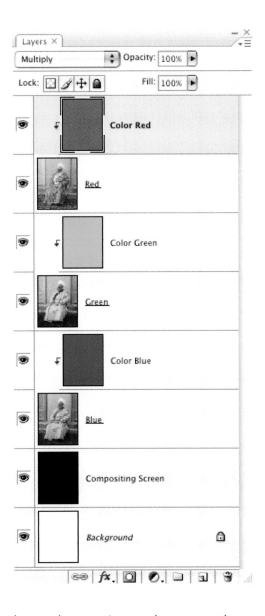

FIG 8.13 Completing the roundup of color additions with the Color Red layer, you are one step away from obtaining full color via filtered layers. When the visibility for all layers is turned on, you'll once again have full color.

This procedure works every time you have grayscale representations of your image … but it isn't likely that you'll soon be out making a custom camera that will shoot separations on a glass plate. Inside every color image there is light, and because there is light, there are light components: Red, Green and Blue. Filtering works to put the color into your image, but a lesson learned from Prokudin-Gorskii is that light components can also be filtered *out* and separated from color images.

📖 An interesting option at this point is to have at the Prokudin-Gorskii image with corrections. You can make a levels correction for starters and a plethora of spot/dust corrections. You might try sharpening, Color Balance, contrast enhancements, and any other technique we've looked at thus far. Doing so can help reinforce those techniques and their application.

Separating a Color Image into RGB Components

Just as Prokudin-Gorskii filtered the light in his scenes for red, green and blue to make his black-and-white 'color' plates, you can reverse the process of adding color and create separations in layers. You might say, 'Oh, we already have channels for that'. But a huge drawback to channels is that they are in a separate palette and you can't work with them nearly as fluidly as you could if you could work them like layers. Let's take a look at the process and then see some of what you can do with separated components.

1. Flatten the Prokudin-Gorskii Composite image. This will commit the changes.
2. Create a new layer, name it Red Filter, and change the mode to Multiply.
3. Fill the Red Filter layer with pure Red (RGB: 255, 0, 0). This will turn the image red and will represent the red light component.
4. Create a Hue/Saturation adjustment layer. Choose Reds from the Edit drop list and push the Lightness slider all the way to the right. You will be left with a grayscale representation of the red light component.
5. Press Command+Option+Shift+E / Ctrl+Alt+Shift+E to copy the visible image to a new layer. Name the new layer Red. Your layers should look like Figure 8.14.
6. Delete the Hue/Saturation layer. Shut off the view for the Red and Red Filter layers.
7. Create a new layer above the Background layer. Name it Green Filter, and change the mode to Multiply.
8. Fill the Green Filter layer with pure Green (RGB: 0, 255, 0). This will turn the image green and will represent the green light component.
9. Create a Hue/Saturation adjustment layer. Choose Greens from the Edit drop list and push the Lightness slider all the way to

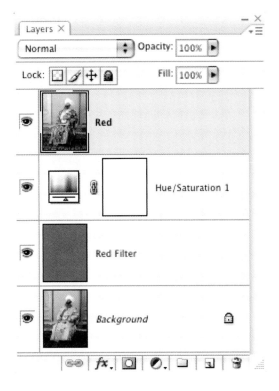

FIG 8.14 **FIG 8.14** Extracting red as the first color component gives you a model for separating the green and blue components as well.

the right. You will be left with a grayscale representation of the green light component.

10. Press Command+Option+Shift+E / Ctrl+Alt+Shift+E to copy the visible image to a new layer. Name the new layer Green (see **Figure 8.15**).

11. Delete the Hue/Saturation layer. Shut off the visibility for the Green and Green Filter layers.

12. Create a new layer above the Background layer. Name it Blue Filter. Change the mode to Multiply.

13. Fill the Blue Filter layer with pure Blue (RGB: 0, 0, 255). This will turn the image blue and will represent the blue light component.

14. Create a new Hue/Saturation adjustment layer. Choose Blues from the Edit drop list and push the Lightness slider all the way to the right. You will be left with a grayscale representation of the blue light component.

15. Press Command+Option+Shift+E / Ctrl+Alt+Shift+E to copy the visible image to a new layer. Name the new layer Blue (see **Figure 8.16**).

16. Delete the Hue/Saturation layer.

FIG 8.15 After creating the Green layer the layer stack looks like this.

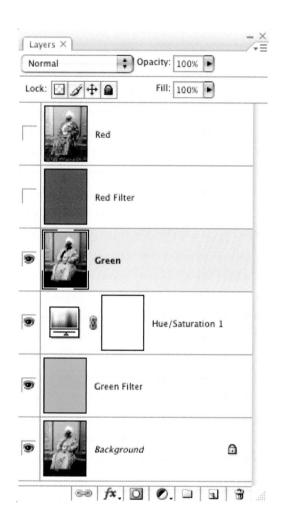

After these steps you should have a Red, Green and Blue layer in your image, all representing grayscale components extracted from the image you were working on. Your next chore is to add the color back to the components to create a color representation while keeping the grayscale components separate. A big hint, look to the earlier part of this chapter where you added color to the Prokudin-Gorskii image to see how to add color back to grayscale separations. Use the Filter layers as the Color layers (that's why I didn't ask you delete them).

Another way to make the separations would be to use the Channel targeting in the Advanced Blending panel.

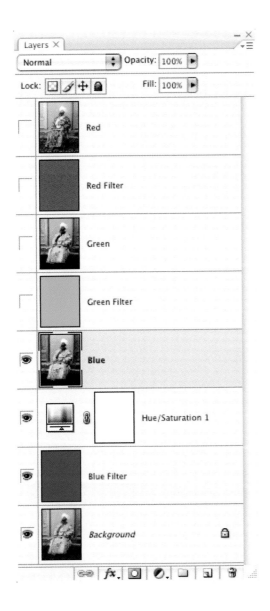

FIG 8.16 The Blue layer gets created with steps almost identical to the others, simply by applying a different color filter.

📖 Try It Now

1. Duplicate the Background to a new image. To do this, click the Background layer to activate it, and then choose Layer> Duplicate Layer. When the Duplicate Layer dialog appears, choose New for the Destination, and name your new image Prokudin-Gorskii New (see Figure 8.17).

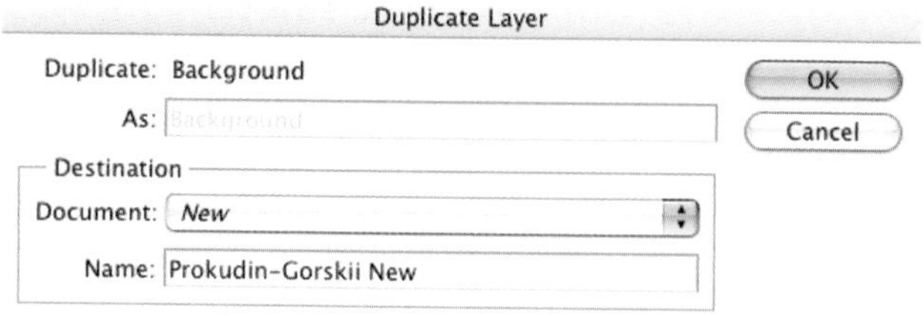

FIG 8.17 Settings for the Duplicate Layer dialog should appear as in this sample.

2. Double-click the Background layer in the new image, and when the New Layer dialog appears, rename the layer Source.
3. Double-click the Source layer and when the Layer Styles dialog appears, uncheck the Green and Blue channels.
4. Create a Hue/Saturation adjustment layer. Choose Reds from the Edit drop list and push the Lightness slider all the way to the right.
5. Press Command+Option+Shift+E / Ctrl+Alt+Shift+E to copy the visible image to a new layer. Name the new layer Red.

This will isolate the Red channel. I'll let you figure out the rest for the Green and Blue. What either of these methods accomplishes is getting your image components on separate layers. Here we have taken apart and put back together your color images – in a fashion nearly identical to the way your images are separated into components and stored, and then reproduced as color from the grayscale channels.

You may think it is a lot of bother to go through to separate out components. That is why I have included some tools on the CD to do it for you. If you load the Separations action set, in it you will find the following tools:

- Complete RGB Separation (duplicates the current image and makes a complete RGB separation following yet another path to separations).
- Blue Component (duplicates the current image and separates out a stand-alone blue component layer).
- Green Component (duplicates the current image and separates out a stand-alone green component layer).
- Red Component (duplicates the current image and separates out a stand-alone red component layer).
- Luminosity and Color (duplicates the current image and separates out Color and Luminosity layers).

- Complete CMYK Separation (duplicates the current image and makes a complete CMYK Separation allowing custom UCR/GCR for black generation).
- *RGBL Components (duplicates the current image and separates out Red, Green, Blue and Luminosity layers).
- *Richard's Custom Black-and-White (duplicates the current image and creates a black-and-white result that works well with many images).
- Simple Channel Mixer (duplicates the current image and sets up a layer-based channel mixing scenario).
- Target Red (targets the current layer to the red channel, unchecks boxes in the Advanced Blending for Green and Blue).
- Target Green (targets the current layer to the green channel, unchecks boxes in the Advanced Blending for Red and Blue).
- Target Blue (targets the current layer to the blue channel, unchecks boxes in the Advanced Blending for Red and Green).
- Target RGB (resets all Advanced Blending channel checkboxes to checked).

📖 We'll be looking at the actions marked with an asterisk in the following section.

Breaking out color components into layers is a very advanced move, and may be something you won't do very often, but it should give you several things, including a good idea of the peripheral power of layers and a good concept of how image information is captured and stored. But what can you do with your knowledge of separations? Follow along into the next section.

Using Separations

Grayscale channels can be used for a variety of highly specialized purposes. First, you can target changes directly to any one of the RGB components by using Adjustment Layers stacked with, and therefore targeted to, specific layer color components. Components can be used for masking, selection and a plethora of alterations, with a freedom in layers that is not accessible to you with channels and channel functions.

Probably one of the most useful and practical applications of separated components is making custom black-and-white conversions. Many people will suggest turning to Channel Mixer, the Black & White function, or perhaps Calculations. The thing each of these functions has in common is that they use separated components to create the image results. However, because these features are pre-defined, there are inherent limitations to the ways they can be combined. You can't, for example, use any of these functions to create a calculation with three components of your choosing in different modes simultaneously. Layer-based calculations and channel mixing allow you complete freedom to use the power of layers however you'd like.

📖 Try It Now

1. Open the Sample13.psd image on the CD (see **Figure 8.18**).
2. Run the RGBL Components action in the Separations action set. This creates the red, green, blue and luminosity components for the image (**Figure 8.19**).
3. Shut off the view for the Luminosity, Red Component and Blue Component. This leaves the view for the Green Component. The flower petals are dark, but they can easily be lightened using the Red Component, as we will do in the next step.

FIG 8.18 A colorful combination leaves some interesting and stark differences between image components after this separation.

FIG 8.19 The range of looks in this separation shows a marked difference that will need to be changed to make a good black-and-white conversion. Clockwise from the upper left we have: red, green, luminosity and blue.

4. Move the Red Component above the Green Component layer in the layer stack. If you view the Red Component by itself (turn off the visibility toggle for the Green Component, turn the visibility toggle for the Red Component on), you will see that it is light in the petal areas but dark in the surrounding greenery. Turn on the visibility toggle for the Green Component, change the mode of the Red Component layer to Lighten and lower the opacity to 60%. This will lighten the flower petal area without a significant impact on the surrounding area.

5. To add back in some of the unique dynamics of the Blue Component, turn on the visibility toggle for the Blue Component layer, change the mode to Overlay and reduce the opacity to 16%.

6. Duplicate the Green Component layer, name the resulting layer Green Component Screen, change the opacity to 70% and be sure the Mode is Screen. This will lighten the area around the petals to create greater contrast.

7. Turn on the Luminosity layer, and change the opacity to 33%. This will mediate some of the extremes that may have been caused by other calculations (see the result in **Figure 8.20**).

Steps 6 and 7 add some calculations that experience has shown will render a better general conversion for almost any image from RGB to grayscale. You can repeat this whole series by using Richard's Custom Black-and-White action from the Separations action set.

You can make adjustments to this result by playing around with the opacity and modes of the component layers. This particular adjustment is one developed after fooling with various possibilities and considering light and color theory. As a conversion, it works fairly consistently over a wide variety of images to produce a pretty good black-and-white image. Give it a try on any color RGB image. This is only one of the infinite possibilities for combining tone. You can fine tune or completely change the result using layer opacity, additional component layers and different layer-blending modes.

The previous example was a result derived from experimentation with the Green Component layer because it is similar to how we perceive brightness. If you start with a component other than the Green Component layer, your goals for changing the image and the calculations you make may be very different than those we used above. For example, if you make the separations and start with the Red Component layer, you could go in an entirely different direction and attempt to make the petals lighter than the background.

FIG 8.20 This combination of layers, components and modes cannot be achieved with Photoshop's native functions, and yet it generally renders a favorable black-and-white result with any image. You need the power of Layers to achieve this.

📖 Try It Now

1. Open the Sample13.psd image on the CD.
2. Run the RGBL Components action.
3. Shut off the view for the Luminosity, Green Component and Blue Component layers. This leaves the view for the Red Component layer. The flower petals are dark but brighter and more contrasty than the background. The background can be darkened, the petals lightened and the contrast enhanced using the following steps.

4. Activate the Green Component layer, and turn on the view. Invert the layer content (Command+I / Ctrl+I), change the mode to Overlay, and reduce the opacity to 24%. This should darken the background and lighten the petals. Inverting the layer changes the content to a negative of the original, in this case making the petals light and the background dark in the Green Component layer.

5. Activate the Blue Component layer, and turn on the view. Apply a Gaussian Blur of 10 pixels, change the mode to Soft Light and change the opacity to 60%. This will serve to smooth out the roughness of the blue component and allow it to be applied to enhance the contrast and soften the image, both at the same time (see the result in Figure 8.21).

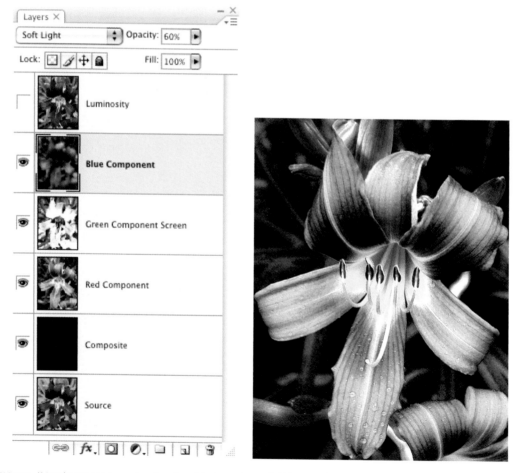

FIG 8.21 Using the same components as from the original procedure with different mode and opacity creates a much different result.

214

This calculation will actually not be likely to produce a good black-and-white conversion on many images. The point is that depending on where you start, how you see an image and how you use the content to make calculations, you can come to very different ends. If you are up to it, try an experiment: start with the Blue Component layer, and see where that leads. See if you can envision the result you want to get and attain it using what you know about layers.

Summary

Separations are the core of another powerful element of Photoshop: Channels. Channels are a powerful tool in their own right; however, when layers are used correctly to their capability, they can virtually make Channels and channel functions unnecessary. Using separated components as described in this chapter gives you tremendous flexibility with the application of components in a more straightforward model than using channels or channel functions. Layering components can help you break away from not only from the limitations of channels, but also of other tools such as Channel Mixer and Calculations.

There is a lot to explore in standard separations of RGB, CMYK, luminosity and color, and perhaps even more to explore with custom separations. That doesn't merely mean that you have an opportunity to explore separations of CMYK where you fiddle with the GCR settings, but that you can create completely custom separations for unique colors. Clever use of custom separations may help you define selections and masks, or create unique black-and-white results. Creating black-and-white images via separations and calculations is not necessarily an endpoint. Black-and-white images offer opportunity for hand-colored effects and redefining the color that makes the image.

At this point we have looked at the power of layers and a variety of applications. We've taken a tour of the process of image editing, defined an approach and process, examined most of the more powerful layer functions, and applied each in turn. As we turn the corner into the final two chapters, we will re-focus on process by taking images through corrective steps from beginning to end with layers as our guide to the result.

For more helpful actions for image adjustments in Photoshop, visit the website for this book at http://www.photoshopcs.com

Tomato

Taking an Image through the Process

We've looked at multiple facets of image correction and adjustment, and now it is time to put them all together. Using a sample image supplied on the CD, we will step through the process of correction and adjustment from start to finish in order to show how the process works in practice.

The base process used for the image will follow procedures suggested earlier in this book, and it may go a step further than you would expect to embellish the image. You don't have to agree with or even like the embellishments, but you should understand the procedures and how they fit into the process of getting to the image result. We will take a critical look at the photo before stepping through the procedures so that we can outline the goals for the image.

Earlier on we looked at various procedures for image editing, and then even ran through corrections of various types on different images, but there has not been an opportunity to put the whole process together as we were still busy exploring layers. The goal of this chapter is to bring together layer techniques that we have learned to see how the procedures apply to a real-world images and real-world editing situations. Seeing the whole process in action should help you to use the concepts and techniques to correct your own images.

The Image

The image in **Figure 9.1** was taken by a long-time friend, Luke Delalio, who does a lot of head shot photography in New York City (lukedelalio.com). He gets outstanding shots of his clients, hand-held, no flash, in natural light – revealing more personality than the standard studio head shots. The image is available on the CD as Sample14.psd.

Luke had other usable shots from this session of his stunning model Carly, but he had passed this one on to me to see if I could do something with it. I could see what he liked in the image: beside the pretty model, there was some interesting lighting, an insolating depth-of-field and a flattering pose. While it is an interesting image, like any image, there are quite a few ways that it can be improved. Shot at a wide aperture at 1/30th of a second, it is almost extraordinary that it is as sharp as it is. While this might never be manipulated to be a terrifically sharp image, it might be a terrific image with a softer quality.

📖 The key to working with digital images day to day is usually not to envision them being something they are not already, but working with what you have to enhance what is there. Enhancement in the form of heroic measures and wild antics are secondary concerns.

Let's review our image-processing checklist (from Chapter 2) before getting together a specific outline of changes to perform.

General Image Editing Steps: A Review

Way back at the beginning of this book we looked at the whole image editing process. By this point in this book, we are concerned more specifically with images than setup issues. The following list of steps is extracted, and somewhat modified from the list of steps suggested in Chapter 2 to target the process. We'll follow this editing checklist in processing the Sample14.psd image:

1. Be sure that your computer system is ready for image editing. Your system is up to speed, your monitor is calibrated, you have set up your preferences and tested your output.
2. Store the original image file safely and work with a copy to do all of your image editing.
3. Have in mind a target range for the resolution and a color mode for the final image.
4. Evaluate the image.
5. Make general color and tonal corrections.
6. Make damage dust and other spot corrections.
7. Make compositional changes, including cropping, compositing and replacing image parts.
8. Make targeted color and tonal corrections to selected parts of the image.
9. Save the layered version of the image. You may want to do some simplifying and optimization at this point.

EXIF Metadata

I didn't take the shot, but I was able to find out some things about it without asking the photographer. All I did was look into the EXIF data that came with the image. So long as you are using a modern digital camera, the camera captures EXIF data (Exchangeable Image File), storing information about the exposures you make at the time of capture. You can access and use this data to refer to exposure information.

To find the EXIF data for your images, open Photoshop, and choose File Info from the File menu (File>File Info). The following data was listed for the sample image under the Camera Data 1 category.

Camera Make/Model: Canon EOS 20D
Date and Time: 11/28/06, 3:28 PM
Shutter Speed: 1/30 second
Aperture: 2.8
ISO: 800

This information can both track what you did to capture the image, give hints as to the quality of the capture, and provide an opportunity for learning. Knowing that this image was taken with a slow shutter, a wide aperture and high ISO, suggesting the image would almost necessarily have a soft quality to it.

Note specifically that this list condenses the setup and computer-oriented issues, as well as the concerns for saving. We will assume at this point that you have taken the initiative to calibrate your monitor, build the ICC profile you need for properly viewing your images on screen, and set up your color management (checklist step 1). The concerns for image storage (checklist step 2) are taken care of by providing the file on the CD. The image on the CD cannot be overwritten, so it is safely archived. We will be processing the image using full size of the provided sample (downsized from the original), which is 9.2 × 7 inches at 200 ppi (checklist step 3). Now we are ready to evaluate the image (checklist step 4).

Applying the Image Editing Checklist

Working through the process of editing will always *really* start with evaluating the image. No matter what you see in an image preview or in Bridge or other viewers, there is no substitute for actually opening the image in Photoshop. So open Sample14.psd and have a good look at the image.

Working with RAW Images

While this image is already converted to JPEG and does not require dealing with Camera RAW conversions, it is worth mentioning what to do with RAW images, and why you might want to consider RAW processing if it is an option.

RAW images are images in their natural capture state – direct off the camera's sensor without any automated in-camera processing. JPEG files, on the other hand, are images that have been processed in camera, converted from the RAW state into something standard and more globally recognized. The advantage of working with RAW images is that you get to control the image conversion from raw data rather than allowing the camera to use some generic processing that only works optimally in run-of-the-mill situations. When it comes to images that are exposure extremes (over- and underexposure), in-camera processing is not an advantage. RAW images offer both more control and a higher bit count than a standard JPEG, which is especially beneficial in processing exposure extremes.

If you shoot in RAW format as a deliberate choice, you add a step to your processing, but you also add some extraordinary leeway with shots that are not exposed optimally. When opening RAW images, you are led to the intermediate Adobe Camera RAW dialog automatically, where you can make a conversion for the image. There are a lot of controls, and with that goes many opportunities for positive change. Some users see this as an opportunity, and some as an obligation. But my suggestion is to not feel too tempted to make changes unless you are positive you can make an advantageous change. If the image is a normal exposure, accept the defaults and go to work in Photoshop where you have the full range of tools and Layers to lean on. Keep in mind that you do not have to do a thing when you pass through the RAW dialog, and are best off only considering making changes when you know the image has exposure issues.

When you decide to make change and corrections in the RAW dialog, consider the histogram display and use it to help keep you from creating bad adjustments. While you may trust your screen to a great extent, the graph helps you see if you are making corrections that are too extreme and actually doing some damage to your images. If you see the graph bunching up and spiking at the right or left in the graph display in the RAW dialog histogram, chances are the image is taking a hit and you are ruining image details perhaps unwittingly. Likewise, if the graph is pulling away from the right or left or forming distinct tails, you may not be making the most of the information you captured. Use these histogram dynamics to help you make intelligent imaging choices.

Automated adjustments selected by Photoshop's Camera RAW dialog don't always make the best choices – they can't see the image. Don't just trust the RAW plug-in to make the choice for you, especially if the preview on screen seems wanting. Play with the possibilities and be careful not to blow out details by being conscious of the histograms provided on the preview. When in doubt, leave the image a little under- or overexposed to save detail so that you can work with it later rather than trying to optimize it all at once in the RAW dialog. You can still fiddle with making changes later, and there may actually be better tools in Photoshop to use when making corrections. Think of the dialog as a helper rather than an all-in-one correction tool.

To examine the image, you might want to do a few simple things, like zoom in to take a look at details (sharpness, graininess, noise), or even take a look at the RGB channels. Sometimes you will find some interesting qualities or the views may suggest specific changes or alterations. For example, you may have a noisy blue channel that suggests a little blurring the blue might help overall, or there might be tonal qualities you'd like to borrow. While you can certainly examine the channels by opening the Channels palette and reviewing the channels, do it the layers way by running the RGBL (Red, Green, Blue and Luminosity) Components action from the Separations action set (from Chapter 8) provided on the CD. After running the action, view the channels by toggling the visibility off for the layers from the top of the layers palette down (see **Figure 9.2**).

Something about the contrast in the blue channel seems interesting, so later in the corrections we'll look at using the blue

FIG 9.2 The RGBL separations show you the tone components that make up your image. From the upper left clockwise we have blue, green, red and luminosity.

channel to enhance the contrast (checklist step 8). Of course we'll want to do an initial Levels correction (checklist step 5). The initial color is fine, but might be a tinge toward yellow or red, and it can use some balance (checklist step 5). Contrast is good, but might even be stronger, playing on the quality of the light in the image. Consider ideas for cropping (checklist step 7). Do you want to get in tighter to the subject? Are there areas around the subject that might be better if removed? What will the image be used for? In this case we have a head shot. It seems the cropping can come in a bit to make the model's head the obvious focus. We've already mentioned that the image is a bit soft, so we'll work with that by playing up the quality of softness to make it more like a soft-focus glamour shot (checklist step 8).

Getting more specific, the midtone to shadow areas may be slightly oversaturated (checklist step 8). The model has virtually no obvious flaws (birthmarks, scars, wrinkles), however underlighting seems to be enhancing a ridge along the upper lip, which can easily be smoothed (checklist step 6). The lighting differs in color between the chest and the face, and that will become more pronounced as the correction progresses. One or the other may need some selective adjustment (checklist step 8). As the face is the focus of the shot, it may help to outline the chin. Muscle structure in the neck and cleavage can be enhanced as well to give the subject more depth (checklist step 8). The eyes and teeth are already white, and a levels correction and color balance will make them whiter still, but you'll need to use care in correction not to blow out detail to make them look fake. We'll look at selective adjustment to these areas to be sure they are optimized and color balanced (checklist step 8).

The final list of corrections per this evaluation is the following, attempting to work from most general to most specific:

- Levels correction
- Color Balance
- Crop
- Enhance contrast
- Add soft-focus effect(s)
- Be mindful of saturation, and adjust
- Enhance jaw line and muscle structure
- Selective balance of lighting between face and chest
- Smooth upper lip
- Hold detail and color in eyes and teeth.

This may seem like quite a lot to do in an image that is already good. Running through the steps using techniques we have already learned or which have been hinted at will make short work of the list. Be aware that as you go you may create additional issues that will require some attention, and at points the image may actually begin to look worse before it begins to get better.

📖 Try It Now

1. Open the Sample15.psd image in Photoshop if it is not already, and make a Levels correction to the image for each channel in the Channels drop list using a Levels Adjustment layer. Name the layer 1 General Levels. See Chapter 3 for a review of the Levels correction. See **Figure 9.3** for the Levels settings used.

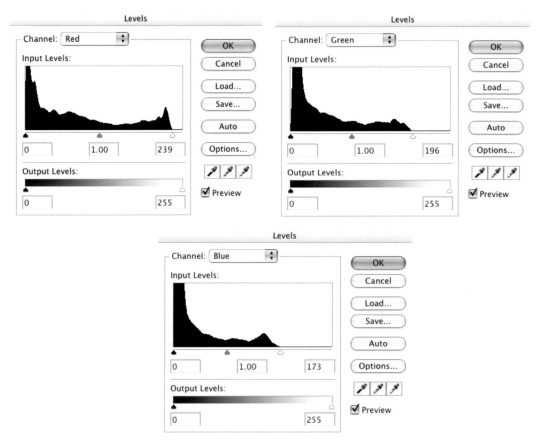

FIG 9.3 For this image there are tails to clip in highlights for each of the channels: Red, Green and Blue.

2. Adjust Color Balance using a Color Balance adjustment layer. Name the layer 2 Color Balance. See Chapter 3 for a review of making Color Balance corrections. See **Figure 9.4** for the Color Balance settings used.

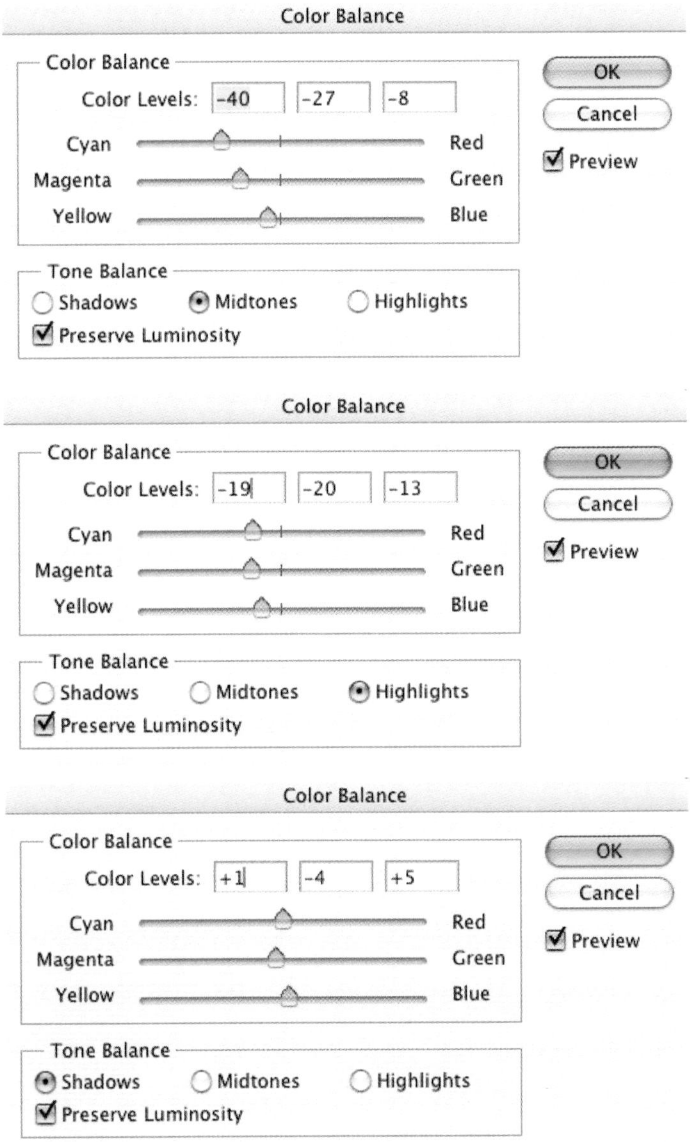

Color Balance

Color Balance
Color Levels: -40   -27   -8
Cyan ———————○—|——— Red
Magenta ———————○—|— Green
Yellow ———————○|— Blue

Tone Balance
○ Shadows   ⦿ Midtones   ○ Highlights
☑ Preserve Luminosity

OK
Cancel
☑ Preview

Color Balance

Color Balance
Color Levels: -19   -20   -13
Cyan ———————○—|——— Red
Magenta ———————○—|— Green
Yellow ———————○|——— Blue

Tone Balance
○ Shadows   ○ Midtones   ⦿ Highlights
☑ Preserve Luminosity

OK
Cancel
☑ Preview

Color Balance

Color Balance
Color Levels: +1   -4   +5
Cyan ———————○——————— Red
Magenta ———————○————— Green
Yellow ———————○————— Blue

Tone Balance
⦿ Shadows   ○ Midtones   ○ Highlights
☑ Preserve Luminosity

OK
Cancel
☑ Preview

FIG 9.4 There are several different light sources to correct for here; you have to achieve the best balance. Depending on how you start the correction and the settings you begin with, your Color balance settings may be very different, but the result should be similar – balancing the color.

3. With the general color and tone corrections complete it is safe to crop the image. Use the crop tool to trim down the image and change the composition (see **Figure 9.5**).

FIG 9.5 You could wait till later in the process to crop, as changes in the image may influence your decisions. I set the crop to 5 by 7 to reflect a standard image size, and cropped with the head a little to the side so the shot was not too centered

4. We will want to borrow back from the original image to get back some skin color. Open the Channels palette, hold down the Command/Ctrl key on your keyboard and click the Red channel. This will load the Red channel as a selection. Click on the Background layer in the Layers palette to activate the Background, then Copy and Paste to create a new layer. Name the layer 3 Load Red; Copy/Paste Background. Press Command+Shift+]/Ctrl+Shift+] to move the layer to the top of the layer stack. Reduce the opacity to 30% (see **Figure 9.6**).

FIG 9.6 The red channel will correspond to highlights and skin in this image. Copying the background will allow you to replace original skin color based on that selection.

5. Duplicate layer 3 Load Red, and name the new layer 4 Duplicate of 3 Blur 20 pixels Opacity 20%. Use Gaussian Blur set at 20 pixels and then lower the opacity to 20%. This will begin to soften the skin and smooth it out.
6. Load the Green channel as a selection by holding down Command/Ctrl key and clicking the Green channel in the Channels palette. Click the Add Layer Mask button at the bottom of the layers palette to add a mask to the 4 Duplicate of 3 layer. This will mask off the darker parts of the layer.

Cropping in Layers

Though you can't really crop in layers, you can create a Crop layer and use it to view the image as if it were cropped. Doing this helps you stay on a path of non-destructive editing:

1. Create a new layer at the top of the layer stack and call it Crop. Fill it with black and set the Opacity to 0%.
2. Choose the Rectangular Marquee tool, set it to 0 Feather. Choose Fixed Ratio and set the ratio according to a standard image size if you want a specific ratio.
3. Make a selection of the area that you would want to crop to. Use the Space Bar to reposition the selection as you create it.
4. Invert the selection (Command+Shift+I / Ctrl+Shift+I [Mac / PC]).
5. Click the Add Layer Mask button at the bottom of the layers palette.

At this point you have your Crop layer. You can turn the Opacity up to 100% and shut off the layer view. As you work, keep the crop layer at the top of the layer stack. You can view the crop by turning on the layer view. You can crop the image by Command+ clicking / Ctrl+clicking the mask for the Crop layer, inverting the selection, and choosing Crop from the Image menu (Image>Crop). This way the crop can also actually be stored with the image as a layer.

7. Duplicate the 4 Duplicate of 3 layer and name the new layer 5 Duplicate of 4 Softlight 100%. Change the layer mode to Softlight and raise the opacity to 100%. Softlight will enhance the contrast of areas that were just softened. It will be masked as well.

8. Create a composite layer, and name it 6 Composite. To make the composite, press Command+Option+Shift+E / Ctrl+Alt+Shift+E.

📖 As we work through here the goal will be to balance a little sharpening with a little softening so that we retain the detail and sharpness while creating the softening effect.

9. Sharpen the image with Unsharp Mask using an Amount of 70% and a Radius of 2 (Threshold 0). You can do this directly to the 6 Composite layer and change the name accordingly to save layers. For this sample, duplicate the Composite, apply the sharpening, and name the layer 7 Duplicate of Composite; Sharpen 70%, 2. Your layers should look like the layers palette in **Figure 9.7** at this point.

10. Duplicate layer 7 Duplicate of Composite and name the new layer 8 Duplicate of 7 Manual Sharpening. We'll come back to this layer in a minute to finish the manual sharpening effect for contrast enhancement.

11. Duplicate layer 8 Duplicate of 7 and name the new layer 9 Duplicate of 8 Color Hold. Change the layer mode to Color. This will lock in the color for the changes below.

12. Activate layer 8 Duplicate of 7, and apply a manual sharpening/Contrast enhancement (for a refresher see Chapter 6). The steps are invert the layer, Gaussian Blur 30 pixels, set the mode to Overlay and the Opacity to 50%. You will see this correction brings her hair out from the shadows.

13. Create a Hue/Saturation layer at the top of the layer stack (above layer 9) and push the Saturation slider for the Master to 30% to compensate for the saturation and click OK to apply the change. This will make much of the color in the midtones and darker quarter tones oversaturated. To adjust that, make sure the hue/saturation layer is active and run the Target Highlights, Half Range in the Blend If actions set provided on the CD. To run the action, click it to highlight, then click the Play button at the bottom of the Actions palette. Change the name of the Hue/Saturation layer to 10 Saturate Highlights.

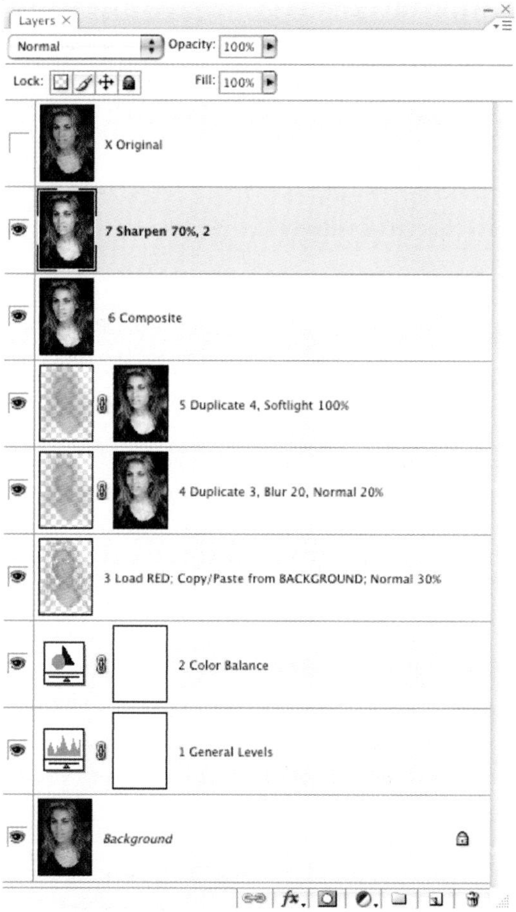

FIG 9.7 At the top of this layer stack is an extra layer. It is just a duplicate of the Background that can be used to quickly compare before and after.

14. Create a Composite layer for the image, and name it 11 Composite (see **Figure 9.8**).
15. Command+click / Ctrl+click on the RGB channel in the Channels palette to load the brightness of the image as a selection. With the 11 Composite layer active, Copy and Paste to extract the highlights and isolate them to their own channel. Name the layer 12 Isolate Highlights.
16. Duplicate layer 12 Isolate Highlights, and name the new layer 13 Duplicate of 12 Blur 20 Pixels. Apply a Gaussian Blur of 20 pixels and change the Opacity to 50%. Command+click / Ctrl+click the Red channel to load it as a selection and click the Add Layer Mask button at the bottom of the Layers palette. This mask will help target the softening to highlights and the skin.

FIG 9.8 The 11 layers you have so far have made the image seem brighter, sharper, with more detail in the hair and a broader range of color than the original. Now that detail is enhanced, we can soften some without worrying as much about losing detail.

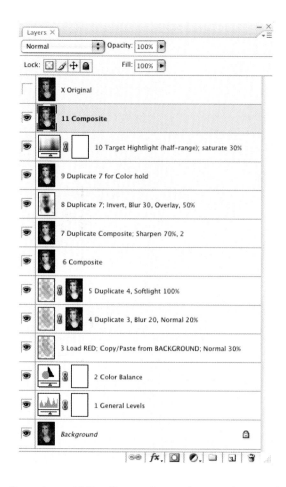

17. Duplicate layer 13 Duplicate of 12 and name the new layer 14 Duplicate of 13 Softlight 100%. Change the mode to Softlight and the Opacity to 100%. Shift+click on the layer mask to disable it, or just drag it to the trash. If you drag it to the trash you will be asked if you want to apply the mask. Click Delete (see **Figure 9.9**). Softlight mode will help enhance the contrast as you smooth out the skin with the blur.
18. Create a new layer and name it 15 Desaturate with Blend If. Fill the layer with black, lower the Opacity to 20%, and run the Target Midtones Full Range action. This will desaturate the midtones 20%.
19. Create a Blue component using the Blue Component action; this creates the component in a new image (a flattened copy of the working image). Play the Target RGB action, which will make the layer target all color components (RGB), turning the

FIG 9.9 The last three steps have added three layers to significantly enhance the softness of the image. A comparison between the original (upper left), pre-softening (upper right) and post-softening (lower left) is shown here.

layer to a black-and-white representation of the Blue channel. Blur the layer with Gaussian Blur at 10 pixels, and set the Luminosity to 30%. This will add a glow of sorts to the image shadows. Name the Blue Composite layer 16 Blue Component to Grayscale Blur 10 pixels Luminosty 30%.

20. Copy the 16 Blue Component layer to the original image. There are several ways to do this from Copy and Paste to click-and-drag. To click-and-drag, for example, be sure both images are visible on screen and that the image with the Blue Component layer is active. Hold the shift key, and click-and-drag the Blue Component layer to the working image. Release the mouse button before the shift key. Close the image copy without saving. The added layer will soften the shadows.

📖 Be sure to release the mouse button before the Shift key when doing click-and-drag to be sure the layer you are moving registers in the center of the image it is dragged to.

21. Duplicate layer 16 Blue Component and name the new layer 17 Duplicate of 16 Soft Light 30%. Change the mode to Soft Light and the Opacity to 30%. The additions of the blurred blue component in Soft Light mode will enhance contrast. See the before and after for adding the blue blur in **Figure 9.10**.

📖 To this point we have done little that requires much free-hand tool skill. Many corrections have been based on understanding of previous chapters, modes, opacity, blending and the advantages offered by light components for quick selection, masking and calculations. We have also taken care of much of the preliminary part of the hit list, including Levels correction, Color Balance, Cropping, contrast enhancement, adding soft-focus effect(s) and being mindful of saturation as it wavered. From here to the end of these corrections, many more of these changes will require some dexterity and individual choice in making more selective corrections.

22. Burn in the jaw line. To do this, Create a new layer, name it 18 Burn in Jaw Line. Choose the Lasso tool and draw a selection around the jaw line, then invert the selection so the active area is off the face – targeted to the area outside the original selection. In this case we are most interested in the neck (see **Figure 9.11**).

FIG 9.10 Working on blur and general enhancement of dynamic range and contrast has begun to give this image a glamour-photo look.

FIG 9.11 Make the selection broad to cover most of the face so that changes painted in have no chance to bleed over the wrong side of the selection. You could actually select the whole face if you wanted just to be safe.

23. Choose the Brush tool and a large, soft brush (200 pixels, 25% spacing, 100% opacity, Normal mode, all fade and other brush dynamics off), then sample a color from a shadow area of the neck. To sample the color, press Option/Alt. Paint in under the jaw line by dragging the brush along the selection line (see **Figure 9.12**).

24. Deselect the selection (press Command+D / Ctrl+D), then change the layer mode to Multiply, and drop the opacity to 35% or so (you may have a different preference). Apply a Gaussian Blur of 10 pixels (see **Figure 9.13**).

FIG 9.12 The selection will mask the painting so it falls just under the jaw. The painting under the jawline should be dark, flat and obvious, but we will adjust it.

FIG 9.13 Blurring helps feather the change in around the jaw line so it isn't terribly abrupt or overdependent on the selection.

25. To make the jaw line harder, we'll add a second, harder accent. Create a new layer, name it 19 Refine Jaw Line. Change the size of the brush to 100 pixels and paint right over the jaw line into layer 19, following the jaw line with the center of the brush. Reduce the opacity of the layer to about 25%, and then add a layer mask. With the mask in place, choose a large (200 pixel) hard (95%) black brush (1% spacing), and paint a mask to define the jaw line. To do this, paint above the jaw line and following the jaw line with the edge of the brush. Apply

a 1 pixel blur to the mask to blend it in. Click the linking icon between the mask and layer thumbnail to unlink the mask and thumbnail, click the layer thumbnail, and apply a Gaussian Blur of 20 pixels. Unlinking the mask and thumbnail will confine the blur to the layer content: you do not want the mask blurring any more than it already is (**Figure 9.14**).

FIG 9.14 Blurring in this case helps feather the change into the previous jaw line shadow, but the blur is restricted over the face by the mask.

26. Create a new layer and name it 20 Burn In Brightspot. Choose a soft, 30 pixel brush and paint in over the bright areas on the viewer's right at the side of the neck still using the sampled color. Blur the result 20 pixels, change the layer mode to Multiply and set the Opacity to 35% or so. This will burn in and darken the lighter area at the side of the neck.

27. Burn in contours on the neck and chest. To do this, create a new layer and name it 21 Burn In Contours and paint in accents similar to what you've done in the previous steps. For this area, try using a brush with a Fade dynamic (Brush: Size 50, Hardness 0%, Check: Shape Dynamics on the Brushes palette, Set the Size Jitter control to Fade and 150). Use paintbrush strokes on the neck to accentuate contours. After all the accents are in place, blur using Gaussian Blur of 20 pixels and set the mode of the layer to Multiply and Opacity to about 35% (or to your preference). See the Fade setting and brush application in **Figure 9.15**.

FIG 9.15 Change the brush size and fade length as appropriate to get better matching on contours. Blurring mode and Opacity will help you blend in the changes effectively.

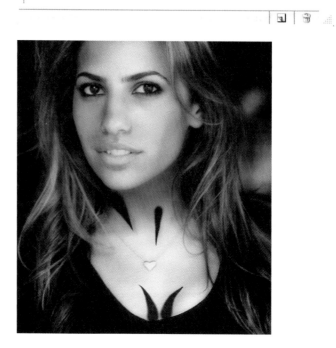

28. Isolate the chest area for adjustment. To do this, create a new layer, name it 23 Mask Chest and composite the changes to this layer. Make a rough selection around the area to be adjusted, then click the Add Layer Mask button. This will create a mask with the selected area. Blur 30 pixels to soften the mask, then run the Target Highlights Full Range action. This will target the highlights within the masked area only.

29. Apply a color adjustment to the 23 Mask Chest layer. To do this, choose Layer>New Adjustment Layer>Hue/Saturation, and check the Use Previous Layer to Create Clipping Mask checkbox on the New layer dialog. Adjust the sliders to improve the matching to other skin tone in the image. Name the layer 24 Color Adjust 23 (**Figure 9.16**).

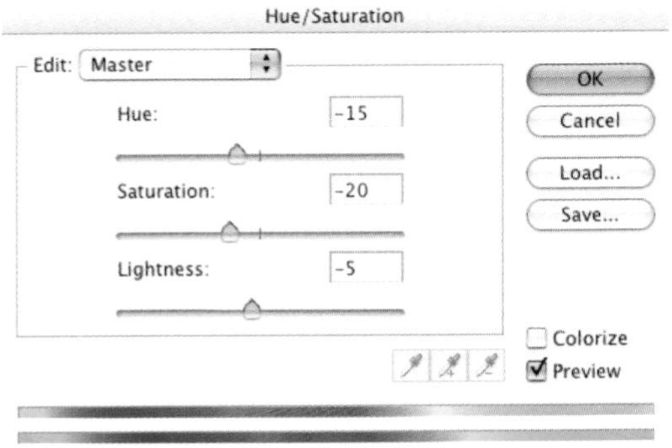

FIG 9.16 There are many other ways to make this adjustment. Hue/Saturation changes shown here reduce saturation, shift the color and slightly darken the result.

30. Retrieve the necklace from Original image to restore it. To do this, duplicate the Background layer, name the duplicate 25 Retrieve Necklace from Original, and move the layer to the top of the layer stack. Click the Add Layer Mask button, and fill the mask with black. Using small hard brushes (95% hard, 25 pixels round for the pendant and about 10 pixels for the chain), change the foreground swatch color to white and paint on the mask to reveal the necklace. Change the mode of the layer to Luminosity and reduce the Opacity as desired. Painting effectively unmasks the old layer's luminosity, darkening the necklace which had faded due to the blurring in earlier steps.

31. Repair the upper lip. To do this, make a new layer and name it 26 Upper Lip Repair. Choose the Healing tool and a small hard brush (10 pixels). Sample from the cheek on the viewer's right to repair the area above the right side of the lip; sample

from the cheek on the viewer's left to repair the left side of the lip. The final result should be a simple smoothing of the shadowed area above the lip. Remember to use the sample all layers setting.

32. Correct the brightness and color balance of the teeth (which have changed partially due to corrections). Isolate the teeth on their own layer by creating a new composite layer, and renaming it 27 Isolate Teeth. Make a rough selection of the teeth, and click the Add Layer Mask button, then blur slightly to feather the mask. Add a Levels layer as a clipping group, and make a Levels correction (see **Figure 9.17**). Rename the Levels

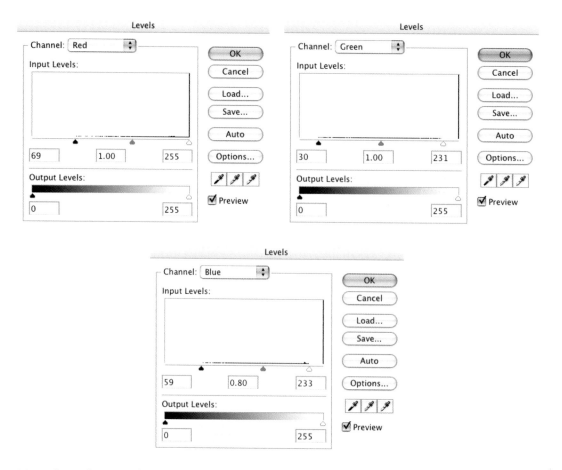

FIG 9.17 In a smaller segmented correction like this, you will be far less likely to cut off tails. Here you want to retain everything or you will blow out details.

layer 28 Levels Teeth Compensation. Adjust the opacity of the 27 Isolate Teeth layer (not the levels layer) to adjust the result (full opacity may seem too bright/white).

33. Correct the brightness and color balance of the eyes. Isolate the eyes by making a new composite layer, making a selection of the eyes and adding a mask as in the previous step. Name the layer as 29 Isolate Eyes, then add a Levels layer as a clipping group and make a levels correction (see **Figure 9.18**). Rename the levels layer 30 Eyes Brighten and Balance. Reduce the opacity of the 29 Isolate Eyes layer to adjust the result to a pleasing look.

FIG 9.18 Brighten the eyes using the center RGB slider.

34. Correct the color and intensity of the lips. Isolate the lips just as you did the eyes and teeth, and name the masking layer 31 Isolate Lips. Use a Hue/Saturation adjustment layer as a clipping group to make a correction. I pushed the Saturation to +30 and adjusted the Hue −4.

35. Do a final Levels check by adding a Levels correction to the top of the stack. You may use the opportunity to brighten or darken the image slightly. Name the layer 33 Levels Check (see **Figure 9.19**).

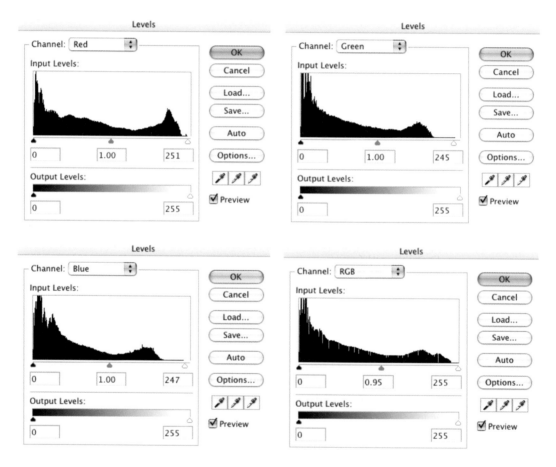

FIG 9.19 I would not cut the tails at this point as it may affect detail in the eyes and teeth.

36. Add a final Color Balance layer to the image and run through the color balance correction. There may be minimal changes at this point, but changes may also more heavily reflect preference over pure balance (**Figure 9.20**).

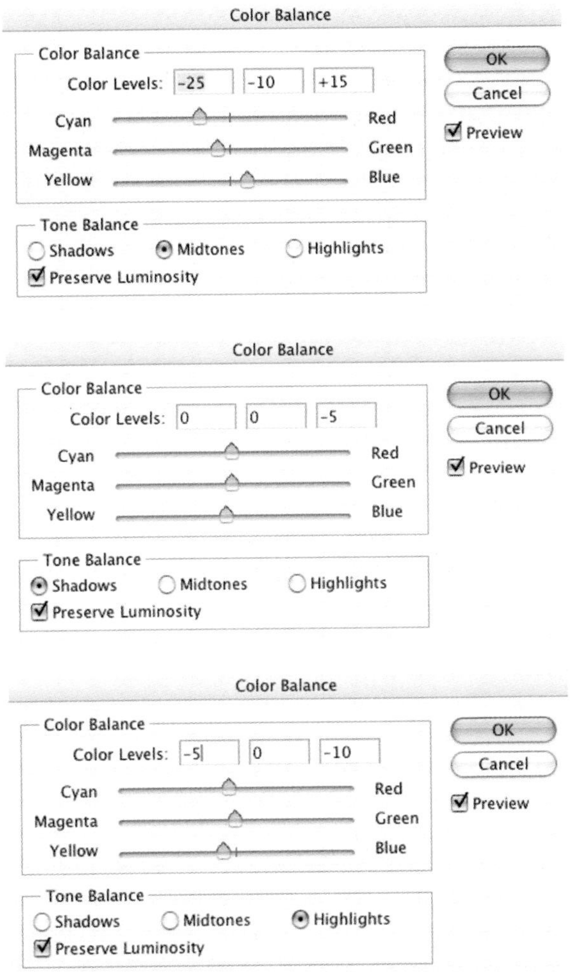

FIG 9.20 I usually like a warmer skin tone, but for this adjustment chose a bit cooler tone. Your corrections may be different.

At this point we have run the gamut of corrections on this image, and – for the purpose of this exercise and the original hit list – we have completed the image correction. We should consider the before and after comparison in **Figure 9.21** as the result.

There may be additional corrections you might like to make or items that you might like to adjust at this point. Of course, you can do more with this image, and experimentation is encouraged. You can examine the sample corrections by opening the Sample14_complete.tif from the CD. This contains all the corrections as they were used for the writing of the exercise. It also contains several groupings as an example of how you might

FIG 9.21 The final image has more color and tone dynamics than the original, and uses the softness to flatter the model.

go back after corrections to group your changes to keep them organized.

Summary

In this image exercise we have used virtually every trick in this book, applying almost every layer capability for practical purposes on an image that reflects the type of day-to-day changes you may make to any image. We've had the opportunity to look at evaluating images, how to apply that to following a plan for corrections and how to apply layers for organizing your path to a result.

If you look at the completed sample image provided on the CD, you can turn off the spot correction layers individually to see how they play into the result. In fact, every layer from layer 12 up can be toggled on and off to view its effect in the final result because they are masked and cumulative changes.

As far as working with these techniques in the future, the ideas we have explored here in layering corrections, sharpening, soft focus and selective correction are applicable whenever you edit images. You are best off, as in this example, working from the general corrections to the more specific, and leaving as many layers intact as you need to accomplish the job. You can always go back later and clean them up, organize them, group into categories, and *learn* from them.

You will note in the sample image that I have noted brush sizes in the layer names, blur radius, and any number of other things that will not be apparent in looking at the content of a layer. In fact even Photoshop's editing log will not record these details. Make smart use of layers and they can provide a wealth of information, convenience and flexibility that can be had in no other way.

In the next chapter we look briefly at an extension of correction in what it means to make collage and composite images.

If you have any questions about the techniques and procedures in this chapter, please visit the website and make your questions known! http://photoshopcs.com.

Making a Layered Collage or Composite Image

We have looked at quite a lot of things that layers can do, and the important thing now is to continue to follow through using the techniques you have learned. We looked at the entire process of evaluating and correcting an image in Chapter 9. One step beyond just working out the issues with a single image is combining images for a finished result.

In this chapter, the emphasis is on considering the idea of collage and compositing, and how to be creative in implementing changes and additions to images using the power of layers.

We have touched on using layers for image correction, adjustment, isolation, masking, and how to use layers to manage and group corrections. In reality, collage and composite are just an extension of that. First we'll look at the idea of composite and collage, and how you go about collecting images for each.

This speaks to the difference somewhat of what collage and composite images are.

What Is a Collage?

Collage is supposedly derived from the French word coller, which means 'to paste'. We started with the simple idea of pasting, and here we come full circle, returning to the earliest techniques to produce the most complex results. A collage is simply a collection of images, used in part or whole or cropped out to specific areas, and combined or pasted together to create a collective visual. In other words, in making a collage you gather source materials and past them together. It's that simple. Simple in idea, but complex, often very complex, in execution.

A collage can be anything from the old grade-school exercise of taking out a bunch of old magazines and cutting out images then pasting them to a larger sheet of paper to far more elaborate adventures in imaging. The photographic equivalent is taking a group of pictures, extracting the interesting parts and combining them to achieve a result. It can be simple collection of images (say a grouping of family photos) to more organized themes, clever compositing, or completely haphazard. It can be humorous, serious, realistic, surreal, artistic and more. When you are bored or have a moment to exercise some creative muscles, it can be great fun.

Guidelines for Collage

Because collage can follow many forms and none are right or wrong, guidelines for making a collage can only be general. You have to supply the image choices and creative direction. Below, find my 5C's of collage:

1. *Collect your images*: You can do this in a variety of ways from going out and shooting new images to rummaging through old files. At the very least you should be using at least two images … there is not really an upper limit except for what time allows.
2. *Create your canvas*: Create a new image about two times the size of the finished project. This will give you some layout space to work with and elbow room for placement of the images. You can crop the image down later (or use a cropping layer as described in Chapter 9) or you may find you just end up filling the space! At the very least this should be two times the width and height of the largest image you plan to use.

3. *Correct your images*: Never neglect to make changes in individual images just because you are going to composite them. Advantages you have for layer corrections especially will be lost if you wait till later.
4. *Clip out and composite*: Like scissors to a magazine, you have the layer tools to start snipping up your images. Make selections and masks to isolate image areas that you will be using in the final collage, and move those components to the canvas created in step 2.
5. *Compose*: With all the images in the new canvas you can spend some time adjusting positions, compositing, blending, correcting and meshing. There is no limit to what you can attempt, and this step can take many hours depending on the complexity of what you are attempting.

Things to keep in mind:

- Collage doesn't have to appear flat and can include effects (e.g. drop shadows) and patterns (like scrapbooking) instead of just images.
- Some image parts, objects or components may have to be built to make any composited part of an image work within the new context.
- Color needs to work together. Color can change! When you isolate image components, you are giving yourself the opportunity to orchestrate the whole scene. Take that opportunity to control the colors and how they fit together as well as the components.
- Be cognizant of light and direction. If you are putting together a wholly new object, you need to note that the lighting and light direction don't conflict with each other. The lighting on all elements of your scene should match or it will appear unnatural.

An Example Collage

Collage can be a great way to find purpose for those images you would possibly otherwise think belong in the digital trash. In a way it can be like cloud gazing where you stare at images until something pops into your head; or you can come at it with a purpose from the outset. The images may not need to be superior or even on a common theme, but shots that can be somehow managed and merged. For example, take a look at the grouping of shots in Figure 10.1.

FIG 10.1 There is nothing particularly connected about these shots, some are common, and some not so good at all . . .

While there is very little central theme to the images selected here, each had something that is central and singular. In this case it is possible set to work just snipping out the objects, and let imagination take over. For example, this might be the source for a somewhat other-worldly scene where the vacuum is given life, adorned with wings from the butterfly, making its rounds to a bright flower with a strangely twisted stem. To create the scene you might start by creating a new image and then by grouping image elements for the butterfly vacuum, and then make the strange flower (see Figure 10.2).

FIG 10.2 Components can be assembled from separate parts before combining them into the whole.

Once the major components are created, they can be fit together in a cohesive whole in the strange terrain. Every one of the techniques required to complete the result was covered in this book. Feel free to open the sample images from the CD and attempt to replicate the result or make your own/different collage with the same photos (Figure 10.3).

📖 I would be glad to see creative collage made either with these sample images or from other groupings. See the website (http://photoshopcs.com) for information about collage contests!

Shooting Multiple Source Images

In times of image trouble one of the greatest options to have is the availability of more than one source image to work with. If you take several shots of the same scene, you are really safeguarding yourself for any corrections you might have to make. For example, if you are taking a posed family shot, taking several images of the same exact setup can give you the source to replaced blinking eyes, turned heads, cliché gestures and the like.

This same philosophy works to help you fix any number of other problems. If you are on a trip to a scenic spot and you think you got the shot, take the same one again. Chances are you won't be coming back all too soon and if you find your hand was a little shaky in the first frame, you'll have possibly saved the shot by squeezing off one more. Other images can be used for patching, copy/pasting and otherwise fixing a variety of things that go wrong.

FIG 10.3 This surrealistic scene was built from the five images in **Figure 10.1**.

Creating a Panorama

Similar to the idea of collage and composite is creating a panorama. You can do this in situations where you don't have a wide angle to tackle the image you want, or to give you greater resolution in the result by stitching together consecutive shots taken in a horizontal or vertical plain. Images shot for a panorama are taken in a series – usually in quick succession – and the series of images are connected to create a continuous landscape. The photos are usually taken in a vertical or horizontal pan to capture a broader or taller area than you would normally get in a single frame with whatever lens you are using. Because you take several overlapping images shot in succession (perhaps using a tilt (vertical movement) or pan (horizontal movement) of a tripod), your resulting image will have more image information once stitched together and can be enlarged more than a single frame of the same scene (Figure 10.4).

Good panoramas are a little tricky to shoot and often tricky to stitch together seamlessly. Lighting conditions change as you pivot the camera, and cameras in any type of auto-exposure mode

FIG 10.4 This series of images can be stitched together to make the complete panorama.

will try to compensate for that between shots. This leaves you with a lot of tone and color changes to correct in post-processing. The obvious solution is to shut off auto-exposure modes and shoot with manual exposure. Taking some care while shooting the source images for the panorama will help simplify processing. Instead of looking forward to corrections, avoid at least a few by switching the camera to a manual mode first – before shooting any of the images. This will keep the exposure setting the same for each frame in your panorama, and will make matching the exposure of the individual frames easier, and your work at the computer a lot quicker later. Setting your camera up on a tripod for the movement can also help by keeping the frames mostly aligned. When you shoot the frames, you will want 30–50% overlap to give yourself plenty of room to blend one image into the next as you stitch them together.

During editing to make these images stitch together smoothly, you will likely have to pull out all the stops and use almost all we've done so far to get a good result. If you open the source images (Sample16.a.psd, Sample16.b.psd, Sample16.c.psd, Sample16.d.psd), you will notice some noise in the images and the color may need a little correction … though it is possible to forgo most of these corrections until after the images are stitched together.

The basic set of steps for completing a panorama are this:

1. *Collect your images*: Purposely shoot a series of images that overlap by 30% or more for the purpose of creating your panorama.
2. *Create your canvas*: Create a new image about two times the height of your images and wide enough to fit all the images in the series. As with collage, you leave some layout space to work with and elbow room for placement of the images.
3. *Compile and collate your images*: Get all the images into the new canvas and order them in series. If the series was shot horizontally, start stacking the images in layers with the right-most image on the bottom of the layer stack, and work left in the panorama as you add layers so they remain organized in the layer stack. If the series was shot vertically, stack from bottom to top. Ordering in layers will help organize your plan.
4. *Blend*: The seam between images can be blended in a variety of different ways. The easiest technique (the panorama plugin in elements is based on this) is simply making a gradient blend at the seam from black to white. Layer masks are recommended. Varying opacity during the blending process can help you see better where edges match.
5. *Correct*: Once you have the panorama stitched together you need to treat it like a single image. You'll want to go through all the steps of correction from levels and cropping to spot corrections to be sure you are making the best image.

You can try stitching together the sample images provided on the CD for this panorama, and you can see the corrections I made in the completed file Sample16.psd. The most telling part of the sample will be the masking used for blending the edges of the consecutive shots. Masking helps make some otherwise tricky transitions simple. Waves – like lines in a topographical map – might not want to easily fit together from shot to shot. But overlaps, masking, blending, and the power of layers can help you create a seamless result.

Summary

This chapter has lacked a bit of direction, quite by design. We have covered some of the basic concepts of composite and collage as a way to think beyond the boundaries of the confines of single snapshots, and have covered the techniques needed earlier in the book. You have been supplied with the images you need and the outline of what to do, and the intent was to leave the details in your hands. If you get stuck, samples on the CD (Sample15.psd and Sample16.psd) should hold a clue to the answers you are looking for. Trying to complete the collage and composites are an opportunity to explore techniques discussed throughout the book before you have to go at it more completely on your own. The core of this chapter lies in taking a broader view of images. Objects and image can be combined not just within their own spatial area, but with other images to expand the borders of what is possible well beyond the scope of viewfinder.

So you see that with panoramas, and blending edges we have truly come full circle. Panorama stitching is quite like trying to put together the pieces of a puzzle, or like blending the edges of a map to stitch together a series of scans – as I told of all the way back in the introduction to this book. Hopefully now that you have seen what layers have to offer and how they can enable you to do things with images that would otherwise be far more difficult without layers, you have a map for your future of working with images in Photoshop.

I like to always think that the end of my books are always just the beginning. As you have time to work with layers, using this book as a starting place and reference, you should grow well beyond what we've looked at to expand your horizons.

As you continue to explore Photoshop layers, please visit the book's website (http://www.photoshopcs.com) and visit the Layer forums online to ask questions, and get answers about layers and other Photoshop issues. This author is bound to be there fairly often as well! I look forward to seeing you there.

INDEX